PELICAN BOOKS

VICTORIAN PEOPLE

Asa Briggs is Professor of History and Vice-Chancellor elect of the University of Sussex. From 1955 to 1961 he was Professor of Modern History at Leeds University. Born in 1921, he took a double first in history at Cambridge. Among his publications are *The Age of Improvement* (1959), *Chartist Studies* (1959), which he edited, *The Birth of Broadcasting* (1961), *Victorian Cities* (1963), a companion volume to this book, *The Golden Age of Wireless* (1965), and *William Cobbett* (1967). Asa Briggs, who is married and has four children, lives at Lewes in Sussex.

 # Victorian People

*A Reassessment
of Persons and Themes
1851-67*

ASA BRIGGS

Penguin Books

Penguin Books Ltd, Harmondsworth, Middlesex, England
Penguin Books Australia Ltd, Ringwood, Victoria, Australia

—

First published in Great Britain by Odhams Press 1954
Published by The University of Chicago Press 1955
Published, with minor revisions, in Pelican Books 1965
Reprinted 1967, 1970

—

—

Made and printed in Great Britain
by C. Nicholls & Company Ltd
Set in Monotype Garamond

Contents

This edition of *Victorian People* is a slightly modified version of the American edition of 1955. The Bibliographical Note has been revised.

A. B.

From the England of Fielding and Richardson to the England of Miss Austen — from the England of Miss Austen to the England of Railways and Free-trade how vast the change; yet perhaps Sir Charles Grandison would not seem so strange to us now as one of ourselves will seem to our great-grandchildren. The world moves faster and faster; and the difference will probably be considerably greater. The temper of each new generation is a continual surprise.

J. A. FROUDE (1864)

CHAPTER ONE

Introduction

I

The period of English history which begins with the Great Exhibition of 1851 and ends with the second Reform Bill of 1867 is one of the least studied and least understood chapters in English history. There are two main reasons for the lacuna: the first, political complexity, a jumble of ministries, and a constant shifting of political alignments; the second, relative quiet in the world of events. The picturesque battles of the nineteenth century fall on either side of the period. On the one side, there are the sharp conflicts of the 1840s, when contemporaries talked openly of class war and imminent revolution, and, on the other, there are the bitter struggles of the 1880s, when Irish nationalism moulded English history and Victorian radicalism overlapped with twentieth-century socialism. The middle years of the century form a great plateau bounded on each side by deep ravines and dangerous precipices.

Yet the plateau has a fascination of its own – a fascination which has increased in recent years, when writers and thinkers of the twentieth century have found far more points of interest in Victorian England than their iconoclastic predecessors. The period from 1851 to 1867 was the period of high-Victorian England; from its social balance it produced a distinctive civilization of its own. The key words of the times were 'thought', 'work', and 'progress'. Clear thinking was preferred to impulse or prejudice and the battle of ideas to the dictatorship of slogans; hard work was considered the foundation of all material advancement; and both clear thinking and hard work were deemed essential to continued national progress.

The stress on thought, work, and progress, carried with it smugness, dullness, and what contemporaries, particularly the bright young intellectuals of the *Saturday Review*, called 'cant'. But it was accompanied also by heightened national pride. The 1851 Preface to G. R. Porter's *Progress of the Nation* catches the mood:

It must at all times be a matter of great interest and utility to ascertain the means by which any community has attained to eminence among nations. To inquire into the progress of circumstances which has given pre-eminence to one's own nation would almost seem to be a duty.

This was the mood of 1851; it survived down to 1867. The period as a whole was a crucial one in the development of English national consciousness:

> Pride in their port, defiance in their eye,
> We see the lords of human kind go by.

Five main influences conditioned the national mood. The first was the direct influence of prosperity. The economic troubles of the preceding generation vanished almost as if by magic. From 1850 there was a rise in prices brought about by the diversion of investment to ventures which yielded their results over a long period of time or, like war and gold rushes, yielded few economic returns at all. Britain was the world's workshop, the world's shipbuilder, the world's carrier, the world's banker, and the world's clearing-house. Free trade was the dominant commercial philosophy of the age, and it seemed as unchallengeable as Magna Carta. Yet landlords retained substantial social and political power, and farmers and workers as well as businessmen shared the prosperity. Although the farmers had been robbed of protection by the repeal of the Corn Laws in 1846, they continued to enjoy the natural protection afforded by geography against imports of cheap food; as much as the manufacturers, they benefited directly from the expansion of the railway system. So too did the workers, for real wages continued to rise as well as prices. The general reduction of taxes on food and the shortening of the length of the working day permitted unparalleled working-class progress. Such a balance of interests and a relative freedom from economic cares made it possible to avoid the political storms of the 1840s or the 1880s, when the interests of landlords clashed with those of manufacturers and when skilled as well as unskilled workers were goaded by 'knife-and-fork' questions into a state of angry revolt.

The second main influence was the sense of national security. Britain ruled the waves, and there was no real outside threat to England's naval supremacy or to the safety of the realm. It was even the boast of Lord Palmerston that 'as the Roman, in days of old, held himself free from indignity, when he could say *Civis Romanus sum*, so also a British subject, in whatever land he may be, shall feel confident that the watchful eye and the strong arm of England will protect him against injustice and wrong.'

Prosperity and security together encouraged a belief in the superiority of English representative institutions. They had withstood the revolutions of 1848, when even English prophets like Carlyle felt that 'their hour had struck', and they continued to stand firm when European countries were swinging from freedom to autocracy and when the United States of America was torn by civil war. Although there were no organic changes in the constitution, there was a movement of unremitting adaptation and reform carried out without violence in

A land of settled government,
A land of just and old renown,
Where Freedom broadens slowly down
From precedent to precedent.

This third influence – trust in institutions – was never seriously shaken. It was an indication of social stability that strong government was considered neither necessary nor desirable.

The fourth and fifth influences reconciled order and change. Belief in a common moral code, based on duty and self-restraint, was shared by most groups in society, including scientists, creative artists, and intellectuals. Institutions like the school, the voluntary organization, the trade union, and, above all, the family emphasized the maintenance of those values which held society together. Even those rebels who refused to accept Christianity demanded that men should be good for good's sake, not God's; and in practice it was difficult to tell the difference. At the same time there was belief in free discussion and inquiry. Men with conflicting points of view were prepared to debate their differences without wishing to exchange blows if they had the worst of the argument. As John Stuart Mill put it in his *Essay on Liberty* (1859):

It is only by the collision of adverse opinions that the remainder of the truth has any chance of being supplied. ... Truth, in the great practical concerns of life, is so much a question of the reconciling and combining of opposites, that very few have minds sufficiently capacious and impartial to make the adjustment with an approach to correctness, and it has to be made by the rough process of a struggle between combatants fighting under hostile banners.

It did not prove possible in the last quarter of the nineteenth century to maintain the balance of the period from 1851 to 1867; even in that period itself the balance was always changing and was never at any moment perfect. Although there was freedom from economic cares, there were years of economic crisis in 1857 and 1866, when there were many business bankruptcies and great working-class distress. Although there was no threat to English security, there were war scares in 1852 and 1859. Although there was a belief in the superiority of English representative institutions, at particulat moments, as in 1854 and 1855, they were more vigorously attacked than at any other period in the nineteenth century. Although there was a common moral code, it was often stretched at the edges or superficially maintained with the support of cant and hypocrisy. Although there was free discussion, the range of the discussion was limited, and many topics were deliberately left unexplored.

It is a mistake to make ambitious generalizations. The unity of the period is somewhat deceptive. The general prosperity did not save large sections of the population from social distress. According to Matthew Arnold, the untaxing of the poor man's bread resulted not only in cheaper food for the poor but in the creation of many more poor men to eat it. Machinery had added to national wealth, but it was continuing to produce 'a multitude of miserable, sunken, and ignorant human beings'. Certainly the convenient distinction between the respectable poor and the rest of the poor obscured any close examination

Introduction

of the origins of poverty. It covered social questions with a comfortable blanket of morality.

Free discussion was possible only because a relatively small number of people took part in it. The free interchange of ideas was for the few rather than for the many, and it was more often conducted in private than in public. Within the limits of debate there was more confrontation of opinions than reconciliation. As one of the first critics of the Victorians, G.W.E. Russell, put it in his *Collections and Recollections* in 1909: 'In all departments of life and thought the Cocksure seem to have possessed the earth . . . . Differing from one another in points neither unimportant nor few, they [the participants in debate] were at one in this – they were sure that they were right.' Russell exaggerated, for there were important elements of doubt in mid-Victorian England, but he did not falsify.

Even the stability of the period can be overemphasized. The instinct for violence and interest in violence remained. The first was satisfied by casual rowdyism, which reached its peak at election times, or by the Crimean adventure and distant struggles in the colonies; the second was satisfied vicariously by reading of crime and horrors, witnessing public executions, or surveying events in Europe. Two hundred and eighty thousand copies of the gruesome ballad written for the murderer Müller's execution were sold in 1864; no single event more powerfully affected the mind of that generation than the 'Indian Mutiny' in 1857.

A more serious threat to permanent stability was the growth of militant radicalism in the cities. There was always a great gulf between the industrial community and the small town or village – a gulf which it was difficult to bridge. 'Suppose you fell asleep tonight and woke up in 1860,' G. M. Young begins one of his essays. 'What is the first thing you would notice?' There is no single answer. It depends where you woke up. The crowds of the cities and the leaders who influenced them were preparing throughout the whole of the period for the great unleashing of popular power, which was made possible by the Reform Bill of 1867. When the urban working classes came into the open to clamour for reform, the intellectual arguments of Robert Lowe were powerless to prevent a complete change in the political balance. In the same way the mixture of reason and dogma which passed for political economy was incapable of explaining or controlling the economic blizzard after 1873. From that date onward, in the words of Robert Browning, it was 'never glad, confident morning again'.

2

A fair appreciation of the unity and form of this mid-Victorian period has only become possible in the middle years of the twentieth century. 'One thing is pretty certain, and in its way comforting,' wrote Leslie Stephen, 'that however far the rage for revivalism may be pushed, nobody will ever want to revive the nineteenth century.' The first historians of the present century echoed his judgement and went further by often succumbing to the temptation of staging a war of the ages. H. G. Wells, for instance, in *The New Machiavelli* (1911), described 'the Victorian epoch' as 'a hasty trial experiment, a gigantic experiment of the most slovenly and wasteful kind'. 'Will anyone, a hundred years from now, consent to live in the houses the Victorians built,' he asked, 'travel by their roads or railways, value the furnishings they made to live among or esteem, except for curious or historical reasons, their prevalent art and the clipped and limited literature that satisfied their souls?' Victorian people were 'restricted and undisciplined, overtaken by power, by possessions and great new freedoms, and unable to make any civilized use of them whatever.'

A very different twentieth-century historian, Lytton Strachey, in *Eminent Victorians* (1918), adopted 'a subtler strategy'. Attacking the Victorian age as a whole, he proceeded not by frontal assaults but by lightning operations in unexpected places – on the flanks or at the rear. The task of the historian of Victorian England was to 'shoot a sudden, revealing searchlight into obscure recesses, hitherto undivined. He will row out over that great ocean of material, and lower down into it, here and there, a little bucket, which will bring up to the light of day some characteristic specimen, from those far depths, to be examined with a careful curiosity.' The bucket was of elegant design, and the characteristic specimens were suitably nasty. Contemporaries were impressed. Strachey's brief and brilliant biographical sketches took the place of the fat Victorian official *Lives*, which he conveniently dismissed as part of the cortège of the undertaker, wearing the same air of 'slow, funereal barbarism'.

Wells and Strachey were men in revolt. They did not foresee, any more than Stephen, that the dusty Victorian biographies would be pulled down from the shelves, while Victorian bric-à-brac would be sold at exorbitant prices. They were so interested in dismissing the Victorian past that they forgot the twentieth-century future.

Interest in the nineteenth century has increased with the growing complexity and insecurity of the contemporary world. The publication of the capacious volumes of *Early Victorian England*, edited by G. M. Young in 1934, was a major landmark in historiography. Since then, the ideas and beliefs of the Victorians have been frequently revalued in an attempt – as a recent radio symposium put it – to shed 'light on matters which puzzle us today'. It has now become fashionable to turn back with nostalgia to the England of the Great Exhibition of 1851; and no one was surprised when a surviving Victorian, Algernon Cecil, claimed in 1953 that he could 'breathe more freely in the Victorian air' than in that of the twentieth century. 'In our own unpleasant century,' another writer, Basil Willey, has said, 'we are mostly displaced persons, and many feel tempted to take flight into the nineteenth as into a promised land, and settle there like illegal immigrants for the rest of their lives.'

Unfortunately, the meaning of the word 'Victorian' remains as vague when it is used by historians of escape as it was when used by historians of revolt. It is no more possible to embrace the whole of Victorian England than it was to battle against it. There was no single Victorian England, and there can be no easy return to the Exhibition of 1851 or to the Jubilee of 1887. The nineteenth century can be understood only when we realize that many of the roads back to it are blocked and that the historical landscape we hope to explore looks at first glance like a *terra incognita*. We can only understand Victorian England by examining particular segments of it, such as the segment discussed in this book. The real continuity of the nineteenth century begins to be apparent only when the unity of the individual periods within it is fully explored.

3

There are various ways of displaying the unity of a period. The greatest historian of mid-Victorian England, G. M. Young, thinks in terms of 'the generation'; his *Portrait of an Age* (published separately in 1936) depicts with brilliant impressionism the hopes and fears of each succeeding Victorian generation. His strongest point was that he never forgot that he was painting a moving picture and not a series of camera stills. 'The sequence of the generations,' he writes, 'is a continuous stream, so that everybody is a little older or younger than somebody else.' The debate between age groups in any period is as important as the debate between rich and poor or between Liberals and Conservatives. 'Culture is not a state but a process. ... The judgements of parents, nurses, governesses, pastors, and masters of all degrees, are, on the whole, the voice of society in equilibrium and bent on maintaining its equilibrium. The judgements of the younger generation are, on the whole, the voice of society dissident and exploratory.' Within each period the unity depends upon a balance; in mid-Victorian England the balance was so nicely adjusted that it permitted order and change. 'Of all decades in our history,' Young concludes, 'a wise man would choose the eighteen-fifties to be young in.'

Writing as foreign commentators, two other historians of the nineteenth century have adopted different techniques and styles. Professor W. W. Rostow, in his *British Economy of the Nineteenth Century* (1948), has divided Victorian England not into early, middle, and late but into 'trend periods' of rising and falling prices. To him, mid-Victorian England acquired its unity through the price rise, 'what is referred to, with some considerable ambiguity, as the great Victorian boom,' running from about 1850 to the financial crisis of 1873. Breaks within the period coincided with shifts in the volume and movement of capital exports and fluctuations in general business activity This analysis is stimulating and suggestive and throws new light on some of the dark corners of the period, but it is of very limited value to the social historian.

Élie Halévy, the most distinguished of all foreign historians of England, has found unity in continuity, in the persistence of the cluster of institutions and attitudes which together made up 'the moral and religious constitution' of England; but his magisterial six-volume study of the nineteenth century (*Histoire du peuple anglais au XIX*ᵉ *siècle* [1912–47]) stops short at the period covered in this book and is not resumed until 1895. By then, conditions had so changed from those of 1850 that he concluded: 'The period between 1895 and 1914 does not belong to the nineteenth century as I see it.' No modern historian can resist the temptation of trying to fill in the Halévy 'gap', for the explanation of the difference in mood between 1850 and 1895 lies in social structure and social adaptation in the middle years of the century.

The method I have adopted in this book is to try to discover the unity of society through a study of selected people who were alive and active in the 1850s and 1860s. In a sense they are 'specimens', as Strachey's characters were, but they are specimens which have not been chosen tendentiously. When Strachey wrote, Victorian people were usually regarded either as ridiculous or as natural targets for satire. Twenty years later they began to acquire a certain 'period charm'. Only today are they accepted as serious and interesting characters in their own right. 'We are coming to see,' as John Holloway has said in his book *The Victorian Sage* (1953), 'that for all their blindness and taboos, and for all their wildness and crudities too, the Victorians made a praiseworthy and fascinatingly interesting attempt to retain and reorganize and even deepen their culture, despite changes in knowledge, technique, and society which set them an impossibly difficult task.'

The people I have chosen are not unknown 'men in the

street' or forgotten personalities; they are men who made a distinctive contribution to the character of their times. Some of them were the best critics of their own age or chroniclers of its history; others were makers of social and cultural values or persuasive advocates of them; a third group were reformers who wished to speed up the processes of change. The selected men include a large majority of politicians, although many of the politicians chosen were only 'part-time' parliamentarians. While Roebuck, Bright, Lowe, and Disraeli were 'full-time' members of Parliament, Hughes, who sat there for several years, is better remembered as author of *Tom Brown's School Days*. It is significant, however, that such was the prestige attached to politics and administration in this period, despite the relative lack of spectacular incidents or issues, that even Trollope, the novelist, and Bagehot, the economist and editor, whom I have chosen for their significance as commentators rather than as actors, made unsuccessful attempts to enter the House of Commons.

The belief that to sit in Parliament should be the highest object and ambition of every educated Englishman has remained widespread and influential even in the twentieth century. The English higher educational system has been geared to this belief rather than to a belief in business success; so, too, have the traditional qualities of the 'gentleman'. The studies of individual people in this book are not designed as miniature biographies so much as explorations of the value judgements and preferences of mid-Victorian society.

The features of that society have considerable interest not only for specialist English historians but for students of society in general. Despite the prolonged business prosperity and the greatly increasing wealth of the businessman in the years 1851–67, England did not become a business society. A Quaker industrialist like John Bright was still cut off from many of the streams of national life; an apologist of occupational success like Samuel Smiles never succeeded in making the creed of self-help the unchallenged gospel of his age. The failure was crucial in the subsequent development of English society and politics. Resistance to the power of businessmen came from three different directions. The small gentry felt only a limited interest in wealth, and through institutions like public schools and universities taught their sons traditional codes of behaviour. The influence of the aristocracy, too, was great, as Bright and, even more eloquently, Cobden often complained. 'So vast is their traditional power,' wrote a shrewd observer, Benjamin Cracroft, in 1866, 'so broadly does it sit over the land, so deep and ancient are its roots, so multiplied and ramified everywhere are its tendrils, and creepers and feelers, that the danger is never lest they shall have too little, but always lest they should have too much power, and so, even involuntarily, choke down the possibilities of new life from below.'

The new civil servant, who usually came from the public school and the university, was expected to be a 'gentleman', just as was the owner of a landed estate. The result, in Young's phrase, was that 'the sudden access of power, prosperity, and knowledge' was confronted in the new civil service by 'a solidly grounded code of duty and self-restraint'.

Finally, the world of labour was unwilling, even in a period when revolutionary or theoretical socialism had little appeal, to accept the attitudes of businessmen or to place individual mobility above class solidarity. The new model trade unions, such as the Amalgamated Society of Engineers, founded in 1851, consisted of skilled artisans who might have been expected to accommodate themselves to a competitive economic system rather than to challenge it. That they did not and instead secured essential trade-union rights of organization and action made far easier the rise of unskilled labour twenty years later.

There was a fourth reason why England did not become a business society, perhaps the most interesting reason of all. The businessmen themselves showed only a limited interest in the values by which they had risen. Many of them were deferential rather than rebellious, snobbish rather than independent, and usually tempered by what Gladstone described as 'a sneaking kindness for a Lord'. The moment quietly arrived in private histories when a new family became an old one and when its members basked in the branches of family trees and forgot that there had been ladders to climb on the way. Self-help was a more convenient philosophy for first than for second generations. If it was not easy for a successful businessman to become a 'gentleman' in his own lifetime, he could have reasonable hopes that his children, educated in the new public schools and marrying sons or daughters of the gentry, would eventually become 'ladies' and 'gentlemen'. He could spend his declining years, if he so wished, 'in hunting up genealogies' and spreading his wings 'for sublime apotheosis among the county families'.

It is a gross understatement to describe mid-Victorian society as undemocratic; it prided itself not on its equality but on its balance, on its nuances of social status, on its varied but converging ideals, and on its inherent superiority to other societies on the continent of Europe or across the Atlantic. Nor was it troubled about its permanence. 'Suppose all our parishioners were put on a level in the scale of society today,' wrote one pamphleteer in 1852, 'before this day twelve months there would be an aristocracy among them, "a nobility without heraldry".' 'Make all men equal today,' wrote Trollope, 'and God has so created them that they shall be unequal tomorrow.' The mid-Victorians still called God into the reckoning whenever they needed Him. It was not only the family which was a 'sacred institution'. Thousands of sermons of every denomination proclaimed that the whole English social system rested not only on divine sanction but on the particular operations of Providence. Sunday school scholars were told to thank God for the 'goodness and the grace' bestowed upon them when He made them 'happy English children'.

My studies in this book are designed to illuminate the nature of mid-Victorian society as it seemed to contemporaries. Each chapter is a separate study, but the chapters are designed to be read consecutively and as a whole. Subsidiary themes play their part – the effects of the Crimean War, for instance, on the climate of opinion and on the contemporary assessment of England's place in the world, and the role of religion in society – although to explore this last theme fully would require a book of equal length to the present volume.

There are inevitable omissions. Although I have said much

about schools, I would like to have said more about relations between young and old. The Victorian maxim, 'Little children should be seen and not heard', was a necessary counsel of prudence in an age when the average Victorian family in 1860 had either five or six children. I should like also to have said more about relations between the sexes and to have included at least one woman in the collection of studies, for women – often 'maiden aunts' – played a leading part not only in family welfare but in the making of Victorian social policy and the practical application of an ideal of service. A community devoted to getting on, and limited at its edges by masculine codes of inherited authority or formalized professionalism, had little to offer women of spirit and ability. Exceptional women like Florence Nightingale, who rejected marriage for service – because marriage did not provide for the promptings of 'a moral, an active nature, which requires satisfaction' – played a really prominent part in the foreground of national life. But many other women, including married women who reacted against the formality and superficiality of subordinate status, were central figures in local life. The place that Florence Nightingale would take in this collection of studies would be very different from that which she takes in Lytton Strachey's; her life has, however, recently been reassessed at length by Cecil Woodham-Smith in one of the best of modern nineteenth-century biographies. No other woman was sufficiently central to the theme of my book, although on a very different plane Lady Palmerston contributed considerably to the size of her husband's majorities in the House of Commons by a judicious distribution of her visiting cards.

4

People are the subject of my book, but it begins with a chapter not on a man but on a year, 1851, and ends with a chapter which is concerned as much with a year, 1867, as with the man who dominated it, Disraeli. The year 1851 is an obvious point to start. It was a year of such excitement that many young Victorians looked back on it with nostalgia for the rest of their lives, and many old Georgians regarded it as the climax of English history. The symbol of the Crystal Palace, built for the Great Exhibition of 1851, dominates the whole period from 1851 to 1867. The building itself seemed so frail that many people were sure that the first hailstorm would shatter it. Instead it was moved from Hyde Park to Sydenham in 1854 and lasted for eighty-five years, until a fire destroyed it on an autumn night in 1936. Its destruction severed one of the most interesting visible links of continuity with the mid-Victorian period: 'It was like watching the burning of a Victorian Valhalla when the gods of our fathers sat in a solemn circle awaiting the end.'

I close my book with an account of the last year of my period – 1867. There was an international exhibition in 1867, too, but it was in Paris, not in London; and in England all the excitement was reserved for the spectacle of the 'leap in the dark' – the granting of the vote to all urban artisans. 'The end of our poor old England', Carlyle called it, and even its supporters admitted that they were taking a very risky gamble. After 1867 the pieces of the mid-century jigsaw puzzle separate out again, and the picture disappears. Within ten years the whole intricate pattern had completely changed.

The people themselves were changing too. Cobden and Palmerston died in 1865; so did Paxton, the Chatsworth gardener who had designed the Crystal Palace. By the end of 1870, Derby and Dickens were also dead; Rossetti had published his first book of poems, and Dilke his first book of politics; Joseph Chamberlain had secured a place on the Birmingham Town Council; and Forster had introduced the first comprehensive scheme for national education. *Tempora mutantur nos et mutamur in illis.* And for some the Victorian age was only just beginning.

CHAPTER TWO

The Crystal Palace and the Men of 1851

These twenty years – how full of gain to us,
  To common humble multitudinous Man;
How swiftly Providence advances thus
  Our flag of progress flaming in the van!
  This double decade of the world's short span
Is richer than two centuries of old:
  Richer in helps, advantages, and pleasures,
In all things richer – even down to gold –
  To all of every class in liberal measures:
We travel quicker now than Isthmians might;
  In books we quaff the veriest Hebe's chalice;
All wonders of the world gladden the sight
  In that world's wonder-house the Crystal Palace;
And everywhere is Might enslaved to Right.

MARTIN TUPPER

I

The year 1851 provides a perfect vantage-point for a survey of nineteenth-century England. The century was half-gone and contemporaries could look back across the 'hungry forties' to the antediluvian world before the railway and the penny post; before steam power, in George Eliot's phrase, had 'driven on every wheel double pace, and the wheel of fortune along with 'em'. They could look forward, too, to long years of progress, to the further expansion of production, and to the further development of distribution – to what satirists contemptuously called 'the cotton millennium'.

An opportunity was given for such an appraisal by the Great Exhibition of 1851, which dominated the year. Its purpose was 'to present a true test and living picture of the point of development at which the whole of mankind has arrived ... and a new starting-point, from which all nations will be able to direct their further exertions.' In its impressive building and in the wide range of exhibits it offered on display, the Crystal Palace proclaimed triumphantly the visibility of human progress. As Henry Cole, one of its leading sponsors, said,

The history of the world records no event comparable, in its promotion of human industry, with that of the Great Exhibition of the Works of Industry of all Nations in 1851. A great people invited all civilized nations to a festival, to bring into comparison the works of human skill. It was carried out by its own private means; was self-supporting and independent of taxes and employment of slaves, which great works had exacted in ancient days. A prince of pre-eminent wisdom, of philosophic mind, sagacity, with power of generalship and great practical ability, placed himself at the head of the enterprise, and led it to triumphant success.

Yet, although the Exhibition was an outstanding success and the pride which it generated was real and lasting, the year 1851 itself was dominated by contrasts and frustration. Economic prosperity and commercial mastery were accompanied by political uncertainty and ministerial instability. At the beginning of the year it was generally expected – and hoped – that Lord John Russell's Whig administration, which had been in power since 1847 but was known to be weak and tending to decline still further, would remain quietly in office throughout a season of carnival. The ministry did not survive peacefully even until the opening of the Exhibition on the first of May. It faced a crisis in February; and, although after a great deal of political coming and going it returned to office intact, its position was extremely precarious and remained so throughout the year. After the dismissal in December of the Foreign Secretary, Lord Palmerston, the way was prepared for its final breakup in 1852.

The Queen and the Prince Consort, more than any other persons in the country, felt both the full thrill of the Exhibition and the strain and inconvenience of ministerial instability. Prince Albert had worked unceasingly to make the Exhibition a success. He had continued his labours indefatigably after the sudden and tragic death of Peel, the most influential political supporter of the idea. Yet in early 1851, when all the preparations were ready, ministerial crisis darkened the sky. 'Altogether it is very vexatious,' wrote the Queen, 'and will give us trouble. It is the more provoking, as this country is so very prosperous.' The same provoking contrast between economic prosperity and political fragmentation was to persist for a large portion of the middle years of the century, and the Queen and Prince Albert came to see quite clearly that the state of the country and the state of the parties were two quite distinct questions.

By the end of 1851 one of the causes of political instability had apparently been removed. Increasing prosperity was influencing the recalcitrant protectionists unobtrusively to drop some of their anti-free-trade slogans of 1846, the year of the repeal of the Corn Laws. Their gradual retreat took the strife out of politics, but it did not come soon enough to provide peace of mind for the royal family in the early months of the year. When Lord Derby told the Queen, in June 1852, that he considered protection 'quite gone', she wrote somewhat wearily that it was a pity he had not found this out a little sooner. 'It would have saved so much annoyance, so much difficulty.'

The annoyance and the difficulty were not entirely the fault of the protectionists, although they had been specially awkward not only about free trade but also about the Exhibition, which some of them condemned as 'the greatest imposition ever palmed upon the people of England'. The year 1851 was one of general pride and prejudice. The continued alarm about papal aggression caused by the Pope's restoration of Roman Catholic dioceses in 1850 roused public opinion to fever pitch and made ministerial politics extremely difficult. Militant Protestantism was stirred to popular action. 'Parties were a good deal confused before thanks to Corn,' wrote Cobden, 'but the Catholic element has made confusion worse confounded.' In his view, that of a small minority, it was unfortunate that England itself, in its violent denunciation of the Pope, should be exhibited in the year of the Exhibition 'as the most intolerant people on earth,' so that 'Europe cries shame on us, and America laughs at us.' The view of the majority was that, in both the Exhibition and the religious crisis, national honour was deeply involved and had to be vindicated.

The Exhibition, the political crisis, the religious hysteria, the commercial supremacy – all contributed to the temper of 1851. Behind the pride and prejudice there were doubts and dilemmas. How could an Englishman welcome crowds of foreigners – most probably Papists – who had come to London to see the Exhibition, while at the same time he thundered out against papal aggression? *Punch* depicted an old Tory who knew one possible answer. He was shown hanging an Exhibition notice outside his house, bearing the words, '*Ici on ne parle pas français.*' Once the Exhibition was over, how could its message of peace and international cooperation be reconciled with the news of Napoleon III's *coup d'état* just across the channel and the knowledge of the alarming 'defenceless state of Great Britain', to which Sir Francis Head had drawn attention only the year before?

Such doubts and dilemmas were as important as the assurance and self-confidence of the men of 1851. The Crystal Palace was no abiding city. The year 1851 was a good vantage-point to take stock of the progress of half a century, but the future was by no means so clear as it seemed at first glance. All that was certain when the survey was complete was, to use a favourite railway metaphor, that the great world was moving for ever 'down the ringing grooves of change'. On pausing to take stock, there were innumerable difficulties in making a final calculation. One might agree with the *Eclectic Review* that 'the year 1851, when compared with the year 1801, is as the Palace of Glass when compared with the houses built under the régime of the window duty,' but one would realize that it all depended upon the choice of time scale. Tennyson's *In Memoriam*, a best-seller for the crowds which attended the Exhibition, was as representative of the times as the glass house of the Great Exhibition itself, but it did not talk, as his *Locksley Hall* had done, of the visible triumphs of industrialization and improvement; it spoke, instead, of vast dimensions of time and space:

> The sound of streams that swift or slow
> Draw down Aeonian hills, and sow
> The dust of continents to be.

2

From a material point of view there were good grounds for optimism.

The statistics of material progress underlined the strength of Britain's industrial position. The Exhibition showed to advantage the nation's undisputed leadership in manufacturing. Its steam engines were the symbols of economic mastery:

> These England's arms of conquest are,
> The trophies of her bloodless war.

Lancashire manufacturers were prepared to welcome exhibits from all countries and to demand 'a clear stage and no favour' because they were in no way afraid of a comparison of British products with those of foreigners. In commerce and finance British supremacy was even more marked.

Yet the merchants, manufacturers, and skilled artisans were only a minority of the population. Despite spectacular signs of progress in trade and industry, over a quarter of the male population of the country was still engaged in agricultural pursuits, and one in nine of all females over ten was employed in domestic service. More men were employed as shoemakers than as coal-miners, and there were only just over a quarter of a million professional workers of all types.

Amid the broad ranks of 'the middle classes', independent small men were the dominant group, not only in retailing, but in commerce and manufacturing. The virtues they prized were those to be acclaimed by Samuel Smiles – self-help, perseverance, duty, thrift, and character. They conceived of self-dependence not only as a ladder to individual success but as the mainspring of social improvement. All men could profit from it.

These values were being taught to other groups in society

not without success. With the relaxation of the tension of the forties and the abandonment of some of the wild projects and dazzling utopias of a long period of conflict, some of the working classes, particularly the 'aristocracy of labour', were reaching up to grasp middle-class virtues. The year 1851 saw the founding, for example, of the Amalgamated Society of Engineers, which claimed that its object was to do nothing 'illegally or indiscreetly, but on all occasions to perform the greatest amount of benefit for ourselves, without injury to others. . . . It is our duty to exercise the same control over that in which we have a vested interest as the physician who holds his diploma or the author who is protected by his copyright.' As the working classes were looking up, some, at least, of the upper classes were looking down. Middle-class ideals set standards for the nation, and, while the aristocracy 'were beginning to live in fear of the grocer and the merchant,' the Queen and the Prince Consort were providing a golden model of respectable and happy family life. South Kensington, the new part of London developed as a result of the Exhibition, was far more congenial to Prince Albert than Ascot or Brighton.

Along with the spread of middle-class values went a rise in middle-class comfort. Austerity did not disappear – in some fields of action it was prized as a virtue – but John Store Smith's *Social Aspects*, a new book in 1851, noted how 'the middle-class family now possesses carpets and hangings, which would have excited great wonderment even at so recent a period as the American War, and not a few of our London middle-class tradesmen possess a better stock of family plate and linen than many a country squire, even of the last generation.' George R. Porter's 1851 edition of *The Progress of the Nation* painted the same picture of the prosperous middle-class household, the walls of their villas covered with paintings and engravings, and the whole setting 'full of evidences that some among the inmates cultivate one or more of those elegant accomplishments which tend so delightfully to enlighten the minds of individuals and sweeten the intercourse of families.'

While the industrial and commercial middle classes were

enjoying prosperity, in the spring of 1851 the landlords and farmers were still disgruntled. Agriculture seemed in the doldrums, and, although it provided employment for a very large proportion of the nation, it was no longer universally considered the backbone of national prosperity. Early in 1851 the division of interest between landlords and manufacturers – the Tory Disraeli's 'unhappy quarrel between town and country' and the Radical Roebuck's 'master-key' to British history since 1832 – was the most important source of conflict within the political arena. A motion by Disraeli in February 1851 which would have produced government action to alleviate agricultural distress was defeated by only fourteen votes, and disgruntled farmers in East Anglia were saying that they would rather march on Manchester, the capital of free trade, than on Paris. In May the protectionists held a giant rally in Drury Lane, where they copied 'the arts and violence of the agitators' which they had so much deplored.

Their economic power was extremely limited. The balance of forces was such that there could be no easy return to any form of agricultural protection. By 1851 one quarter of the people's bread was foreign. These immense imports of foreign grain and flour were consumed, as the free-trader Sir James Graham did not fail to point out, 'by millions of mouths that otherwise would not have been fed.... Though Peel is dead, he still speaks, and from the tomb I hear the echo of his voice.' Wise Tories could not ignore these figures, and clever politicians could not afford to overlook one essential element in all political calculations – the strength of what had become over the previous five years a free-trade tradition. It was clear that, if the protectionists came back into office determined to reverse the decisions of 1846, the threat of a new agitation outside Parliament, on the lines of the Anti-Corn Law League, would produce vigorous and ultimately successful reaction. The North of England was still on the alert. As the *Manchester Guardian* put it, 'The moral effect of Free Trade supplies a theme which years of agitation have not stayed, nor the eloquence of Mr Cobden exhausted.'

By the end of 1851, after a good harvest, there were unmistakable signs of that agricultural revival which was to persist throughout the middle of the century; protection seemed less and less necessary. Granby, a prominent Tory leader, visited Hughenden in November, staying just long enough, Disraeli wrote, to have time to ask the village butcher whether any land had gone out of cultivation in the neighbourhood. 'The astonishment of Redrup, who had just sold his barley for 30s. a quarter, may be conceived.' It was not only Disraeli and his friends who were beginning to think that protection was dead. A little later even the ultra-Tory *Quarterly Review* wrote that 'the prospects of British agriculturalists are not of a nature to lead to despondency' and explained with largeness of gesture that protectionism did not mean protection of landlords but protection of the interests of the poor, of the labour of young people, and of the Christian character of the state.

The year 1851 was a critical one in the reshaping of British agricultural prospects. It ushered in a period of agricultural prosperity largely dependent upon the opening-up of the railway system and the increase in incomes generated by industry. Industry indeed boosted agriculture; the middle years of the century were to be years of prosperity for both farmers and businessmen.

Contemporaries in 1851 saw the new gold discoveries in California and Australia as the cause of the rise in prices and the boom in the economy as a basic force giving, in the words of *The Times*, 'an electric impulse to our entire business world'. While the crowds at the Exhibition admired a piece of gold from California, at the other end of the Empire, in Australia, the gold rush was 'drawing even clergymen to the exciting scene' – nor, as one commentator said, 'did they confine themselves in every case to their calling.' In excited anticipation of a new period in history, Ashley wrote in his diary that California had led the way and Australia followed. '*Auri sacra fames*. What no motive, human or divine, could effect, springs into life at the display of a few pellets of gold in the hands of a wanderer. This may be God's chosen way to fulfil his commandment and "replenish the earth".'

In the period after 1851 many people thought that they

caught a glimpse of the Promised Land. Certainly much of the
tension disappeared from the relations between both landlords
and captains of industry and between masters and men. The
way was prepared for a balance of interests, for what Professor
W. L. Burn has called 'the age of equipoise'.

The fiction of the day reflected the change as much as the
politics. There was a significant shift in writing from 'novels in
which the basic structure of society was discussed in terms of
bitter satire and deep passion to those in which personal problems were discussed against the background of a society whose
structure was assumed to be sufficiently stable.' There was a
new tendency to introspection, to 'the dialogue of mind with
itself', rather than a preoccupation with 'the condition of
England' question, which had been the great social issue of the
forties.

In such conditions the big issues of politics withered away –
not only questions of the Corn Laws or protection, but also
questions of parliamentary reform and the granting of the vote
to the working classes. Abortive skirmishes between pressure groups absorbed more energy than struggles concerning
large measures of constitutional or social change. There were
squalid intrigues, for example, between the vested interests of
private water companies and the General Board of Health, and
battles in Parliament about the incidence of taxation on different sections of the community. Income tax, standing at seven
pence in the pound, was considered 'inquisitorial' and 'bur-
densome', and, when the Chancellor of the Exchequer Wood
tried to introduce a new tax on houses in place of the hated
window tax which he managed to abolish, his proposal was defeated by a conjunction of some of his own supporters with his
enemies. The men who defeated the government were neither
fiery extremists nor Manchester men wedded to the creed of
Cobden and Bright. They were, as the *Daily News* remarked,
'the quiet, steady representatives of mercantile communities,
who are, in general, chary of extremes.' They were the men
who were to count most in the period after 1851 – men frightened of taxation and suspicious of government. As trade remained buoyant and agriculture improved, they felt that they

could rely upon themselves to secure what they wanted far more than upon politicians.

There was in consequence an underlying distrust of government, which continued to determine the shape of politics until after the passing of the second Reform Bill in 1867. Self-help came first; government, except as an agency for dealing with foreign relations and for facilitating self-help, came very low on the list of daily preoccupations.

3

It certainly came below religion. Religious questions shared the headlines with news of the Exhibition throughout the first half of 1851. There was a sustained religious crisis – as it was called by contemporaries – which began with Wiseman's announcement, 'given out of the Flaminian Gate of Rome' in 1850, of the papal decision to divide England into Roman Catholic dioceses and restore a regular Catholic hierarchy. Russell, the Prime Minister and 'historic champion of religious liberty', made himself the spokesman of indignant Protestant exasperation. The noise and excitement of the public reaction to the Pope's decision surprised even the Evangelical Ashley, who had long foreseen a religious crisis of this type. 'What a surprising ferment!' he wrote. 'It abates not a jot; meeting after meeting in every town and parish of the country.... It resembles a storm over the whole ocean; it is a national sentiment, a rising of the land! All opinions seem for a while submerged in this one feeling.' Other less partisan observers remarked that there had been no similar popular outcry since the brief period in 1831 and 1832, when the first Reform Bill was considered to be in danger, and that in 1851, as then, the middle classes, 'those who were usually the calmest and more reflecting section of the community', were at the heart of the movement.

The flames were fanned by those who pointed not to the external but to the internal danger – the threat, from within the Church of England itself, of traitors attempting 'to lead their flocks step by step to the verge of the precipice' of Rome and of ritualists like William Bennett, forced from St Paul's, Knightsbridge, in 1851 to an obscure and quiet living in Somerset. The influence of the Catholic revival was in full swing, and many clergymen of the Church of England seemed to be assisting it. *The Times* warned against 'the terrible danger of the renegades of our national Church' restoring 'a foreign usurpation over the consciences of men to sow dissension within our political society.' Even while Parliament was debating legislation against papal aggression, Archdeacon Manning, one of the leading figures among the younger Anglican clergy, was moving over from the Church of England to the Church of Rome. 'Lord, purge the Church of those men,' wrote Ashley in his diary, 'who while their hearts are in the Vatican, still eat the bread of the Establishment and undermine her.' Gladstone himself told a friend much later in his life that, when the news of Manning's conversion reached him, it seemed like an act of personal injury. 'I felt,' Gladstone said, 'as if Manning had murdered my mother by mistake.'

Russell realized the strength of the Protestant cry in the country and in February 1851 introduced his Ecclesiastical Titles Bill in an effort to curb papal claims by legislation. In its original shape it forbade the assumption of any episcopal or territorial title without the authority of Parliament and the circulation inside England of papal bulls. Strong though the bill was, it was too mild to satisfy militant Protestant feeling inside as well as outside the House of Commons. But at the same time the very idea of legislation on this topic alienated the Catholic Irish group in Parliament, on whose votes the fate of the Whig ministry depended. Irish members were lobbied by their constituents against the measure just as strongly and strenuously as were English members in its favour. The member for Cork, for instance, described how his constituents, 'who were as calm as a summer sea when compared with the excited inhabitants of other parts,' had passed a resolution calling upon him to vote against the Whig government on every occasion, no matter what the principle involved. Such congenial advice was willingly accepted by most of the 'Pope's Irish Brass Band', who found a leader for the occasion in 'the pocket O'Connell',

John Sadleir. It was the loss of Irish support which was the most important factor weakening the Whig government in 1851. Russell found himself in an impossible parliamentary situation; nor could any other leader have done better, for, as Cobden wrote, 'any government that perseveres in the anti-Papal policy will be opposed by the Irish members on every subject, and if an Administration were to come in to do nothing against the Pope, they would, I suppose, be turned out by the English. So that we are in a rather considerable fix.'

The Ecclesiastical Titles Bill was indirectly responsible – through the defection of the Irish – for the defeat of the government and the ministerial crisis. It also prevented the Whigs, during and after the crisis, from coming to terms with the Peelites, the group of anti-protectionist conservatives who remained loyal to the principles of Sir Robert Peel after his death in 1850. There could be no broad coalition, for both the Peelites and some of the Radicals, particularly John Bright and J. A. Roebuck, were resolutely opposed to legislation concerning ecclesiastical titles. If the Peelite *Morning Chronicle* had been the property of Cardinal Wiseman himself, wrote one Protestant, it could not have advocated his cause more thoroughly or with more apparent zeal. The Peelites gave as their main reason for not joining a coalition their opposition to new legislation on the Catholic question. 'Who could now assert that the Pope has no power in England?' asked Ashley. 'He has put out one Administration and now prevents the formation of another.'

When the Whig ministry returned unchanged after its political crisis in February, Russell shortened and modified the Ecclesiastical Titles Bill, leaving it, as Sir Robert Inglis said, rather like the play of *Hamlet* with the part of Hamlet left out. The second reading of the measure, in its mutilated form, was carried by the enormous majority of 438 to 95, but in committee it met with many vicissitudes. With the Irish contingent 'significantly and ostentatiously abstaining' from speaking and voting, the Protestants succeeded in carrying extreme amendments against the government. Frederick Thesiger, the Protestant leader, whose arguments were described by his opponent

Gladstone as 'formidable indeed', proved himself a more effective tactician than Russell. The bill, as amended by the Protestants, was finally carried by 263 votes to 46.

There were spirited protests from the Peelites and a handful of Radicals. Gladstone made the most telling speech against it. He said that, while he had disliked 'the vaunting and boastful character' of the papal pronouncements, he disliked the bill even more. It was hostile to the institutions of the country on four counts. It would teach the established religion to rely on other support than that of its own spiritual strength and vitality which alone could give it vigour. It would undermine and weaken the authority of the law in Ireland. It would disparage 'the great principle of religious freedom upon which this wise and understanding people had permanently built its legislation'. Finally, 'it would destroy the bonds of concord and good will which ought to unite all classes and persuasions of Her Majesty's subjects'. Another member, Grattan, went further and suggested that the title of the measure should be amended to read: 'A Bill To Prevent the Free Exercise of the Roman Catholic Religion in the United Kingdom'.

These opposition opinions were far from representative of feelings outside Parliament. Most people in the country would have agreed with Lord Winchilsea that the bill did not go far enough and merely attempted to vindicate 'the wounded honour of our illustrious Queen' in pounds, shillings, and pence. Although the Queen herself regretted 'the un-Christian and intolerant spirit' abroad in the land and 'the violent abuse of the Catholic religion', there was little she could do to damp it down. Even a large number of nonconformists, who disliked the Establishment as much as they disliked the papacy, and stressed the 'Dissidence of Dissent' alongside 'the Protestantism of the Protestant Churches', proclaimed themselves Englishmen first and attacked the idea of a foreign potentate – 'be he Pope or King – assuming to divide our kingdom according to his pleasure.' Charlotte Brontë complained that, with the arrival of Cardinal Wiseman in England, 'London will not be where it was, nor will this day or generation be either *what* or *where* they were. A new Joshua will command the sun not merely to stand still, but to go back six centuries.' The panic persisted. In less oracular vein Scholefield, one of the members of Parliament for Birmingham, claimed that cells were being built in Newman's seminary 'for the forcible detention of some of Her Majesty's subjects'. He was not convinced when Newman replied that the 'cells' consisted merely of a larder and a kitchen.

The manifestations of hysteria were probably shared by many who were not troubled at all by profound religious convictions. Indeed, the *Ecclesiastic*, a magazine favouring Catholic tendencies within the Church of England, warned the Evangelicals that their alliance with the 'godless crowds' of the large towns could at best offer only a temporary source of strength and that before very long anti-Catholicism might turn into anti-Christianity. Certainly, even in 1851, despite the excesses of religious enthusiasm, there was a submerged mass of religious apathy and indifference. The religious census of 1851, which presented statistics of the numbers of people attending churches and chapels on a random Sunday, 30 March, showed that more than half the population had not been to a church or chapel at all and that only twenty per cent had attended an Anglican service. Furthermore, what was more serious, had they wished to go, there was seating in the churches and chapels for only 58 per cent of the population – in Birmingham for only 28.7 per cent of the population and in London for 29.7 per cent. However easy it might be in a wave of national emotion to justify England to the Pope, it was more difficult, in Charles Kingsley's phrase, 'to justify God to the people'.

The blackest areas were the working-class districts of the large cities, where there were large groups of people scarcely touched by Christian influence at all. These were the people outside the pale of both church and constitution, with few opportunities to become either members of the *pays légal* or sons of the church. They had been offered cheap food in 1846 and little else; and it was left to the *Eclectic Review*, a nonconformist journal, to point out there was no necessary connexion between the repeal of the Corn Laws and a religious revival. Indeed, in a rapidly changing world, politics and religion might pull in opposite directions. Kingsley's novel, *Alton Locke*, published in 1850, was raising these and similar questions. 'It is the book of an age,' wrote one reviewer; 'it is a kind of concrete thrown up from the vast cauldron of civilization, in which luxury and filth, brutality and art, virtue and intellect, tyranny and wretchedness seethe tumultuously together.'

4

It was against such a background of light and shade that the ministerial crisis of February and the Great Exhibition stand out. The first was an affair of private meetings and secret conferences; the second, a festival of crowds, bustle, and publicity.

But the ministerial crisis does not make sense if it is left entirely unrelated to the general national background. It was reaction to the budget which made the government tremble; it was the Ecclesiastical Titles Bill growing out of the national religious panic which robbed Russell of essential Irish support. It was parliamentary reform, the threat to the balance of the whole constitutional structure, which, in Lansdowne's phrase, provided 'the last drop which made the cup flow over'.

On 20 February the government was defeated on a Radical motion, which proposed that the conditions of franchise should be the same in the counties as in the boroughs. This 'simple, moderate, and practical plan' was suggested merely as the prelude to a great and comprehensive measure by Russell himself. The mover of the motion claimed that it would crown the victory of 1846 by finally destroying the political bastions of protectionist privilege in the countryside. And was not protectionism still a dangerous threat to society, 'akin to communism in its worst shape, for Protection might be regarded as the few taking from the many, and communism as the taking from all'?

Russell attacked the proposal. Simple it might profess to be, but in reality it was opposed to the spirit of the 1832 Reform Bill, on which all reform of the franchise should be based. Conditions of the suffrage in town and country had been deliberately left different. 'We should not attempt to construct a new and fanciful edifice, but endeavour to add to the symmetry and convenience of the old.' He pledged himself, however, to bring in a reform bill of his own during the next session, if he were still in office. The Radicals, who normally supported the Whig Russell, paid little attention to such a promise and divided the House. Most of the Irish and protectionists stayed away, and the government was defeated by 100 votes to 54. According to Lord Stanley, the leader of the Tories (who succeeded his father as the fourteenth Earl of Derby later in the year), the minority consisted of 17 protectionists, 27 'official men', tied to the government in various ways, and only 10 'independent' Whig members.

There was general surprise in the House of Commons when Russell chose to resign on this defeat. 'Not a creature in or out of the House,' wrote Greville, 'expected he would regard such a defeat as this as a matter of any importance.' The ministers themselves were divided about the propriety of going out of office. The Queen, however, understood the cause and sympathized.

Though it was not a question *vital* to the Government, Lord John feels the support he has received so meagre, and the opposition of so many parties so great, that he must *resign*! This is very bad, because there is no chance of any other good Government, poor Peel being no longer alive … but Lord John is *right* not to go on when he is so ill-supported, and it will raise him as a political man, and will strengthen his position for the future.

The position of a Whig prime minister was, had been, and was yet to be an extremely difficult one; and this particular crisis was symptomatic of a chronic weakness in the mid-Victorian structure of politics. For this it deserves close attention. The Tory *Quarterly Review* offered a shrewd, if one-sided, analysis of the problem. In the first place, a Whig prime minister always faced the dilemma of being at one and the same time the leader of a 'movement and agitation party' and the head of a government, 'the essence of all government being restraint and resistance'. Apart from the extreme Radical tail, which normally but not always supported the Whigs, there were many 'Independent members' among the Whigs who were unwilling to support the government in all circumstances merely because it was a Whig government. They might be won over by patronage, as they were won over later by Lady Palmerston's visiting cards, but patronage could not at this time meet all the demands made upon it. From 1846 onward, Russell had governed precariously 'from hand to mouth – that is, by what the Treasury *hand* puts into the *mouth* of the hungry member.'

Where patronage could not be offered or would not work, temporary expedients were constantly necessary. From the Reform Bill of 1832 onward Irish support had been essential for Whig power; so too had been the intermittent support of the mixed group of Radicals. As a result of constant recourse to such expedients,

what was called *governing* the country came to be nothing else than the art of keeping this heterogeneous and discordant body together and in any kind of discipline – which could only be accomplished by a constant subterraneous traffic of patronage with private jobbers, and by frequent sacrifices of Church and Constitution to Dissenters and Radicals. This was the real difficulty of the case and the cause of every Ministerial crisis.

The condition was a chronic one and could not be attributed to any single individual or to any particular sequence of events. It was to produce further crises in 1852.

Russell's resignation in February 1851 led to several days of hectic excitement. 'Such was the confusion of the Ministerial movements, and political promenades,' wrote *Punch*, 'that everybody went to call upon everybody. The hall porters were never known to have had such a time of it, but though knocking at doors continued throughout the whole day, nothing seemed to answer.'

The Tories were unable to form a ministry of their own. However right the *Quarterly Review* was in its thesis on Whig weakness, there was no doubt at all about the even weaker position of the Tories. They were not only a minority in Parliament; they were clearly a minority in the country. The Whigs could claim on their side two great advantages: experience of office – the knowledge that they could form a government of seasoned ministers – and the slogans of free trade and progress which kept them aligned with 'the spirit of the age'. When free trade was threatened from outside, they knew that they could not only close their own ranks but also widen the basis of their support. 'Upon the first proposition of a Stanley Government,' Aberdeen and Graham, the Peelite leaders, told the Queen, 'the junction of the Parties would be contemplated, and there would be only *one* strong Opposition.' The cry of 'Free Trade in Peril' would rouse the country and make the work of a protectionist government impossible. 'I am *l'homme impossible*,' the Tory Stanley told Russell when the crisis was over.

If the continued identification of the Tories with protection handicapped them in the eyes of the outside world, their lack of experience and their differences of opinion about tactics led to division and paralysis in their inner councils. With the notable exception of Disraeli, they were neither prepared for nor willing to accept the responsibilities of office. 'It was by no act of mine or one of my friends that the late Government fell,' Stanley told the House of Lords. 'I felt no exultation at the event, and I felt no undue anxiety to seize the offices they had held.' He begged the Queen, indeed, that 'he might not be called upon to take office except as a *dernier ressort*.'

The Tories could not form a ministry; the position of the other major political group, the Peelites, was a different one. They were richly endowed with administrative experience, but by themselves they were impotent; nor at this time did they feel disposed to join in a coalition with the Whigs. In the negotiations with Russell they raised so many issues besides the Ecclesiastical Titles Bill that it seemed as if some of them 'did not wish to complete any combination'. They were unwilling to reach any understanding with Stanley and the Tories, for, apart from the shadow of Peel and the barrier of free trade, they felt that the Crown and the country were only safe, 'in these days, by having the Liberals in office, else they would be driven to join the Radical agitation against the institutions of the country.' Throughout the crisis, however, they talked of the possibility of joining the Whigs at some unknown date in the future on terms favourable to themselves. They were in fact waiting for another and bigger crisis, for, as the

Quarterly Review remarked, 'coalitions of this [Whig–Peelite] nature are reluctantly taken in cold blood. They are taken out of a *mêlée* rather than a *pas seul* or a *pas de deux*.'

The Queen tried all possible existing combinations. She was not in favour of a dissolution of the House of Commons and a new general election as a means of breaking the political deadlock and refused to give Stanley a positive assurance that she would dissolve, saying that 'she would discuss the question when the emergency arose'. She was anxious, as were many other people, to avoid a dissolution in the year of the Exhibition; but, quite apart from this special consideration, she feared stirring up electoral commotion in the country before it was strictly necessary. The Queen's attitude was widely shared, particularly by members of Parliament who did not wish to have the expense of appearing before their constituents again, and there was little public interest in an 'appeal to the country'. After the crisis was over, Greville claimed that the only possible influence which would obtain anything like forbearance for the restored government was 'the general dread of a dissolution and the anxiety of members to stave it off'.

The only possible answer to the deadlock was to follow the advice of the aged Duke of Wellington and restore the Russell ministry to office. They came back on 4 March, not triumphantly but as a *pis aller*. They were

damaged, weak, and unpopular. . . . No bonfires were lighted, no bells were rung, no living man, save those personally interested, rejoiced in the fact. The administration had worn out the endurance of the nation; not a particle of enthusiasm remained. Amongst its followers a dull dead feeling of indifference prevailed. . . . The country was incredulous. They could not believe that the Ministry, *as a whole*, were reinstated.

The return of Russell marked no final solution of the par liamentary deadlock. 'It is the unique distinction of the prese dilemma,' wrote *The Times*, 'that it was always foreseen, that in similar circumstances, it must inevitably recur. exists no political party competent, at the usual challe receive from others the reins of power. We po

Opposition convertible into a Government, and we feel the effects of the privation in the negligence and imperfections of a Ministry so long as it acts, and in the absolute paralysis of the State when it can act no longer.'

There were three possible interpretations of the recurring crisis. A reader of the *Quarterly Review* or indeed a thinking Tory of any kind would see the dilemma of 1851 as part of the price of the Reform Bill of 1832, a permanent feature of the new constitutional framework. 'How can the Royal Government be carried on?' Wellington had asked. The answer was that it could not, except through a series of perpetual compromises and surrenders. A Peelite – and the Queen shared Peelite views on this question – would see the deadlock as largely personal, in terms of the disintegration of the Peelite party and the premature death of 'poor Peel' himself. A Radical would see it as a chapter in an unfinished political revolution. 'The family *côteries* of Whiggery require to be broken up,' wrote the *Eclectic Review*, 'and what has occurred will hasten this. . . . What we have witnessed is only one of the many scenes which will be enacted before the common right of Englishmen in the business of legislation is admitted. . . . The times for oligarchical rule are passed. We have as yet seen only the initial struggle. The real contest is to come . . . We must secure talent and public virtues by whomsoever exhibited, and in whatever class seen, without regard to the interested cliques which claim a monopoly of political wisdom.' According to this view, so long as cliques controlled politics at Westminster, they would while away their time in merely factious struggles, irrelevant to the progress of the nation.

Caught among all these interpretations of the crisis, Russell was in his usual uncomfortable position. He had always been a politician who seemed to get into mischief. 'His mishaps have almost exhausted metaphor,' one writer put it. 'One day *e overturns the coach*, another day he *swamps the boat*, then *breaks down*, then he *blows up*, in council he is *squirrel minded*, finally, it is *impossible to sleep soundly while he has command watch*. Admiral Byron did not better deserve the sobri- *Foul-weather Jack*.' And his troubles were by no means over. Although he was to ride safely into a new year, at the heavy price of losing his Foreign Secretary Palmerston, he met his tit for tat in 1852. The fall of Palmerston from office in December 1851 had more important political consequences than the February crisis, for it was Palmerston and not Russell who was to dominate politics in the middle years of the century. It was Palmerston who discovered the art of managing the Commons, thereby imposing some sort of order and continuity on half-reformed English politics. And it was by inducing sympathy for his foreign policy rather than by offering new doses of parliamentary reform that Palmerston was to cast his spell.

5

Between the February crisis and the fall of Palmerston in December came the Great Exhibition. To Disraeli, with both eyes fixed on parliamentary prospects, it was 'a godsend to the Government ... diverting public attention from their blunders'. To those less interested in the promptings of political ambition it was a national triumph. The *frondeurs*, like Colonel Sibthorp, who had ridiculed both the idea and the site of the Exhibition in 1850 – 'an industrial exhibition in the heart of fashionable Belgravia to enable foreigners to rob us of our honour' – prophesied public indifference and financial failure. As events proved, there were over six million visitors between the opening and closing days. Even Colonel Sibthorp himself visited 'the showy bauble' once before the summer was out. Cheap excursions insured the success of the enterprise. Visitors poured in from all parts of the country and overseas. Never had such quiet and orderly crowds been seen in London before. They made the most of the occasion. 'I never remember anything before that everyone was so pleased with, as is the case with this Exhibition,' wrote the Queen.

Part of the delight lay in the inspiration of the glass mansion itself designed by Joseph Paxton, who more than any other Englishman deserved the title of 'man of 1851'. The enormous conservatory of glass and iron which he designed was really an immensely magnified version of the Lily House at

Chatsworth, where he had been head gardener; but it was designed to capture the public imagination. It was 1,848 feet long, 408 feet broad, and 66 feet high – with transepts 108 feet high so constructed as to contain indoors some of the finest elms growing in Hyde Park. The young Edward Burne-Jones might find it 'cheerless' and 'monotonous' and John Ruskin dismiss it with impatient contempt, but most visitors were delighted and surprised:

> As though 'twere by a wizard's rod,
> A blazing arch of lucid glass
> Leaps like a fountain from the grass
> To meet the sun.

Joseph Paxton had won the prize for the design of the Exhibition building in face of 254 designs and specifications sent in by professional architects from all parts of the world. His adaptation of the Chatsworth conservatory, which he had begun in 1837, when glass was still heavily taxed, was a triumph of imagination. As Sir John Summerson has said, 'Paxton was a type of creator as new and as characteristic of the Age as the building he had designed.' Paxton, the expert gardener, the observer of nature, the man of affairs, the engineer, the railway director (he had sketched his first rough drawing of the proposed building on blotting paper at a meeting of the directors of the Midland Railway), the promoter of newspapers and magazines, seemed as much the 'complete man' of Victorian England as Alberti had been of Renaissance Florence. He was the epitome of self-help, and the whole of his career from the time when he became head gardener at the age of twenty-three illustrated, as the Queen remarked, how the lowest were able to rise by their own merits to the highest grade of society. When his building was being erected and unofficial visitors were not allowed to inspect the developing site, an exception was made for the Duke of Devonshire, the owner of Chatsworth, to whose 'fostering hand' Paxton owed his advancement, solely because the Duke was a partner in 'Paxton and Company'.

The building itself was thought to offer a solution to the

difficult problem of finding a distinctive nineteenth-century style in architecture. 'We have been saved from a hideous and costly mass of bricks and mortar,' wrote one commentator, 'and have a graceful and beautiful creation in its stead, and a new and suggestive *fact*, a step taken along a fresh track. . . . Architecture had had to wait for help from a botanist. Quite in keeping is the building with the age. It is the aesthetic bloom of its practical character, and of the practical tendency of the English nation.' 'Practical' and 'magical' were not considered incompatible. Glass was one of the newly freed commodities from which a prohibitive tax had just been lifted; it was also the substance which more than any other dazzled and sparkled and glittered. 'We shall be disappointed,' wrote *Punch*, 'if the next generation of London children are not brought up like cucumbers under a glass.' Disraeli was more romantic. Caring little for the philosophy of the Exhibition, he called the building itself 'that enchanted pile which the sagacious taste and the prescient philanthropy of an accomplished and enlightened Prince have raised for the glory of England and the delight and instruction of two hemispheres.' Douglas Jerrold's brilliant name 'Crystal Palace' was the perfect designation; it seemed to catch not only the workaday realities but also the hidden dreams of England in 1851.

The Crystal Palace was a symbol of the age. It suggested at the same time both fairy tale and success story. Behind the glitter there was human thought and human work. From the first flash of the bright idea it took Paxton just over a month to draw up the blueprints, from 11 June to 15 July 1850. The achievement of the contractors was equally remarkable. The ground was handed over to them on 30 July; the first column was raised on 26 September. Within seventeen weeks of the start, nearly a million feet of glass had been fastened on to the weblike structure of thirty-three hundred columns and twenty-three hundred girders. The secret of the speed of construction was prefabrication. All material used on the Palace was interchangeable: the girders, columns, gutters, and sash bars were identical throughout the whole building. Even before the Palace was completed, the exhibits themselves started to pour in, and on 1 May, the official day of opening, the only exhibits which had not arrived were those from Russia. The planning had been perfect.

There were over thirteen thousand exhibitors, one half of the total Exhibition area being occupied by Great Britain and the colonies, and the other half by foreign states, of which France and Germany were the most important. The exhibits were classified according to a scheme of the young scientist Lyon Playfair, one of the rising men of 1851, an industrious professor who was also an outstanding public servant. Rejecting elaborate systems of classification based upon Continental abstraction, he divided the objects on show into four groups – raw materials, machinery, manufactures, and fine arts.

Taken as a whole, the objects suggested the meeting of old and new. Machinery was in the ascendant, but handicrafts were not yet in general eclipse. Alongside a sewing machine from the United States and cotton machines from Oldham there was fine black lace from Barcelona and pottery from Sèvres.

> Harvest-tool and husbandry,
> Loom and wheel and enginery,
> Secrets of the sullen mine,
> Steel and gold, and coal and wine....
> All of beauty, all of use
> That our fair planet can produce.

The Machinery Court was the noisiest and most popular spectacle inside the Crystal Palace. Crowds of farmers in smocks could be seen admiring the agricultural implements, which included a pioneer reaping machine from the United States; mechanics from Leeds and Birmingham gathered round the Jacquard loom and De la Rue's envelope machine; the Queen herself was specially interested in a medal-making machine, which produced fifty million medals a week. She marvelled, too, at the electric telegraph and sent appropriate messages to her loyal subjects in Edinburgh and Manchester. Many of the machines displayed were more clever than useful. For example, among the gadgets on view were 'an alarm bedstead, causing a person to arise at any given hour', and a 'cricket catapulta, for propelling the ball in the absence of a first-rate bowler'.

Pride in ingenuity, as Professor Nikolaus Pevsner has said, often took the place of aesthetic appreciation in the response of contemporaries to the exhibits of 1851. There were no accepted canons of appreciation and no single accepted style. It was possible to conceal a predilection for generous curves and proliferation of ornament behind many different stylistic disguises: 'Louis Quatorze' vied with 'Louis Quinze' and both with Renaissance Italy and even ancient Egypt. One engine designed to drive cotton machinery was complete with scarabs; one large 'Elizabethan' sideboard was made entirely out of rubber, 'gutta-percha' as it was then called. There were some contemporary critics of 'the mass of ornament' and 'the sins committed against good taste', but most visitors to the Exhibition seem to have felt as enthusiastic about the objects as about the building which housed them. Bulgy curves and intricate relief appealed to a generation which found comfort in the richness and permanence of worldly possessions.

The only contemporary artist who believed that there should be one single style, just as there was one single faith, was Pugin. His Gothic gloom was fashionable in 1851. Set aside from the rest of the Exhibition, 'looking dark and solemn', was Pugin's Medieval Court 'for the display of the taste and art of dead men'. Gothic gloom or Crystal Palace: 1851 had two faces. It was possible to look either forward or backward. While Dr Whewell, Master of Trinity, and Charles Babbage, the mathematician, looked longingly to machines and interchangeable spare parts to create an age of mass production, Pugin lingered contentedly in the fourteenth century. When the Queen visited the Guild Hall in July to celebrate with the City of London the success of the Exhibition, supper was served in the crypt, which was fitted up for the occasion as an old baronial hall. Lights were carried by figures in medieval armour.

Candles and gaslight and dreams of electricity; medieval armour and Birmingham hardware; pyramids of soap and massive ecclesiastical ornaments, which made the commissioners afraid of cries of 'No Popery' – all these were part of 1851.

And many recent writers who have made it fashionable to admire Victorian Gothic have considered that the medieval pre-occupations of the men of 1851 were at least as fruitful as their confident expectations of continued material progress. It is difficult to judge. Of two young men who visited the Exhibition, one, William Whiteley, aged twenty, was so inspired by the glass building that he began to dream of large retail stores, 'universal providers' shops', with plate-glass fronts. The other, William Morris, three years younger, was moved sufficiently by the Exhibition to call the whole display 'wonderfully ugly'. His revolt not only against mid-Victorian design but against mid-Victorian society demonstrated the sharp change of mood in the later nineteenth century.

Both old and new, revival and anticipation, had to be adequately represented if the Exhibition were to fulfil the objectives laid down by its great architect, the Prince Consort, and his indefatigable colleague, Henry Cole, who has been properly described as 'a Prince Consort on a lowlier plane'. Their ambitious project of an international exhibition developed out of very humble origins. The Royal Society of Arts, which had exhibited its prize awards for agricultural and industrial machinery since 1761, held two special tiny exhibitions in 1844 and 1845; it was interested in the possibility of 'wedding high art with mechanical skill'. Cole, a civil servant with a taste for administrative centralization, submitted a model of a tea set and not only won the silver medal but became a leading member of the society. He infused an energy into the society's projects which justified the use of the motto on the title-page of his biography: 'Whatsoever thy hand findeth to do, do it with thy might'. He and the Prince Consort, working first through the Royal Society and then through a royal commission, were directly responsible for the scale and magnificence of the final Exhibition. 'For the *first* time in the world's history,' Cole told the members of the Society of Arts, 'the men of Arts, Science, and Commerce were permitted by their respective governments to meet together to discuss and promote those objects for which civilized nations exist.'

The Exhibition had a moral as well as an industrial purpose.

It was intended to be a running commentary on the age interrupted at regular intervals by object lessons. Two themes were repeated more than the rest – the gospel of work and the gospel of peace.

The gospel of work came first: the Exhibition was designed to honour 'the working bees of the world's hive' and to cast tacit reflection on the drones. 'The workers, of all types, stand forth as the really great men.' The Exhibition medals bore the words: *Pulcher et ille labor palma decorare laborem.* In such a festival not only the captains of industry but also the manual labourers had to be remembered. The Prince Consort had become president in 1844 of the Society for the Improvement of the Condition of the Labouring Classes. In 1851 he commissioned Henry Roberts, who had already built model working-class houses, to build a model house for the Exhibition on a patch of vacant ground close to the Knightsbridge Cavalry Barracks. Concern for the condition of life of the poor was to be forced upon visitors. Indirectly, then, the Exhibition focused attention on the same set of problems as had been raised in *Alton Locke*. 'Shall we ostentatiously show off all manner of articles of luxury and comfort, and be ashamed to disclose the condition of those we have to thank for them?'

This was a question which could no more be dodged than the other great question of the day – the divergence and the reconciliation of material and moral progress. The prayers uttered by the Archbishop of Canterbury at the opening of the Exhibition were the prayers of a successful people whose God had 'multiplied on us blessings which Thou mightest most justly have withheld,' but could all doubts be shelved? 'For what shall it profit a man if he shall gain the whole world and lose his soul?'

The gospel of peace was stressed with as much fervour as the gospel of work. There had been many industrial exhibitions before 1851. The special feature of the 1851 Exhibition was that it was universal. 'Paxton, go forth,' *Punch* depicted Prince Albert as saying, 'take glass and iron, and, beauty wedding strength, produce the Industrial Hall of Nations.' Out of the honest rivalry of industry and skill, countries would find a new brotherhood. The Crystal Palace was thought of as a temple of peace where all nations would meet by appointment under the same roof and shake each other by the hand. *Paxton vobiscum*.

The tree of trees to be planted is a gigantic olive that is expected to take root in the Paxton Palace of Hyde Park; an olive strengthened, sheltered, and protected by the glass walls and roof, that admit the commercial trophies of all the world – a veritable Peace Congress, manufactured by the many-coloured hands of the human family. We do not see why there should not be an Order of the Olive. Will Prince Albert think of it?

The emphasis on peace was coloured by two philosophies or by what many people felt were two facets of the same philosophy – Christianity and free trade. While newspapers reminded their readers of the connexion between the repeal of the Corn Laws in 1846 and the hope of international business harmony in 1851, the Archbishop's opening prayers recalled to the first distinguished visitors not only that all wealth came from God but also that England could be specially thankful for mercies received, particularly for 'the peace that is within our walls and plenteousness within our palaces'. The visitors should pray together that God might help them in their noble purpose of 'knitting together in the bonds of peace and concord the different nations of the earth'. The earth was the Lord's and all that dwelt therein. Queen Victoria was pleased with a 'nice sermon' which she heard three days after the opening of the Exhibition, when the preacher alluded to the ceremony and took as his text, 'And he hath made of one blood all nations of men to dwell on the face of the earth.'

The hopes of peace were soon dashed. They had seemed too grandiloquently phrased for many of the writers of the time. The *Eclectic Review* referred to 'stern facts weltering beneath the rose pink surface' and pointed out how the 'federation of the universe' propaganda of the French Revolution had served, at a previous moment of optimism, as a prelude to a generation of war. 'The "tears of joy" were turned to tears of blood, and with their plenteousness watered the earth.' These words were not intended to suggest that similar terrors were imminent; but it was perhaps an omen that the closing day of the Exhibition was wet and depressing and that, by the end of the year, scarcely before the contractors had begun to dismantle the fabric of the Crystal Palace, events in France rudely shattered the confidence in the new world. At the same time also, they shattered the summertime equilibrium of Russell's government.

6

The Great Exhibition had been designed not only to establish the superiority of British manufactures and to proclaim the gospel of free trade and universal peace but also to reveal to foreigners the attractions of the British constitution. 'We are all agreed,' the Duchess of Gloucester wrote to the Queen the day after the opening of the Exhibition, 'in rejoicing that Foreigners *should* have witnessed the affection of the *People* to *you* and *your Family*, and how the *English people* do *love* and respect the *Crown*.' Foreigners did not appear to learn the lesson very easily. On 30 September the Queen wrote to the king of the Belgians that the position of princes, which was difficult in those times, 'would be much less difficult' if they would behave honourably and straightforwardly. To give the people gradually those privileges which would satisfy all the reasonable and well-intentioned 'would weaken the power of the Red Republicans . . . . Instead of that, reaction and a return to all the tyranny and oppression is the cry and the principle – and all papers and books are being seized and prohibited, as in the days of Metternich.'

The Queen and the Prince Consort held strong views concerning not only the duty of princes but also the methods and responsibilities of foreign secretaries. They had clashed frequently with Palmerston, the Foreign Secretary, in 1850, the Queen persistently urging Russell to transfer him to a different office or to remove him from the cabinet. On European questions their viewpoint was diametrically opposed. The February crisis seemed to offer an easy opportunity for getting rid of Palmerston, but Russell refused to consider any immediate change. 'Our party is hardly re-united,' he wrote, 'and any break into sections, following one man or the other, would be fatal to us.' He knew and confessed that he, Russell, was the element of weakness in the government, and Palmerston the element of strength, and that to remove the Foreign Secretary would break up the administration. He promised that he would try to get rid of Palmerston during the Easter recess but, when Easter came, declared that this was again impossible. Palmerston's departure was indefinitely postponed, and the Exhibition overshadowed all other questions.

It had scarcely come to a close when the visit of the Hungarian nationalist exile, Louis Kossuth, to England led to a renewed antagonism between the Queen and the Foreign Secretary and to open conflict between the Foreign Secretary and the Prime Minister. The visit of Kossuth was one of the big popular events of the year. He met with enormous cheering crowds wherever he went, in the provinces as well as London, and fulsome tributes were paid to his eloquent defence of liberty and to his masterly presentation in fluent English of the salient features of the international situation. The Queen feared a meeting between Palmerston and Kossuth, and Prince Albert feared that, if that did not happen, 'something worse' would. When Russell 'positively requested' Palmerston not to receive Kossuth, the Foreign Secretary replied tartly that he did not choose to be dictated to as to whom he might or might not receive in his own house. 'I shall use my discretion.... You will, of course, use yours as to the composition of your Government.' The cabinet backed Russell; and Palmerston did not see Kossuth, but he did receive radical deputations from the London suburbs who used colourful language in his presence to praise the brave fight of Kossuth and to discredit the actions of the emperors of Austria and Russia, enemies of Hungarian independence.

The Kossuth affair was still being discussed when news of Napoleon's *coup d'état* reached London. Louis Napoleon, president of France, dissolved the Assembly and asked for full powers. The *politique de bascule* was over in Paris; midnight military violence had taken its place. The 'Man of December', as Napoleon came to be known, had arrived. Behind a carpet which had been shown at the Exhibition, twelve persons were killed. England could not escape the impact of the French crisis, the last big event in the sequence of revolution and counter-revolution which followed from the events of 1848. 'We are destined to feel the electric shock of every explosion or convulsion that France undergoes,' wrote the *Quarterly Review*.

News of the *coup d'état* reached England by the recently constructed electric telegraph. There were immediate rumours in the *Daily News* that Palmerston, who was known to sympathize with Napoleon, had quarrelled with his colleagues: 'Along with the alarming dispatch from Paris has come a report that Lord Palmerston is no longer in the Cabinet.' The rumours were soon forgotten, however, and on 16 December the newspapers reported that ministers were quietly leaving London for their Christmas holidays, 'congratulating themselves, no doubt, on the very comfortable state of things in England compared with France'.

Beneath the surface things were very far from comfortable in the cabinet. Two days after the coup, Queen Victoria wrote to Russell, explaining that it was of very great importance to instruct Normanby, the British ambassador in Paris, to remain entirely passive and to take no part and make no comments on what was happening. The Queen's advice came too late. Palmerston had already expressed 'private' approval of the *coup d'état* to Walewski, the French representative in London, and was writing to Normanby, rebuking him for his hostility to Napoleon and telling him to report more sympathetically on the course of events in Paris.

Normanby's brother-in-law, Colonel Phipps, was the Prince Consort's secretary, and Lady Normanby plied him privately with information concerning Palmerston's peculiar and 'most flippant' conduct. He had behaved more wildly than ever before. 'He ridicules the idea of the Constitution; turns to scorn the idea of anything being done to the Members of the Assembly; laughs and jokes at the [English] Club being fired into, though the English people in it were within an ace of being murdered by the soldiers; says that Normanby is pathetic over a broken looking-glass, forgetting that the same bullet grazed the hand of an Englishman, "a Roman citizen"...' How could one reconcile such conduct with the brave defence of all English interests which had been urged so powerfully by Palmerston himself in his famous 'Civis Romanus sum' speech in the Don Pacifico debate only a year before, when he had defended the rights of a Gibraltar Jew who happened to be a British subject?

On 13 December the Queen wrote to Russell, enclosing a Normanby dispatch about Walewski's conversation with Palmerston, and asked, 'Does Lord John know anything about the alleged approval, which, if true, would again expose the honesty and dignity of the Queen's Government in the eyes of the world?'

Russell received an extremely unsatisfactory explanation from Palmerston, offered him the lord lieutenancy of Ireland in place of the Foreign Office, and, finally, after Palmerston had refused this greatly inferior position, replaced him by Lord Granville, 'the Polite'. Granville was a friend of the Prince Consort, with whom he had worked closely on the Royal Commission for the Exhibition. He was *persona gratissima* with the royal family, and, although, as the son of an English ambassador to France, he seemed well equipped for the Foreign Office, he had graduated, as it were, not through the embassies but through the Crystal Palace. The public knew less about Granville than did the court; it was Palmerston who was the popular idol. It was two days after the cabinet decided on 22 December to back up Russell that the news of Palmerston's fall was announced in *The Times*. Despite the previous rumours of resignation, the news came as a shock. 'The change had been made, and all but formally ratified, with the secrecy and celerity of the Parisian *coup d'état*.' Many people did not believe the report in *The Times* and waited for the evening's *Globe* to see if a mistake had been made.

The cause of the dismissal of Palmerston was not immediately announced to the public. The *Morning Chronicle* spread the report that it was because he had quarrelled with the Austrian and Russian ambassadors about England becoming 'a place of asylum' for foreign refugees. The Kossuth question was still in the air. It was not until a little later that the news came through; first, that the French question had led to a 'divergency of action, amounting to the opening of two distinct and discordant channels of communication with the French government,' and, second, that, of late, 'Lord Palmerston assumed an independence and singleness of action altogether inconsistent with the fact that the whole Cabinet shared the responsibility of his acts'.

While the readers of the press were bewildered and perturbed by the fall of such a popular Foreign Secretary, the Queen was delighted with this ending, or apparent ending, to what she thought was a long chapter of recklessness and disaster. 'I have the greatest pleasure,' she wrote to the king of the Belgians on 23 December, 'in announcing to you a piece of news which I know will give you as much satisfaction and relief as it does to us. Lord Palmerston is no longer Foreign Secretary.' Seven days later she philosophized about the news. 'It is too grievous to think how much misery and mischief might have been avoided. However, now he has done with the Foreign Office for ever, and "the veteran" statesman, as the newspapers call him, to our great amusement and I am sure, to his infinite annoyance, must rest upon his laurels.' This was one occasion upon which Queen Victoria was amused, although the amusement did not last for long.

The Queen and the Prince Consort felt themselves strengthened by Palmerston's fall; Lord John Russell's administration was undoubtedly weakened 'unto death'. Russell chose the occasion of Palmerston's fall with as much care as he could, and he acted swiftly. As Disraeli wrote maliciously to Lady Londonderry: 'The success of Napoleon seems to have given Johnny a taste for *coups d'état*.' Russell hoped that not all the Radicals would adopt the same friendly approach to the new French government which Palmerston had done and that their opposition to bloodstained dictatorship would more than counterbalance their faith in Palmerston as a Radical bulwark in European politics. He hoped further – and in this he was right in the very short run – that Palmerston's waywardness towards his colleagues and, though it could not be said too openly, towards the Queen would meet with general disapproval. But all these optimistic hopes could not cover over the loss of the one powerful personality in the government who was capable of winning the loyalty of both Radical and 'Independent' members. 'Palmerston's good nature, courtesy, and hospitality,' wrote one of the cabinet ministers, 'made him many friends, and he was able to turn away the wrath of opponents as no other member of the Government can do.' He even contrived during the change-over to be friendly and cooperative with his successor, Granville.

In the last few months of 1851 all the paradoxes in the Radical support of Palmerston had been strikingly demonstrated; for, while he was listening to addresses referring to the emperors of Russia and Austria as 'odious and detestable assassins' and 'merciless tyrants and despots', he was resolutely opposing Russell's plans for a new reform bill, the long-awaited Reform Bill which Russell had promised in February. The fate of the Reform Bill became very problematical after the fall of Palmerston, and so did the fate of the government. Lord John realized that, if he abandoned 'finality', standing by his Reform Bill of 1832, and proposed a new measure of reform, he would be confronted with an impossible situation. If he proposed a comprehensive reform bill in such quiet times, it would be talked out or thrown out; if he proposed a mild bill, the 'movement party would spring at him like hounds'. Disraeli knew the answer to that dilemma: 'He ought to resign.'

The only way of averting defeat and resignation was to explore yet again the rejected alternative of the crisis of February 1851. The one thing which stood out after December as a political necessity was a Whig–Peelite coalition, but it did not prove possible to secure it at once. The failure to secure it immediately led to the downfall of Russell. February again proved a cruel month, and the Prime Minister was forced to resign in February 1852, when Palmerston threw his weight against him. This time the protectionists took office, although Palmerston would not join them. By gradually abandoning protection, the cause for which they nominally stood, they were freed from thraldom to a dogma and were able to take the first step in the long and difficult process of becoming a popular party. That first step was a necessary condition for a return to a two-party system in English politics, which had been broken in 1846; so too was the ultimate absorption of the Peelites in a broader Whig–Liberal party. Until such a two-party system began to function again, executive government was bound to be weak, and parliamentary reform was bound to seem calculated to make it weaker. The Queen's great fear in contemplating Russell's reform proposals of late 1851 was whether 'the strengthening of the Democratic principle will upset the balance of the Constitution, and further weaken the Executive, which is by no means too strong at present'.

7

The weakness of the executive at the end of 1851 might alarm the Queen, but it cheered large sections of the community. They had no reason for hankering after strong government. They wanted to be left alone. While the Queen rejoiced in the fall of Palmerston, at Christmas 1851 the community as a whole rejoiced in a year of prosperity and progress. '1851 would long be remembered,' wrote Macaulay, 'as a singularly happy year of peace, plenty, good feeling, innocent pleasure and national glory.'

The *Manchester Guardian* interpreted the events in the spirit of the year for the benefit of its Christmas readers.

The best contribution that anyone can make to the happiness of the Christmas circle is to show its members that they have good grounds for satisfaction, for hope, and for self-approval. We are glad, therefore, to be able to say that English society has never a better right, than at the present moment, to sit quietly under a sermon with that pleasing moral. In all our relations, we have at least as much, if not more, substantial reason for contentment and thankfulness, than at the close of any past year in our history.

It went on to give the reasons for this happy state of affairs. First, there was cheap food in plenty and with it 'clothing, fuel, shelter, and transition from place to place – within the

reach of all, except those whom demerit, or extraordinary misfortune, has reduced to complete destitution'. Second, 'we
have complete domestic tranquillity, and as much amity abroad,
as is compatible in these days, with the maintenance of self-
respect.' Third, the tone of the country was right, and it was
set on a road of boundless progress. 'The last twenty years
have witnessed an unprecedented growth of good feeling
among our widely separated classes, a great improvement in
national manners and public morality, the introduction of a
more humane and popular spirit of legislation, and, in general
terms, a patient, but earnest desire of progressive improvement
in all ranks of the people.' Finally, but not least, 'it would be un-
seasonably invidious to institute a minute comparison between
our own and our neighbour's pudding; but we cannot refrain
from saying that there are few Christmas parties in Europe to
which we can turn a momentary glance, without greatly height-
ening the satisfaction with which we turn again towards home.'

There is an underlying smugness in this catalogue of national
blessings, but the qualifications it introduces are important in
catching the spirit of 1851. The phrase 'except those whom
demerit, or extraordinary misfortune, has reduced to complete
destitution' recalls once again the submerged ranks of the
nation, those who were not able to help themselves. They were
no longer big enough to be regarded as a second nation in themselves, as Disraeli had regarded them a few years before; at
the same time they could not be ignored, even by those writers
who tried to dismiss them in the name of social theory or inevitable accident. They were the hungry at the feast, always
socially insecure, liable as one of them put it to pass through
'the smallest accident' from a life of 'comparative happiness
to irredeemable misery'.

The phrase 'as much amity abroad as is compatible with
the maintenance of self-respect' recalls the limit placed by
contemporaries, even in this year of peace, on national appease-
ment. There was a recognition in the words of Prince Albert
that 'we are entering upon most dangerous times in which
Military Despotism and Red Republicanism will for some time
be the only Powers on the Continent, to both of which the

Constitutional Monarchy of England will be equally hateful. That the calm influence of our institutions, however, should succeed in assuaging the contest abroad must be the anxious wish of every Englishman.' The calm influence of institutions was clear enough in 1851, but could the English people themselves always be relied upon to be as calm as Prince Albert had suggested? It was the Prince's friend, Henry Cole, who called the English people 'the richest in the world, and, I fear, the most pugnacious', but who went on to trust that

the Exhibition will have tended to make ourselves a less quarrelsome and meddlesome people with other nations than we have accustomed to be, and will have taught us that our true policy in international disputes, should they unfortunately arise, is to stand on the defensive, and in that attitude to be as well prepared as possible, and to be content with being so.

The recognition of dangerous times ahead on the Continent did not go far enough in 1851 to disturb the mood of self-satisfaction. As Sir Llewellyn Woodward has said, 'The Victorians were living dangerously, far more dangerously than they knew. The world was much stronger than their machinery, and the nature of man more fragile and at the same time more unfathomable.' The elements of doubt had not yet been fashioned into a pattern of self-criticism. That was to be the work of the future. Although the main features of the social system were to remain substantially unchanged through the middle years of Victorian England, the Crimean War was to provide a jolt to easy complacency.

CHAPTER THREE

John Arthur Roebuck and the Crimean War

Roebuck has lived before the world for nearly half a century, and his public life has not been lacking in consistency. But if it comes to talk about honour and usefulness, it suggests the inquiry whether the wasp is an honourable and useful factor in daily life. Roebuck has been a political and Parliamentary wasp, and I never heard of the bees insisting upon doing honour to this member of the hymenopterous family.

HENRY W. LUCY (1878)

I

The gospel of peace proclaimed at the Great Exhibition did not capture public opinion for long. The Queen had spoken in 1851 of 'this peace festival, which unites the industry of all the nations of the earth', but three years later inflamed opinion was clamouring for war against Russia. The Exhibition had been popular, but the Crimean War, even before it officially began, was more so. Only a small group of Manchester School Radicals, the apostles of peace and free trade, stood completely aloof from the supporters of the struggle and called the Crimean War a crime; for their refusal to identify themselves with the nation they were pilloried in the press and even burned in effigy by the crowds in Manchester itself. They were a very small minority, smaller than the band of protectionist malcontents, like Colonel Sibthorp, who refused to associate themselves with the Exhibition. For the most part the nation – Radical, Liberal, and Conservative – was one, though it was the Radicals who were the noisiest supporters of the war and the people least anxious to see it come to a conclusion. 'There is scarcely a man to be found from Land's End to John o' Groats but would like another year of war,' exclaimed one Radical speaker in 1856. 'There is a general impression that now we are fully prepared for it, another year's war would show the world that there is that in Englishmen which would conquer every difficulty.'

The war was popular not only with the crowds, particularly the urban crowds, and the politicians, particularly the Radical politicians, but also with most of the poets and writers of the times. The new poet laureate, Tennyson, who had caught the mood of 1851 in *In Memoriam*, was equally successful in catching the mood of 1854. *The Charge of the Light Brigade* was representative even down to the phrase 'some one had blundered', while the greater poem *Maud* did not scruple to condemn Bright as 'the broad-brimmed hawker of holy things'. In the experiences of war Tennyson discerned a purging of base ambitions, an escape from selfish individualism, and even a strange but relentless moral necessity:

> For the peace, that I deem'd no peace, is over and done,
> And now by the side of the Black and the Baltic Deep,
> And deathful-grinning mouths of the fortress, flames
> The blood-red blossom of war with a heart of fire.

'War goes on famously,' wrote Robert Pemberton Milnes, an English squire, to his son Richard in 1854, 'and I would have it go on – wars are serviceable, as thunderstorms are – there would be no breathing at Crewe Hall between Manchester and the Potteries, but for them.'

The contrast between the moods of 1851 and 1854 seems less sharp if the Exhibition itself is placed in its proper perspective. The talk of peace in that year was a little forced. Only a year before, Palmerston had appealed in the famous Don Pacifico debate not to love of peace but to self-assertive national pride. Throughout 1851 itself there was an undercurrent of vociferous nationalism. In 1852, as Napoleon III consolidated his power, France once more assumed the shape of the national enemy, and the Volunteer Movement was launched to enlist unstinted middle-class patriotic enthusiasm. The dreams of the free-traders of 1846 and the makers of the Exhibition of 1851 were already fading into the background, and Tennyson's 'Hands All Round', 'incomparably the best convivial lyric in the language', was accusing the dreamers of peace of deriving their idealism merely from the desire to sell more cotton goods overseas:

> Tho' niggered throats of Manchester may bawl,
>> What England was, shall her true sons forget?
> We are not cotton spinners all,
>> But some love England and her honour yet.

In the same year the death of the Duke of Wellington, the hero of Waterloo, was an impressive military spectacle; influential writers were roused to complain that 'this nation is a great deal enervated by a long peace, by easy habits of intercourse, by peace societies, and by false economies.' Even while they were complaining, it was becoming clear that the 'enervation' was creating its own reaction.

Between 1852 and 1854 the restless mood persisted, although France, the enemy of 1852, became the ally of 1854, and Russia became the enemy. Without this shuffling of friends and foes the war could not have been so popular. Russia as an enemy mobilized the ill-will of the greatest possible number of the population. Indeed, popular enthusiasm for the war can be explained in terms both of a general reaction to a long period of peace and of a specific reaction to the 'threat' of increased Russian power. Tsarist Russia appeared not only as a national rival endangering the balance of power in Europe and British security in India but also as a despotic tyrant, the gigantic obstacle to European freedom and liberation. Behind the events of 1854 were the revolutions of 1848, the flight of the European exiles, and the dreams of a new European order; behind them also were the facts of Russian expansion in central Asia and the fears of Russian domination of the Middle East. Whigs, Tories, and Radicals could each see the conflict in acceptable but different terms. Respectable Whigs and Peelites could be anti-Russian because they wanted to have the claims of public law vindicated against the ambitions of an aggressor; Tories could tremble with rage at the policy of 'sap and mine' by which

Russia was increasing its power; Radicals could look to Moscow as the centre of international reaction and call upon Hungarian, Polish, and Italian exiles to prophesy for them that 'the state of Europe, and the dispositions of the *active* party everywhere, are such as to make us foresee that a supreme struggle will take place between Right and Might before a long time has elapsed.'

The roots of Russophobia in England lay deeper than the revolutions of 1848. Between 1815 and 1830, writers like Sir Robert Wilson and George de Lacy Evans had argued that the Russian objective was Constantinople and that, once Constantinople was captured, universal dominion lay within Russia's 'easy grasp'. They familiarized important sections of the reading public with the view that only enslaved peoples anxious for their own liberation could drive the semi-barbarous Russian despots back into the steppes of Asia. Nothing fundamentally new was said by pamphleteers about Russia in 1854 and 1855 which had not been said by 1830. But, between 1848 and 1854, Russophobes stirred not limited sections of the reading public but large crowds of people. One of the strongest Russophobes was Karl Marx. 'In this instance,' he wrote, 'the interests of revolutionary Democracy and England go hand in hand.' Russia was the one great menace to civilization. The message of all the European exiles was the same; as Kossuth wrote to David Urquhart, a sympathetic English Radical, in the year of the Exhibition from his temporary shelter in Turkey: 'There is something in my mind, which tells me we are on the dawn of great events and must everywhere prepare to meet them in the best manner we can. We must crush Russia, my dear sir! We must, and headed by you we will.'

Urquhart was only capable of heading a noisy conspiracy, but he saw mass opinion in the cities move between 1852 and 1854 to a position not very different from his own. Turkey's welcome to the revolutionary exiles of 1848 disposed Radicals to regard even the sultan as a friend. As Victor Hugo put it, 'What now glitters in the desperate grasp of Turkey is not the old dented scimitar of Othman, but the brilliant lightning of revolution.'

Only very few Englishmen cared to contemplate a revolution, but many warmed to a national cause, which had about it a distinctly 'Radical' flavour. The domestic wounds of Chartism, which had divided the country as recently as 1848, were healing, and the appeal of nation became stronger than the appeal of class. A representative Radical like G. J. Holyoake talked of 'an unknown and unsuspected instinct of race stirring in his blood' and confessed an undiscriminating patriotism while the war was in progress. He was 'for the success of England right or wrong', and, when the peace was declared, he refused to illuminate his office in Fleet Street, preferring to display a large placard bearing Elizabeth Browning's verses on the continued plight of Poland, Italy, and Hungary.

He was not alone. In all the large cities of the country – particularly in Sheffield and Newcastle – there were many public meetings and special new organizations to arrange them. Speakers from Polish democratic committees were as welcome as proved local orators. The countryside, however, and the small market towns were relatively unaffected; they were almost as impervious to the clamour as they had been to the fiery rhetoric of Chartism in the previous decade.

Almost as impervious, but not quite, for there was one important difference between the noise of Chartism and the war fervour. The press, which for the most part had opposed the Chartists, did as much as the public meetings to create a war atmosphere. The press, or, at any rate, *The Times*, its leading organ, penetrated middle-class homes in many quiet parts of the country. With a circulation of over forty thousand copies, it was the leading newspaper not only of England but of Europe: 'It is a well-known fact,' wrote the Whig, Lord Clarendon, 'that *The Times* forms or guides or reflects – no matter which – the public opinion of England.' *The Times*, which vacillated between peace and war in 1853 and early 1854, soon forgot its doubts; so too did Clarendon. When the war had not been long in progress, he was proclaiming, 'We are not now engaged in the Eastern Question, but in the battle of civilization against barbarism, for the independence of Europe.'

2

Despite the popularity of the war and the bold simplicity which its issues assumed in the eyes of the general public, the leading statesmen of the day were unable to give any clear or consistent account of the reasons why it had broken out or of the purposes which they hoped it would secure. Napoleon III was far more clear than the English Prime Minister Aberdeen, a well-known lover of peace, who watched his own cabinet drift into war through a series of halfhearted measures of which he only half-approved. A Peelite, he had come into power as Prime Minister of a Whig–Peelite coalition in 1852 after the failure of the protectionists to establish their ministry. One of his main purposes was to avoid war. On the opposite side of the ring, Nicholas I, the Tsar of Russia, was not so much plotting as blundering his way into an impossible position; he had no desire for an international war of any kind.

Even now the causes of the Crimean War cannot be adequately stated. It is usually claimed that it grew out of a local squabble between Roman Catholic and Greek Orthodox monks for the control of the holy places in Jerusalem. The Russian tsar was the protector of the Greek church; Napoleon III considered himself the protector of the Catholics and used the occasion to maintain the ancient French patronage of the Catholic church. The two countries fought a diplomatic battle to acquire influence at the court of the 'infidel sultan' in Constantinople. In May 1853 Nicholas demanded that the Turks should recognize his authority not only over the Jerusalem monks but also over the whole ten million Greek Orthodox Christians in the Turkish Empire. When the Turks refused, Russian troops marched into the Danubian provinces of Turkey. The first reaction of the great powers – France, Great Britain, Austria, and Prussia – was to try to hammer out a compromise. By this time the Turks were unwilling to accept such a solution, and in October 1853 they declared war on Russia.

These colourful incidents were not accidents; they sprang from an increasingly unstable power situation. The fact that the Ottoman Empire was 'the sick man' of Europe, incapable of reform, sharpened existing differences and eventually forced Britain and Russia into opposite camps. Neither country was certain what to do with what was called the 'Eastern Question' or what the other country would do. 'When *we* are agreed,' Nicholas had told Seymour, the British ambassador, at a party in January 1853, 'I am quite without anxiety as to the rest of Europe. It is immaterial what others may think or do.' The two countries drifted into open war through a welter of misunderstanding and false estimates of each other's intentions rather than through a deliberate policy on either side.

When fighting broke out between Russia and Turkey in October 1853, Aberdeen was still most anxious to prevent it spreading and, far from feeling pro-Turk, strongly disliked any idea of propping up the Ottoman Empire. 'The beastly Turks have actually declared war,' wrote his Foreign Secretary, Clarendon. Much of the press supported Aberdeen at this stage, for he was, after all, the respected leader of the coalition which had finally emerged as the 'natural' alignment to secure a more stable administration. Although his cabinet was divided and his 'leadership' was never accepted within it, there was no opposition to the resort to negotiation between the powers as the means of dealing with the situation. 'We cannot see how any man who holds himself responsible for his words and actions,' wrote a representative provincial newspaper in Sheffield, 'and gives the smallest thought to the consequences of war, can urge upon us such a mad and murderous enterprise.'

The advocates of war were held back until, at the end of November 1853, the tense international situation, described by a recent historian as a 'nineteenth-century cold war', suddenly became critical. The Russian fleet attacked and destroyed an inferior Turkish squadron at Sinope, on the Black Sea. Although the action was a legitimate operation of war, it blasted away any lingering British doubts about the need for a 'firm stand'. The national temper was roused. 'Sinope,' wrote *The Times*, 'dispels the hopes we have been led to entertain of pacification. . . . We have thought it our duty to uphold and defend the cause of peace as long as peace was compatible with the honour and dignity of our country ... but now war has begun in earnest.'

Officially, however, war did not begin until 28 March. In the meantime the British and French governments, now acting as allies and backed by an enraged British public opinion, ordered their combined fleets into the Black Sea. On 6 January 1854 a British frigate appeared before the walls of Sebastopol. Aberdeen might still waver and complain that 'some fatal influence must be at work' jeopardizing the cause of peace; but, the more he hesitated and wavered, the more divided his cabinet became, and the more determined became public opinion. The same Sheffield paper which in July 1853 had talked of peace and sung the praises of Aberdeen was demanding war in December. 'Mere talking to the Tsar will do nothing ... now the time does appear to be at hand when we must act so as to dissipate the evil designs and efforts of Russia.'

The conflict between hesitating statesmen and militant makers of opinion drove a wedge between government and people even before hostilities began. Once they had begun, there were two further reasons for increasing domestic antagonism. First, the diplomats – to the annoyance of the critics of 'secret diplomacy' – remained as important as the soldiers. While negotiations for terminating the conflict continued almost without cease throughout the whole of its course, public opinion in Britain was unwilling at all points to countenance a premature peace; and in 1855 there was an increasingly wide gap not only between government and people but also between the English people and their far less enthusiastic French allies, who by then were prepared, under Napoleon himself, to seek peace.

Historians of the Crimean War have, for the most part, been more interested in what happened in diplomatic negotiations in Vienna than in what happened in Manchester or Sheffield, yet the unpopularity of John Bright in Manchester, when he opposed the war, and the wild popularity of John Arthur Roebuck in Sheffield, when he supported it, reveal more of the England of their time than the elaborate accounts by ministers of the aims and purposes of the struggle. The war itself was without a real decision in the field of international politics, but it left a profound impact on British politics, government, and society. As the American Nathaniel Hawthorne noted, the war gave the country 'a vast impulse towards democracy'. Changes on the home front were always more important than on the narrow front in the Crimea.

There was a second and bigger reason for the antagonism between government and public. As the war continued, it revealed daily evidence of 'mismanagement'. When war was declared, there was little realization, at any rate among members of the public, of the difficulties and dangers which lay ahead. 'The long, long canker of peace' was over, it was believed, and war would once again vindicate the qualities of the English soldier and the English people. But it soon began to be clear in the hard Crimean winter of 1854–5 that, while the individual soldiers were heroic, military leadership was incompetent and military administration chaotic. Forty years of peace and public economy campaigns had run their course, and the invincibility of the army had become a matter of faith rather than of organization.

The war undermined confidence in the military and administrative system at the same time that it enhanced the prestige of the individual soldier, who was considered a crusader in the cause of right. There was shame and anger at his sufferings as they were described in the press. War correspondents, particularly William Henry Russell of *The Times*, sang the praises of the 'thin red streak topped with a line of steel', while old Chartists talked not of the six points of the people's charter but of a new soldiers' charter. The bravery of the soldiers was demonstrated during the storming of the heights of Alma in September 1854; but, as the winter advanced, 'the failure of the system' was equally vividly demonstrated by the failure of the army to capture the city of Sebastopol. The besiegers rather than the besieged were forced on the defensive, and, though the battles of Balaclava and Inkerman showed that heroism was still alive, the small British army had to face a cruel winter, suffering from want of shelter, clothes, food, and medicine. It was not until September 1855 that Sebastopol fell, and by that time public opinion at home had passed from whole-hearted enthusiasm for the war to scathing criticism of its mal-administration. 'Efficiency' became a Radical slogan, and the general sentiment of the country was indicated by the title of a pamphlet, *Whom Shall We Hang?* By then the Russians were a far less accessible enemy than the English generals and the 'aristocrats' behind the scenes at Whitehall.

The mid-Victorians liked to expose 'scandals', with the press as a necessary intermediary, and in 1854 it carried out its task with what to many conservatives was frightening effec-tiveness. John Delane, the editor of *The Times*, prepared for the outbreak of war with more foresight than the govern-ment. An army of correspondents, paid and unofficial, provi-ded him with information. In consequence Delane could thunder so ceaselessly against those whom he held responsible for military and administrative blunders that it was a brave man who dared to challenge him. One man who did, the Earl of Winchilsea, had to preface one of the rare open attacks on *The Times* in the House of Lords by giving thanks to Provi-dence that he was not deficient in moral courage. W. H. Russell, Delane's chief correspondent, was on his way to the Crimea when war broke out; once it had started, he was in a privileged position compared with correspondents before or since. He had the newly invented telegraph at his disposal, but he had no censorship to cramp his style. He and the other 'crouching tigers' of the press began to realize during the war that publicity was their trade and that their readers welcomed sensational revelations more enthusiastically than bare factual information.

Such a realization shocked conservatives of all sorts, who were alarmed by the new manifestation of newspaper strength. Whigs and, in particular, Peelites suffered. Lord John Russell, who was not one of Delane's heroes, talked of the 'vile tyranny' of *The Times* and claimed that it aspired to be 'not the organ but the organizer of government', while Greville wrote in his famous diary in February 1855, that for the first time in his life he was

really and seriously alarmed at the state of affairs. The press with

The Times at its head is striving to throw everything into confusion and running amuck against the aristocratic elements of society and the Constitution. The intolerable nonsense and the abominable falsehoods it flings out every day are none the less dangerous because they are nonsense and falsehood, and backed up as they are by all the vulgar Radical press, they diffuse through the country a mass of inflammatory matter the effect of which may be more serious and arrive more quickly than anybody imagines.

The public attack by the Radicals began with a convincing barrage of criticism directed against the archaic military system which was hopelessly split up between a variety of military and civil departments. There was really no system at all, merely a division of responsibility. At least eight authorities, whose co-operation was necessary to get anything well done, worked independently of each other. As Prince Albert remarked in a carefully prepared memorandum:

We have no generals trained and practised in the duties of that rank; no general staff or corps; no field commissariat; no field army department; no ambulance corps; no baggage train; no corps of drivers; no corps of artisans; no practice, or possibility of acquiring it, in the combined use of the three arms – cavalry, infantry, and artillery; no general qualified to handle more than one of these arms; and the artillery kept as distinct from the army as if it were a separate profession.

Even when the necessity for reform was accepted, improvements were always limited by the feeling that 'it is never prudent to push changes one inch beyond the length it is absolutely necessary'. Red tape and worship of routine often turned confusion into deadlock, and by the end of 1854 *The Times* was writing powerfully of 'the decline and decay of our great expedition' as a result of 'grossest mismanagement' by 'that huge impostor, our military system'. England was 'on the verge of ruin', and the 'national reputation' had been completely destroyed.

The administrative confusion was made even worse by the physical conditions in which the troops were bound to live in the Crimea. Only one-sixth of the deaths in the Crimean War were caused by battle; disease was always more destructive than the actual fighting, and at first little was done to alleviate it. After the Battle of Alma there were no splints and no bandages, and, when *The Times* commented some weeks later that the manner in which the sick and wounded were being treated was 'worthy only of the savages of Dahomey', there was a surge of public rage at home.

Florence Nightingale's mission to the Crimea was undertaken in response to the challenge of this 'tremendous crisis': contending against military prejudice, medical jealousy, and even religious controversy among her nurses, she showed indomitable courage and determination. More than any other single person she interested the public in the magnitude of the task to be carried out in and behind the battlefield. A Crimean veteran recalled her passing his bed with some doctors who were saying, 'It can't be done,' and her replying quietly, 'It *must* be done.' 'There seemed,' he said, 'to be no appeal from her quiet conclusive manner.'

But no 'quiet conclusive manner' could regulate the position in England from which, as she herself saw, 'the grand administrative evil emanates.' The more news came through of difficulties and disappointments in the Crimea, the more was the public roused to an angry demand for wholesale changes. The higher command was criticized at first, then the whole system of military promotion, and finally aristocracy itself. Favour, incompetence, and stupidity seemed to be 'revelling and rioting' in the camp at Sebastopol. Lords Raglan, Lucan, and Cardigan, three of the chief officers, were subject to widespread attacks – Lord Cardigan, 'the Noble Yachtsman', was commanding the Light Brigade from a luxurious private vessel in Balaclava Bay; his superior officer, Lord Lucan, his brother-in-law, with whom he had been on bad terms for years, was christened 'Lord Look-On' by his own troops; Lord Raglan, the commander-in-chief, admitted to be 'the kindest, calmest, and most gentlemanly of men', had provided positions on his staff for five of his nephews. Living in the past, he was unable and unwilling to substitute talent for connexions. He proved incapable of managing either the war or the private dispute between Lucan and Cardigan, who were aptly described by one of their captains in words which shocked his conventional parents: 'Without mincing matters, two such fools could hardly be picked out of the British Army. And they take command. But they are Earls!'

It is not surprising that critics at home asked whether it would be possible to turn for effective leadership from the aristocrats to

the great railway administrators and contractors, the men who manage lines of packets, who own and direct successfully the operation of whole fleets of merchant ships ... men who, conducting their own operations with unfailing regularity, look with scorn on the miserable and repeated proofs of official blundering, which has so grievously misdirected and wasted unbounded resources?

Why not dismiss the aristocrats and appeal to the businessmen; why not get rid of the politicians and accept the services of the experts? Victory, on which such high hopes were centred, seemed to depend not only on the overthrow of the pacific Aberdeen's 'weak' government but on a searching examination of all traditional English institutions and a purging of the 'leaders' who were undermining the best of them.

3

It was against such a setting that John Arthur Roebuck emerged as a 'tribune of the people'. On 23 January 1855, 'deeply moved' by events in the Crimea and convinced that they 'cried aloud for investigation', he asked the House of Commons to set up a select committee to inquire into the condition of the army before Sebastopol.

Roebuck, unlike several of the active critics of the government, had no detailed knowledge of the Crimea or of the Near East. His fellow-critic, Henry Layard, was the excavator of Nineveh; Roebuck was merely the member for Sheffield. But his nickname was 'Tear 'Em', and even as late as 1936 the phrase 'Don't John Arthur Roebuck me' was still used in Sheffield if one felt that a person was getting the better of one, somewhat tendentiously, in a heated argument.

Roebuck was not an expert but a public accuser. He dealt in denunciations and judgements more happily than in proofs or

arguments; his favourite word was 'sham', and he used it frequently. 'Placing unbounded confidence in himself and troub-
ling his mind very little about anyone else,' A. W. Kinglake,
the historian of Crimea, said of him, 'he had a hardiness beyond
other mortals.' A very small man in height, he had a loud
voice, considerable powers of oratory, and a bundle of vehement opinions. Although he was ill in 1855, he had by no
means lost his energy, and he had already established his reputation of being one of the few members of Parliament who
dared to use plain speech and who showed no fear of great
persons, whether in the cabinet or at the court.

His independence was his greatest asset. When he entered
Parliament in 1832, he was, in his own words, 'neither Whig
nor Tory.... I went into the House of Commons determined
to advocate that which I believed to be for the interest of the
people, without regard to party considerations.' Such independence he did not find incompatible with a strong and growing distaste for Whiggery, which he had always considered an
even less congenial political philosophy than Toryism. Born in
Madras and reared in Canada, Roebuck had a natural dislike of
all government by 'connexion'. 'The Whigs have ever been
an exclusive and aristocratic faction,' he wrote in 1852, 'though
at times employing democratic principles and phrases as weapons of defence against their opponents.... When out of office
they are demagogues: in power they become exclusive oli-
garchs.' Such a sharp distrust of the Whigs strengthened,
rather than weakened, his position in 1855, when distrust of
'Whig aristocracy' was one of the great levers of public
agitation.

Roebuck was never a conformist, but his political training
and background fitted him in 1855 to be a vocal representative
of the urban middle classes. His great-grandfather had founded
the Carron Iron Works in Scotland and was given a place of
honour in Smiles's *Industrial Biography*. He himself was a friend
of John Brown, the Sheffield steel king. He had little sympathy
with the doctrines of the Manchester School, particularly with
the views of foreign policy which they expressed, but he had
been a vigorous Benthamite in his youth and a close personal

friend of John Stuart Mill, the first friend the precocious young Mill ever had. Roebuck, like all Benthamites, loathed privilege, particularly inherited privilege. 'All political power which exists in the shape of privilege has a tendency to be mischievously corrupt,' he once wrote. Although Professor Trevelyan likes to call him 'a pseudo-radical', there was no deficiency of radicalism here.

Behind Roebuck in 1855 was the turbulent city population of Sheffield, the great Yorkshire steel town, the population of which was untouched by Whiggery and little affected by the philosophy of the Manchester School. Roebuck had been chosen in 1849 as one of the two members for the city and was a good judge of its moods. At one of its great annual institutions, the Cutlers' Dinner, in September 1853, he described the recent Spithead naval review as the greatest peace meeting of the year. 'To be prepared for war,' he went on, 'is the best preservative of peace.' Roebuck was a patriotic Radical before most Radicals became patriotic. Even in 1850 he was the private member of Parliament who, by proposing a vote of confidence in the government's foreign policy, gave the opportunity for Palmerston to make his famous Don Pacifico speech, claiming that, wherever a British subject might be, the watchful eye and the strong arm of Britain would protect him. The 1853 crisis in the Near East inspired no new patriotism in Roebuck, although his fellow-member of Parliament for Sheffield, Hadfield, was a follower of Cobden and Bright, anxious at first to keep out of the Eastern question altogether, and only later moving round to a modified support of the war. In January 1855 he was willing to second Roebuck's motion. Sheffield was united.

The *Sheffield and Rotherham Independent*, which, like *The Times,* had swung round from sincere support of Aberdeen to vigorous approval of the war – 'war will probably give us a better route to India via Syria and Mesopotamia. All Asia lies before us' – praised Roebuck in January 1855, for trying to break through 'the fetters of routine of aristocratic preference. ... We are glad that the public voice has found a spokesman in the House of Commons so able and fearless as our Member ...

and Ministers must make a wonderfully cogent answer to Mr Roebuck before they can satisfy either the House of Commons or the country that their duty has been done, and that our whole system of administration does not need a radical change.' Another Sheffield newspaper, the *Iris*, went further:

It is not at all improbable that if the popular voice had been heard through the means of large public meetings in the manufacturing districts as early as the end of last November ... two months of trifling at home and misery abroad might have been spared. ... Let Mr Roebuck take heart; his burning words cannot express the deep-seated shame ... with which the disgraceful past is viewed in Sheffield, nor the firm resolve which exists to bring the authors of our loss to exposure and punishment. We trust he will persevere, be the consequence what it may.

Even with Radical opinion behind him, and with the support of many people in the large cities of industrial Britain, Roebuck appeared to more than one observer rather like David confronting Goliath when he moved for his select committee in January 1855. That he not only got his select committee but also brought down Aberdeen's government was the result not so much of his zeal or ability as of serious divisions inside Aberdeen's cabinet. When he hurled his stones at the government, it was already shaking at the knees.

The first result of Roebuck's announcement of his motion was the resignation of Lord John Russell, who had long felt unhappy and frustrated as an ordinary member of a coalition ministry headed by the Peelite Aberdeen – 'the worst government I ever belonged to', he called it. Throughout 1854 Russell had threatened resignation so often that Prince Albert kept a special file marked in his own hand, 'Concerning the part which Lord John Russell took in breaking up Lord Aberdeen's Government, Nov. 1854–Feby 1855'; this time the resignation was pressed just at the moment when opinion outside the House was most critical of the administration.

When the Whig–Peelite government, robbed of Russell, tried to resist Roebuck's motion, it was defeated by the surprisingly heavy margin of 305 votes to 148. The House was so amazed at the size of the majority that, when the figures were announced, they were greeted not with the usual cheers but with profound silence followed by derisive laughter. The government had been condemned, in the words of a contemporary, to 'the most ignominious end recorded of any Cabinet in modern days'.

All the groups which were dissatisfied with either Aberdeen or more particularly with Newcastle, his Secretary of War, took the opportunity of bringing the government down. The lines of division showed how unreal party labels were in the 1850s and how little the main features of the general political situation had changed since 1851. Although Whigs and Peelites had come together in the long-expected coalition which had proved impossible in 1851, they had only done so in terms of group interest, not in terms of 'a coalition of party sentiment and feeling'. 'Everybody's principles had united with nobody's opinions,' said one Conservative. Their tepid cooperation was effected in a House of Commons elected in 1852 which nobody expected to last for more than a month or two. 'It will be an impossible Parliament,' one of the Peelite leaders, Sir James Graham, had written to Gladstone just after the election. 'Parties will be found too nicely balanced to render a new line of policy practicable without a fresh appeal to the electors.' No such appeal was made, and the Parliament lasted until 1857, but it only did so because there was a perpetual shifting of groups, a desperate hunt for places, and a general dislike of dissolution. In 1855 the situation was so serious that Matthew Arnold, meditating on the tombstones in Haworth churchyard, could turn from the Brontës to politics and write of

> This ignominious spectacle,
> Power dropping from the hand
> Of paralytic factions, and no soul
> To snatch and wield it.

The failure to take Sebastopol made the political situation seem desperate. Ordinary members of Parliament and disgruntled people everywhere were asking for 'a War Cabinet, constituted with the single purpose of prosecuting hostilities with energy, of repairing past errors, and of saving the remnant of our army'.

Yet the crisis did not end with the defeat of the Whig–Peelite coalition. When Aberdeen's government fell, both Derby, the protectionist, and Russell, the Whig, found it impossible to form a ministry. Derby's failure, which made Disraeli sullen and bitter, recalled his failure of 1851. He was willing to serve if Palmerston and some of the Peelites joined him, but he was clearly unwilling to draw too close to Radicals like Roebuck, with whom Disraeli was on very friendly terms. Russell, too, failed to form a ministry. After his resignation from the government he was generally discredited; his late colleagues would not serve under him.

In such circumstances only Palmerston was left. He had served as Home Secretary under Aberdeen, and he was the one minister of the Aberdeen government whose reputation had not been impaired by the military disasters in the Crimea. Tories might consider Derby to be *l'homme nécessaire*, but Palmerston became *l'homme inévitable*. Roebuck could claim that he had put him there, and public opinion was prepared to endorse the change only if it meant a strengthening of government and a reform of the administration. The aim was not to shuffle political personalities but

to put strength into the place of weakness, courage and resolution in the place of timidity and fickleness, and enlarged and enlightened views respecting the true interests of the empire, in the place of paltry and narrow ideas, which naturally led their owner to cherish a profound reverence for despots and despotism.

Palmerston, in February 1855, was the creature of the people rather than their master. There were doubts at the time among the Radical extremists whether the aristocratic 'whiskered wonder' of over seventy was likely to lift the war out of the quagmire into which it had been forced by 'the aristocratic system, a system of total incapacity'. Disraeli played on the doubts with the same consummate skill that he had played upon Tory doubts in 1846. 'Palmerston is really an impostor,' he wrote to a friend, 'utterly exhausted, and at the best only ginger-beer, and not champagne, and now an old painted pantaloon, very deaf, very blind, and with false teeth, which would fall out of his mouth when speaking, if he did not hesitate so in his talk.' To John Bright he was equally candid: 'You may see the breed, but the action and power are gone.' Bright did not need to be told. 'Palmerston – Prime Minister!' wrote Bright in his diary. 'What a hoax! The aged charlatan has at last obtained the great object of his long and unscrupulous ambition.'

Responsible opinion accepted Palmerston because of his popularity in the country, his experience in Parliament, and his supposed favour in the counsels of France. If Disraeli did not think much of him, it was confidently believed that Napoleon III did. Even the Queen and Prince Albert were influenced by these considerations. But he soon lost ground after taking office. His first night was 'a failure', and 'the House was bewildered and disorganized'. Roebuck refused, despite the change of ministry and despite pressure from Palmerston himself, to abandon his intention of securing a select committee. The change of government, he said, had not even meant a complete change of ministers; Palmerston was still surrounded by guilty men, and inquiry was as urgent as it had been when Aberdeen was in command. There was no incompatibility between Palmerston's proposed reforms of the administration and continued inquiry by members of Parliament into the origins of disaster.

Nothing but the authority of the house could enable the official chief to overcome the *vis inertiae* in the atmosphere of office. He should move his committee [said Roebuck], as an assistance to the Noble Lord, in infusing new vigour into the constitution of the country, which he would not do with his unaided efforts.

Roebuck got his committee, even though its constitution was a little different from that which was originally planned, and the political position of Palmerston was further weakened. By attempting to suppress the Sebastopol committee, he had aroused popular suspicion; by eventually giving way, he forced the resignation of his three remaining Peelite ministers, Graham, Gladstone, and Sidney Herbert. The old Whig combination of 1851 was restored, and, though the Peelites were discredited both as administrators and now as politicians, it was clear that, as Disraeli said, the only effect of the crisis had been that 'we have replaced a Cabinet of All the Talents by a Cabinet of All the Mediocrities'.

Palmerston's position remained weak throughout the spring and early summer of 1855. When Russell, who consented to go to Vienna in February to take part in peace talks, got caught up in a web of intricate double-talk and intrigue, there were many people, dissatisfied with the whole state of affairs, who sighed for 'men who had no party considerations, who cared not for aristocratic influences, who went out determined to sacrifice those who were guilty, regardless of persons, and who did so'. Russell, whose erratic course had precipitated a crisis in 1854, was even more erratic in 1855. He spoke in Vienna as a peacemaker and in London as a warmonger, and, when it became clear that he preferred his Vienna performance to that on his own soil, he was totally discredited:

> I went like a fairy plenipotentiary
> To the town of Vienna, to settle the war,
> But they'll not believe me then, they vow I've deceived them,
> And call me the friend of the great Russian Tsar.

The Tories took the lead in moving a vote of censure on his conduct, and, when Palmerston told them in defence of his old rival that 'they were making much ado about nothing', Sir Edward Bulwer Lytton replied pertinently that '*Much Ado* came next after *The Comedy of Errors*.' Before Parliament could pass a vote of censure on Russell, he resigned his special position on 13 July 1855. Palmerston was now the only commanding figure left in English politics, but he was still subject to the close scrutiny of the Commons and the press. 'The country is in a peculiar temper and looks for victory,' the *Illustrated London News* had written a month or two before. 'Until that be achieved, it will be difficult for any statesman, or set of statesmen, however great their genius, or pure their characters, to conduct its affairs with much profit or satisfaction. Sebastopol must be taken, or discontent will grow into a danger; and many things more precious than the existence of a Ministry, or of a Parliament, will be called into question.'

4

It was in this period of political uncertainty that Roebuck's select committee set to work to examine the origins of mismanagement. The establishment and continued existence of the committee marked an interesting innovation – of a very temporary character – in English government. The English parliamentary system has never, unlike the American system, relied on committees to carry out its work. The supporters of a committee of investigation might claim a precedent in the Walcheren Committee during the Napoleonic Wars, but in fact the existence of an active tribunal of inquiry considering a wide variety of administrative and political questions was something new. Radicals always employed the select-committee technique to explore specific questions, but this was the only occasion on which a committee with such wide terms of reference investigated government as a whole. Roebuck, on one previous occasion in 1843, had tried to have such a committee appointed to investigate the causes of a war in Afghanistan. On that occasion he had referred to the war as 'unjust and impolitic' and had spoken of Lord Palmerston's 'mischievous meddling and more pernicious influence on our foreign policy'. In 1855 he approved of the war and accepted Palmerston, and he got his committee because there was a general demand for it outside Westminster.

Indeed, in many parts of the country there were local foreign affairs committees attacking the whole conduct of 'secret diplomacy'. The most important of them was in Newcastle, where the members were proclaiming with satisfaction that the 'deluge seems to be at hand' and that 'the time is ripe and rotten for a change'; the Sheffield committee was almost as important and was sufficiently strong to intimidate both Hadfield and Roebuck. The Sheffield committee, while welcoming the appointment of Roebuck's committee, wanted to go much further and to set up 'a Standing Committee of both Houses of Parliament, to have a surveillance of foreign affairs, on the principle of similar standing committees in the United States'.

The influence of the local foreign affairs committees would have been even stronger had they not split into factions, particularly into two groups, one supporting David Urquhart, and the other violently opposing him. Urquhart, by now a wild and eccentric Radical, unbalanced and paranoiac, believed in conspiratorial terms that Palmerston himself was a Russian spy, accepting gold from the tsar. He managed to persuade many workingmen that this melodramatic thesis was tenable, but for every convert he won he made several sceptics and several violent opponents. Roebuck told the supporters of Urquhart in Sheffield that he did not believe for one moment that Palmerston had designedly betrayed England, although he had made many mistakes; for taking this point of view, Roebuck himself was accused of complicity with the Russians by the Urquhart group. 'Lord Palmerston,' they said, 'has woven a spell, against which no British politician has the talisman; the spell is crime.' Roebuck did not fear Urquhart. 'That such a person looks upon me with suspicion,' he wrote to the press, 'is, I think, a circumstance rather in my favour.'

The supporters of Urquhart were masters of innuendo and smear, but they could not influence politics in Parliament, and in Parliament Roebuck was as extreme a Radical as that institution was capable of nurturing. For proposing his committee and persisting in carrying out the investigations he had demanded, he was subject to constant criticism from Whigs and Peelites.

All the difficulties involved in 'government' by select committee were pointed out by the Peelite former ministers before the committee met. Graham asked whether it would be open or secret. Either way there would be many problems to face. If it were to be secret, the persons implicated by the evidence would have no opportunity of defending themselves in public, of examining the witnesses, or of rebutting false accusations. If it were to be open, the evidence would be published each day in the press and would be published in such sensational form that morale would suffer and the winning of the war itself would become more difficult. In any case there would be no appeal from any member of the committee to the House until the committee had presented its report, and this would afford a serious threat both to personal liberty and to the constitution. Roebuck had already referred to Lord Raglan, the commander-in-chief, as 'the prisoner in the dock'. 'I warn the House distinctly,' said Sir James Graham, 'that it is delegating its powers, unaccompanied by any check or control, to the chance medley of six out of eleven gentlemen, and that it may thus involve the country in the most fatal consequences.' He added that he would have preferred an inquiry at the bar or, if there had to be a select committee, the presence of a minister of the Crown on it as a full-time member.

Graham's arguments were cogent, but they were characteristically Peelite; they were tinged with an administrative rather than with a political colouring. It had never been Graham's forte to understand the movement of public opinion or to sympathize with public vituperation. The Peelites had drifted further and further away from the public since 1851, when they had set themselves firmly against the rising tide of anti-Catholic prejudice. By 1855 no one really cared what they said; they were on their way out of English politics as a separate group. Little attention was paid to Gladstone's statement – and in 1855 Gladstone was still a Peelite – that the committee, not being a committee of punishment or a committee of remedy, must therefore, if it were anything at all, be a committee of government, taking away from the executive the most important of its functions. Gladstone's reputation in the House was greater than his reputation in the country, and at this time he was more interested in the reform of the University of Oxford than in the Crimea. This did not, however, stop the *Sheffield Times* from dismissing him as one of the Russian party in England.

The House itself rejected the Peelite arguments and followed the lead of lesser-known members like the Tory, Sir John Pakington, who became a member of the committee, and George F. Muntz, the bearded manufacturer from Birmingham, who protested against arguing from precedent in a case where there was no precedent. Palmerston himself, somewhat cynically, accepted the committee on the grounds that, if he resigned, there would be nobody left to take his place. The possibility of a parliamentary solution of the difficulties of the country would then have been exhausted, and the way would have been open for the emergence of an institution more like a French committee of public safety than a select committee of Her Majesty's Faithful Commons. He realized that there might be inconvenience in an inquiry, but, confronted with such a strong body of opinion in favour, he thought that he had better give in gracefully. Very properly he believed that there would be a greater inconvenience still 'in this country presenting the spectacle of a Government in abeyance at a period so critical'.

Once Palmerston had accepted the committee, the debate on whether it should be secret or not became more spirited. Pakington and Roebuck, supported by most of the committee members, preferred secrecy, for they felt that the difficulties of the task of investigation beset them like rocks on every side. Only Lord Seymour, the Whig member, who had done his best to hold back public health reform a few years before, preferred open to secret sessions. But Parliament as a whole was less friendly to 'a hole and corner' committee. 'The House loses its powers over the Committee if it be secret,' Graham said. 'Witnesses will be more guarded in their statements, and Members in their questions, if it be open.' When he went on to argue that a secret committee would be an inquisition unworthy of a free and generous people, Disraeli accused him of indulging in 'the oratory of terror', but the alarm was not merely a rhetorical flourish. Roebuck himself, seeing that the House was seriously divided on the matter, showed sufficient judgement to withdraw the request for secrecy. Common sense triumphed over doctrine.

The open committee continued its sessions until June in an atmosphere of great public excitement. The meetings were always well attended, and a large crowd always gathered outside seeking admission. Only a small fraction of those wishing to attend could be accommodated in the space allotted to the public. The evidence was published each day and could be followed by readers of the newspapers in all parts of the country.

Most of the witnesses were willing to give full and explicit evidence and showed conclusively that the blame for mismanagement fell not upon individuals but on the system for which both political parties and Parliament were responsible. The most distinguished witness, the Duke of Cambridge, stated in his evidence that, at the very moment when a cabinet minister was assuring the House that the number of men fit for duty was thirty thousand, the real number was only twelve thousand, and that *The Times* had been right in exposing the deficiencies of food, medical equipment, and clothing. It soon became clear that Aberdeen and his ministers, including Newcastle, had been unjustly blamed for offences of which they were innocent; the causes of administrative confusion lay buried in the whole structure of government, not in the incompetence of particular people. 'I felt corruption round about me,' wrote Roebuck, 'but I could not lay my hand upon it.'

As the committee moved towards such a conclusion, extreme Radicals became more active in demanding army reform and administrative reform. The system in the army of promotion by purchase was so vigorously condemned that the reforms of 1871 would have been carried out in 1855 or 1856 if the war had continued. One of the leading supporters of army reform was Viscount Goderich, the son of a former prime minister and an advanced Liberal who supported cooperative workshops and even trade union strike funds. Merit alone should be the test of a commission, he claimed. If improvements were introduced and young sergeants were allowed to become subalterns, an intelligent class would enter the army. De Lacy Evans, an army officer himself and an early Russophobe, told stories of Peninsula veterans still rotting as lieutenants while aristocratic newcomers were pushed straight to the top. The Duke of Wellington, he said, had believed that the maintenance of an aristocracy was more important than the maintenance of an efficient army. 'Those who have more friends get up to the higher ranks of the Army; but if there is a question of selecting someone for the command of a corps or of an army, the answer is – "Oh! such a man is not of such a class" and "Don't talk to us of him".'

It was clear that inherited notions of hierarchy and status were breaking down under the impact of unsuccessful war, but Parliament as a whole was not anxious to change the system too radically. The Tories helped Palmerston to defeat Goderich's proposals by 158 votes to 114. They were as strongly opposed as was Palmerston to the 'radicalization' of the army, for many of their own members were army officers. They produced curiously modern-looking arguments to defend their point of view, such as that former rankers would find things more difficult in the officers' mess or that an army without social cement would not be able to maintain discipline. There was also one final argument which was not much used in public – that to touch the army certainly meant friction with the Crown.

The most important consequence of the defeat of Goderich's motion was the conversion of the demand for army reform into a more general demand for administrative reform, culminating in a bill for the opening of the civil service to competitive examination. Many administrative reform associations were set up in the country in cities like Birmingham and Manchester, designed 'to destroy the aristocratic monopoly of power and place in the Civil Service'. They found ammunition in the famous *Report on the Organization of the Civil Service,* which was prepared by Sir Charles Trevelyan and Sir Stafford Northcote and which stated that admission to the civil service was eagerly sought for, but mainly by the unambitious, the indolent, and the incapable. 'Those whose abilities do not warrant an expectation that they will succeed in the open professions ... and those whom indolence of temperament or physical infirmity unfit for active exertions, are placed in the Civil Service, where they may obtain an honourable livelihood with no labour and little risk.' Reformers contrasted the hard work, the careful attention to duty, and the reserves of energy and ability of the industrial manufacturing classes with the sloth and incompetence of the departments. The London Administrative Reform Association, which staged great demonstrations in Drury Lane, had Samuel Morley, the great hosiery manufacturer, as its president and Charles Dickens, then associated with the *Daily News,* as one of its speakers. The nonconformist Morley had been a wealthy backer of the Anti-Corn Law League and of the disestablishment of the Church of England; Dickens had always been an administrative reformer, and it was he who went on to create the picture of the 'Circumlocution Office' and the aristocratic breed of Titus Barnacles inhabiting it.

There were many members of Parliament who sympathized with the demand for administrative reform as businessmen rather than as politicians. Samuel Laing, for instance, contrasted private concerns, where merit was the mainspring, with government offices, where merit passed unnoticed. The reason why the *system* was wrong was the mediocrity of the people who were managing it. Mediocrity succumbed to system; only ability could dominate it. The Tories joined with the Radicals in Parliament on this issue, and both Ellenborough and Derby agreed that, unless there had been good grounds for administrative reform, men of high mercantile character would never have plunged into such keen discussions on such a subject. But the chief supporters of administrative reform were Radical politicians, particularly Layard, and it was he who introduced the question in the House of Commons in June 1855.

The debate on his motion – that the House viewed with concern the sacrifice of merit and efficiency to party and family influences and to blind adherence to routine – was a most interesting one. Layard claimed that the government was a closed monopoly of a few families, that the army was a stronghold of favouritism, that the consular and diplomatic services were private preserves of a small group of people, and that the civil service needed to be opened to competitive examination. On the last point he was strongly supported by Gladstone, who demanded the opening-up of all the departments. Palmerston showed himself very sceptical. Examinations must not be trusted too far, nor would throwing them open to all entrants always secure first-rate men. The brightest and most promising young men would always be attracted to more lucrative professions.

Two of the most interesting speeches in the debate were made by the Tory, Sir Edward Bulwer Lytton, and by the Independent, Henry Drummond. Both enjoyed the oratorical opportunities of the war to the full. Lytton claimed that it was the Prime Minister who had made this question the subject of a popular platform agitation by the injudiciousness of his resistance and the levity of his acquiescence and by his scattering of pleasant jokes and flowery epigrams. Though he did not identify himself with Layard's attack on party or the social system, he did condemn the combination of families and privileged houses 'with which the Whig party had chilled the enthusiasm and energy of the people'. Drummond, who had supported the setting-up of Roebuck's select committee, was far more outspokenly independent in his views. He asked whether it was true that the middle classes were better or more 'pure' administrators than the aristocracy. They had not even succeeded in draining the great cities in which they lived.

See what a precious mess they have made at Manchester. Filled as that town was with Radicals and philosophers, they could not drain it. And yet there was hardly a town in the kingdom which could be more easily drained; for it stands upon two hills and any man of ordinary common sense would have at once said, 'Cut a ditch from the top to the bottom and so drain it.'

Drummond added that the cry for administrative reform was a delusive cry and that the dream of replacing all those who had ever been concerned in the government of a country by shipbrokers, stockbrokers, and railway directors could only lead to disaster. Drummond's sarcasm was extremely effective, and Layard's resolutions were defeated by 359 votes to 46.

The matter was not shelved, however, and remained important until the end of the war. There was a further debate in July in which the opponents of competitive examinations were less successful than they had been a few weeks previously. Gladstone contended that the civil service system as it existed at the moment not only did not provide the country with the best men for the job but created a vast mass of collateral evils connected with the dispensation of patronage, which kept a large class of men in a state of expectancy, wasting their lives in solicitation. At the end of this debate even Palmerston admitted that competition might be usefully introduced in some spheres of the administration.

While these parliamentary debates on the system of government were continuing and public excitement remained high, Roebuck's committee was still in session, influenced naturally by the general temper of Commons and people but unable to find convenient scapegoats. On 18 June 1855 the committee presented its report.

It was not so damning a document as it might have been, for Roebuck's draft was turned down and a far more gentle document by Seymour accepted in its place. It found that insufficient care had been taken in looking after the welfare of the soldiers in the Crimea and that particular departments, especially transport, had been grossly mismanaged; but it exonerated the Duke of Newcastle, who had been the chief target of criticism in January. It was only on the casting vote of Roebuck that the committee accepted the sentences containing its most decisive denunciation –

that the sufferings of the army mainly resulted from the circumstances under which the expedition to the Crimea was undertaken and executed. The Administration which ordered that expedition had no adequate information as to the armament of the forces in the Crimea. They were not acquainted with the strength of the fortresses to be attacked nor with the resources of the country to be invaded. They hoped and expected the expedition to be immediately successful, and, as they did not foresee the probability of a protracted struggle, they made no preparation for a winter campaign. . . . Your Committee will now close their report with a hope that every British army may in future display the valour which this noble army has displayed, and that none may hereafter be exposed to such sufferings as have been recorded in these pages.

Some members of the committee and most members of the House would have been content to let the inquiry terminate with the publication of the report, but Roebuck insisted on moving a motion in July 1855, visiting 'with severe reprehension every member of that Cabinet whose counsels led to such disastrous results'. The moment seemed propitious for a sharp bout of political excitement, for, between the publication of the report and the debate on Roebuck's motion, Russell had

resigned for the second time, 'shaking the confidence of
the world in the whole of British political stability.'

But it soon became clear that the House on this occasion was
less disposed to support Roebuck than it had been in January.
His short speech was far less effective than his very short speech
earlier, which he had been compelled to cut because of illness.
Simply reading out the motion was, as Disraeli remarked, the
most effective piece of rhetoric in January. By July members
felt that Roebuck was flogging a dead horse in attacking Aberdeen's defunct cabinet. There was little support for impeach-
ing Lord Aberdeen, and, although Roebuck presented petitions
from Birmingham and Bradford, praying that Aberdeen's ministers might be impeached, he did not press the point. Lord
Palmerston and half his cabinet would have been compelled to
resign if the motion had been carried, and only very few members of Parliament in July 1855 were prepared to contemplate
another change of government.

Many members of Parliament in the course of the debate on
Roebuck's motion expressed dislike of Roebuck's 'acrimoni-
ous and vindictive personality'. His spell of influence had been
broken. 'He evidently delights in casting charges upon everybody,' said Russell, 'and indulging that abundant vituperation
which is evident in his nature.' 'His speeches,' he went on,
'began with a strong exordium and ended with an admirable
peroration, but lacked proof or substance in the middle. . . .
These are the beak and talons of the bird of prey, but the inside
is nothing but straw.' In any case, 'was it prudent to exaggerate the difficulties of a constitutional government by severity
of scrutiny and too great animadversion upon failures?'

John Bright dealt very effectively with Russell, and it was
ironical that on this occasion he was one of Roebuck's warmest
supporters; the peace Radical and the war Radical once again
joined hands. But neither of them was fully alert to the change
of mood. Bright was regretting that Lord Derby had not taken
office, and Roebuck was looking beyond Westminster to Sheffield; but it was Palmerston who was beginning at last to establish a position of complete ascendancy. He attacked Roebuck

for trying to persuade the House to pass a vote of censure upon the existing government on account of the transactions of a government which no longer existed, but he had a far stronger argument which looked to the future rather than to the past. The army had been in a bad condition in December 1854, but it was in a good condition in July 1855. Indeed, it was in as fit a condition as any army that had ever existed. Victory was round the corner. Why spend time brooding on history?

Roebuck's motion was not formally rejected but shelved. General Peel, a member of the committee and a brother of Sir Robert, moved the previous question and carried the House by 284 votes to 182. Government by select committee had come to an end.

Sheffield, however, and the large industrial cities stood firm behind Roebuck. When one writer dared to call him a 'failure in public life', the *Sheffield Times* wrote: 'If the honest advocacy of innumerable measures intended for the welfare of the people at large . . . constitutes a "failure", then perish from the scroll of immortality all the Howards and Hampdens that glorify humanity.'

5

The summer and autumn of 1855 saw a further strengthening of Palmerston's position. June was a hot and feverish month, with three successive days of rioting by London mobs in Hyde Park to add to the excitement; yet the rioters were demonstrating not against the government or its military policy but against a private member's proposal – Lord Robert Grosvenor's bill to put down Sunday trading in the capital. Fussy Sabbatarianism and the threat to personal liberty of eating and drinking in London seemed a more lively menace in the summer of 1855 than crypto-Russians at court or in Parliament.

Party warfare was still being carried on at Westminster with what Whigs described as 'recklessness of consequences' and their opponents as 'unceasing vigilance', but Palmerston was beginning to stand out in the Commons as 'a Triton among the minnows'. As the military situation improved, he began to receive a large share of the credit for winning the war. The more conservative sections of the middle classes were beginning to abandon their more violent language, to lose some of their strident radicalism, and to look with suspicion on new extreme Radical organizations such as the State Reform Association, which dispensed with the guinea subscription of the Administrative Reform Association and included manhood suffrage and universal education in its programme as well as reform of government departments. It seemed as though the political volcano which had heaved and vomited forth its lava throughout the early months of 1855 was at last becoming dormant or, at any rate, that the damage it brought was being checked. But there was to be one final eruption. In September news of the capture of Sebastopol reached London by telegraph. The great military objective, which had been expected to fall during the first few weeks of the war, was at last in allied hands.

Far from improving the domestic situation, the fall of Sebastopol complicated it. There was relief at the news, but the important question of whether to go on with the war or not was now forced to the forefront. Many members of Parliament wanted peace, and, more important, so did the French. Indeed John Bright at this stage began to turn to Napoleon III as the hope of the future, while the Tories were divided and uncertain.

Palmerston himself was anxious to carry on the war to the point of resounding victory: Sebastopol had fallen largely as a result of a French and not an English assault, and England needed a victory of its own if it were to emerge from the war with its national pride satisfied. The militant Radicals went even further, still holding to the view that only the continuation of the war

would force upon the Government the necessity of making those changes in our naval and military systems which alone can give real effect to the valour of our soldiers and sailors and enable us to reconquer the *prestige* which we have lost, so that we may once again become a truly great and independent power instead of disgracefully hanging on to the coat-tails of the usurper of France.

The wheel was turning full circle. Tsar Nicholas had died in March 1855: now, even before the fighting ended, the emperor of France was beginning to assume the more familiar features of a national enemy. And the dreams of freedom for the down-trampled nationalities of Italy, Hungary, and Poland were still alive. 'If peace is to be really preserved,' wrote the *Sheffield Times*, 'it must be placed on some new basis. The progress of civilization is altogether incompatible with the preponderance of two or three despotisms on the Continent of Europe, always capable of disturbing the tranquillity.'

Palmerston found it impossible, however, to continue the war without the support of the French, and, after many secret negotiations, peace talks began in Paris in February 1856. The Treaty of Paris was signed at the end of March. There was no public enthusiasm; the settlement was generally regarded as 'a botchery and a sham', and the heralds who proclaimed it were hissed at Temple Bar.

In Sheffield, when the proclamation of peace was announced, it met with 'the very reverse of a hearty response'. There were hisses from the crowd, and 'the most uncomplimentary terms were everywhere exchanged by spectators, whom curiosity had attracted to the route as the procession passed them'. The windows of the embassies in London were brilliantly lit for the occasion, but the sober citizens of Sheffield were advised by the *Sheffield and Rotherham Independent* that the peace was not glorious enough or the prospect of its continuation so sure 'as to make it wise to spend our time in processions or our money in gas lights.'

The war had not lasted long enough to provide a complete inoculation against exuberant nationalism. Even though the leaders of the Manchester School were trying to persuade the working classes that the high price of corn in 1856 was the result of the continuation of hostilities, 'dear bread' did not become an antiwar slogan. Rather the public provisions societies, which were set up in some of the large towns like Birmingham, were anxious to rally opinion to enthusiasm for a continuation of the fighting. 'There is no pretence of having gained anything,' wrote another Sheffield newspaper; 'the cry is simply *Peace* as two years ago it was *War*. A maniac nation has exchanged its hatchet for a halter.' Nothing had been gained either by the fighting or by the peace. 'We are going to close a discreditable war by an inglorious peace,' wrote Richard Monckton Milnes; 'we shall have 10 p.c. income tax and 0 p.c. benefit to mankind.'

Once peace had been signed, however, there was a sharp decline in Radical vigour, and Palmerston more and more won the support of public opinion. In 1856 the Queen, while assuring Clarendon, the British representative at the peace talks, that the settlement was due 'to *him* alone', conferred on the Prime Minister the first garter bestowed on a member of the House of Commons since the time of Castlereagh. A year later the public showed its appreciation – an appreciation Palmerston greatly preferred – by overwhelmingly supporting him in the general election. The election was forced by a coalition of all his opponents in Parliament – Russell, Gladstone, Disraeli, Graham, the Cobdenite Milner-Gibson, and Roebuck. The issue was Palmerston's 'bellicose' handling of an incident at Canton in China, and Palmerston, who was accused by his enemies of bellicosity, boldly appealed to the electorate over the heads of all his opponents. He demanded a plebiscite rather than an election and gained a triumph 'greater than that of any minister since 1832', as great indeed as any of Napoleon III's triumphs across the channel. The leaders of the Manchester School were routed, the Peelites were broken up as a group, and the Prime Minister, who had appealed from a factious Parliament to a united nation, could claim that he, not Roebuck, had now become the Tribune of the People.

Roebuck was one of the few of his opponents who did not lose his seat. Sheffield held firm and returned both him and Hadfield at the top of the poll. A great public meeting offered him a handsome testimonial and a gift of eleven hundred guineas collected by subscription. His services during the war were extolled as a lesson for posterity. 'The example of his Committee,' one of the organizers of the testimonial claimed, 'will be a standing terror for years to come to careless administrators. It shook even Lord Palmerston into seriousness.' But it did not keep Palmerston serious for very long; he was one of the first subscribers to the fund collected for Roebuck. Indeed, he continued to need men like Roebuck in the years after 1857 to give him substantial independent backing, for he always preferred Radical enthusiasm for foreign questions to Radical demands for reform at home.

Roebuck became more interested in foreign affairs the older he got and less and less of a radical reformer. He was not alone in following this line of development. No other politician ever showed his zest for incompatible foreign causes, but many were increasingly indifferent to big questions of reform. The mood was changing after 1857, and, as it changed, the nature of Palmerston's appeal to the public altered. When peace was signed in 1856, *Reynold's News* complained that 'a great nation' had been 'ruled, thwarted, flouted, plundered, and dishonoured' by Palmerston, 'a man not naturally of a capacity superior to the average churchwarden'. By 1858 many Englishmen were showing that they preferred average churchwardens to eccentric demagogues. Cantankerous individuals continued to expose scandals, often with savage zest, but the mood of national exuberance had passed. The music of the guns was fading into the background, and the stage was set for the England of Bagehot and Trollope.

CHAPTER FOUR

Trollope, Bagehot, and the English Constitution

There never has been a *structure* in English political society: every man has not walked by the light of his own eyes: the less instructed have not deemed themselves the equals of the more instructed: the many have subordinated their judgement to that of the few. They have not done so blindly, for there has always been a spirit of discussion in the air; still they have done so – opinions have always settled down from the higher classes to the lower; and in that manner, wherever the nation has been called on to decide, a decision that is really national has been found.

WALTER BAGEHOT

I

Once the Crimean War was over, the English people could settle down without too many anxieties to live through the great mid-Victorian peace. 'Rest and be thankful.' The two writers who most surely described the essentials of life in the late fifties and sixties were Trollope and Bagehot. Indeed, two of the labels which have most frequently been attached by tidy-minded historians to the middle years of the century have been 'the age of Bagehot' and 'the age of Trollope'. The brilliant diagnosis of Bagehot's *English Constitution* and the steady observation displayed in the forty-seven novels of Trollope point to a common set of interpretations and conclusions. Both writers described the same superficially secure and comfortable England; for both of them Young England had passed into the world of dream and Chartism into the world of nightmare. The Crimean War left only lingering memories, and they were memories of what happened at Westminster rather than what happened at Sebastopol. The fire of the forties had burned out.

So too had much of the social fervour of the Great Exhibition and the social criticism of the middle fifties. As far as politics were concerned, 'a sense of satisfaction permeates the country, because most of the country feels it has got the precise thing which suits it'.

Neither Bagehot nor Trollope would have chosen the particular labels attached by their enthusiastic disciples. For both, the central political figure of their time was Palmerston, and the age they were describing was 'the age of Palmerston'. Palmerston had survived the gloomy prophecy of the Queen in 1851 and the popular assaults of the enraged Radicals of 1855 and 1856; he even survived the disintegration of his own triumphant majority of 1857. From 1859 to 1865 he was Prime Minister of a powerful coalition of Whigs, ex-Peelites, and Radicals, the ministry from which the Gladstonian Liberal party was formed. Yet Palmerston in these years relied on accumulated experience rather than on anticipation of the future. He carried forward into the sixties aristocratic grace and ripe experience, and one of his nicknames was 'Lord Evergreen'. 'His older popularity,' wrote Argyll, 'was entirely founded on foreign affairs, in which the British public are rather fond of games of bluff. But now, when in the multifarious transactions of his office as Prime Minister his moderation and good temper came to be often felt, he was becoming more and more a universal favourite.'

Characteristically, Trollope and Bagehot did not pitch Palmerston's claims too high. They did not consider him a hero as much as a symbol. Bagehot found the secret of his success in the fact that, though he was not a common man, a common man might have been cut out of him. 'He had in him all that a common man has and something more.' Trollope, who wrote a little-known biography of Palmerston which appeared in 1882, said similarly that 'he was by no means a man of genius and was possessed of not more than ordinary gifts of talent. . . . He was a man who from the first was determined to do the best with himself; and he did it with a healthy energy, never despairing, never expecting too much, never being in a hurry, but always ready to seize the good thing when it came.'

Palmerston was supreme precisely because he never expected too much. 'He was a statesman for the moment. Whatever was not wanted now, whatever was not practicable now, he drove quite out of his mind.' He was more interested, in fact, in his own age than in the past or the future.

The normal politics which both Bagehot and Trollope described were the politics of the period of Palmerston's ascendancy. From 1850 to 1867 fortune favoured the politician who left rapid improvement alone; so too did the economic situation, which allowed for the minimum interference by government. It was the business of politics not to define political issues but to provide honest leadership and sound administration. In Trollope's *The Prime Minister* the Duke of Omnium is disturbed when the restless leader of the Commons suggests that the government might be well advised to find a policy for the new session. He is a Treasury official and not a politician; like his eighteenth-century predecessor, he is immersed in the intrigues of influence and place rather than in programmes or policies. It soon becomes clear, however, that Sir Orlando Drought has no policy to propound, save a mild increase in armaments, to which people would not bother to object. Sir Orlando himself goes on to confirm that the main work of Parliament is not to legislate but to raise supplies. 'When that has been done with ease ... Ministers are very glad to get rid of the Parliament. ... To get a session over and done with is an achievement and delight.' Bagehot presented the same picture. The legislative aspect of the work of Parliament came not first but third in normal times, subordinate in importance to the executive management of the state and the political education its debates provided for the whole nation. While the governments were anxious to avoid contentious legislation, the members of the House of Commons were loath to seek frequent dissolutions. Elections were expensive and violent, and too regular contact with constituents was demoralizing. And so the politically experienced Palmerston, who had learned how to lull rather than to arouse the minds of his followers, became the dominating figure in the life of his age.

'Dear old Brock,' says one of Trollope's characters, 'he was the very model of an English statesman. He loved his country dearly, and wished her to be, as he believed her to be, first among nations. But he had no belief in perpetuating her greatness by any grand improvements. Let things take their way naturally, with a slight direction hither or thither as things might require. That was his method of ruling.... He never broke his heart because he could not carry this or that reform. What would have hurt him would have been to be worsted in personal conflict. But he could always hold his own, and he was always happy. Your man with a thin skin, a vehement ambition, a scrupulous conscience, and a sanguine desire for rapid improvement, is never a happy and seldom a fortunate, politician.'

Fortune is usually more fickle in its dealings with politicians than Trollope suggested, but it was consistent enough in the middle years of the century. Scrupulous consciences operated in private rather than in public. They called upon the active service of the voluntary body rather than the state. Sanguine desires for rapid improvement were at best tinged with expediency. The great cry of parliamentary reform, for instance, which had divided England in the early nineteenth century, was kept alive in these years, as John Bright once suggested, by its enemies as much as its friends. Its survival as an issue between 1852 and 1865 is best explained in terms of a delicately balanced situation within the House of Commons rather than in terms of sustained pressure from outside or of the persistent attraction of a fundamental theory. The reform bills of ministers were less triumphant vindications of principle than useful political manoeuvres which had the special advantage of being very unlikely to come off. 'Lord Robert Grosvenor's Bill against Sunday trading,' wrote one contented Conservative, 'created five times more popular agitation and excitement than all the Reform measures united.' Another Conservative, more critical and less contented, complained that 'in politics, at least, the old antithesis of principle and expediency is absolutely forgotten. Expediency is the only principle to which allegiance is paid.'

Some writers claimed that the dominion of expediency had

begun with Peel's acceptance of free trade in 1846 against the wishes of a substantial section of his own party. Trollope suggested this in a bitter aside in *The Three Clerks*. Other writers claimed that it was not the betrayal of Peel but his death that had taken the backbone out of English politics. Whatever the cause, party fragmentation and social compromise maintained politics in a state of truce, of arrested development. Even during Palmerston's ministry of 1859–65, which prepared the way for the emergence of the Liberal party, the American Henry Adams could write: 'Never had the British mind shown itself so *décousu*, so unravelled, at sea, floundering in every sort of historical shipwreck.' Or, as Gladstone exclaimed in 1860: 'We live in anti-reforming times. All improvements have to be urged in apologetic, almost supplicating terms.' It was only after the death of Palmerston and the passing of the Reform Bill of 1867, which could be regarded either as the crowning triumph of expediency or as the belated victory of principle, that politics took a new turn.

2

Both Bagehot and Trollope recognized that the peculiar characteristics of the English constitution in the middle years of the century depended upon a social as well as a political balance. The two main features of the social balance, as Bagehot stressed, were 'old deference' and the appeal of the 'dignified parts' of the constitution, 'parts, that is, retained not for intrinsic use, but from their imaginative attraction upon an uncultured and rude population.' Deference and dignity were safeguards of parliamentary government in a society in which 'primitive barbarism lay as a recognized basis to acquired civilization.'

Deference meant unthinking and habitual respect for social superiors. Even during the storms of the Crimean War, when urban radicalism battered against the aristocratic system of government, Gladstone had claimed that, 'if this country is more aristocratic . . . than it ought to be, it is not owing to any legal privileges possessed by the aristocracy, nor is it owing to any exclusive legislation; but it is owing partly perhaps to the strong prejudices in favour of the aristocracy which pervade all ranks and classes of the community.' In the small towns and villages the challenge of the Crimean War had been far less real. Gladstone's words would have passed as a platitude in a cathedral close, a senior common room of a college, or a country house. They became one of the most popular platitudes of the late fifties and sixties. On the eve of the second Reform Bill even those writers favourable to reform had to admit that, although the prestige of the aristocracy was 'growled at' occasionally, it was 'on the whole conceded, and even, it must be owned, secretly liked by the country at large.'

Dignity was equally important. It was the dignity of the constitution which impressed the public more than its efficiency or inefficiency. The press, particularly *The Times*, might influence the reading public, but the ceremonial and theatrical elements in government impressed the unreading multitude.

That which is mystic in its claims; that which is occult in its mode of action, that which is brilliant to the eye; that which is seen vividly for a moment, and then is seen no more; that which is hidden and unhidden; that which is specious, and yet interesting, palpable in its seeming, and yet professing to be more than palpable in its results; this, howsoever its form may change, or however we may define it or describe it, is the sort of thing – the only sort – which yet comes home to the mass of men.

Dignity and loyalty as well as deference lay at the heart of the mid-Victorian constitution.

Deference and dignity were more than safeguards of social peace and political tranquillity; they were necessary conditions.

A deferential community, even though its lowest classes are not intelligent, is far more suited to a cabinet government than any other kind of democratic country, because it is more suited to political excellence. The highest classes can rule in it; and the highest classes must, as such, have more political ability than the lower classes. ... A country of respectful poor, though far less happy than where there are no poor to be respectful, is nevertheless far more fitted to the best government. You can use the best classes of the respectful country; you can only use the worst where every man thinks he is as good as every other.

The qualification 'though far less happy' provides the key to the social philosophy of Bagehot; whereas the Utilitarian Jeremy Bentham had taken 'the greatest happiness of the greatest number' as the unchallengeable aim of government, Bagehot considered happiness neither as a precondition nor as a prior objective of 'the best government'. The 'best government' was that based on discussion; it was most effectively managed not by the many but by 'a select few', men who had enjoyed 'a life of leisure, a long culture, a varied experience, an existence by which the judgement is incessantly exercised and by which it may be incessantly improved'.

The 'select few' were the members of Parliament. Although some of them were 'the finest brute votes in Europe', they were prepared for the most part to debate wisely and above all to choose responsible members of the cabinet. They were never eager 'to press the tenets of their party to impossible conclusions'. Together, they made up 'a deliberate assembly of moderate and judicious men'. They chose rulers 'as we wish rulers to be chosen. If they did not, in a speaking and writing age, we should soon know.'

Trollope accepted the social presuppositions of Bagehot and explored them very fully in his novels. A more convincing impression of what everyday life was like in England in the middle Victorian years can be gathered from their pages than from any other source. It is true that Trollope did not describe the turbulent industrial North, but he was a faithful reporter of the shires, the small boroughs, and the metropolis. Against a social background which he understood instinctively, he posed the problems and dilemmas of his individual characters. Distrustful, even cynical, about society, he was curious and optimistically sympathetic about individual people. In his distaste for theory and missionizing, he reflected his age; indeed, there is no more shrewd judge of Victorian people. At a time when it was fashionable to decry his achievements, James Bryce wrote (1904) that, even though it would be impossible to predict that he would be read in fifty years, whoever did read him would catch the flavour of his age more satisfactorily than anywhere else.

Trollope maintained with no hesitation that Bagehot's 'select few' should always be 'gentlemen'. He was sensitive on this point and laboured it both in his novels and in his *Autobiography*. 'He would be defied to define the term "gentleman" – and would fail should he attempt. But he would know what he meant, and so very probably, would they who defied him.'

Both Bagehot, the essayist, and Trollope, the novelist, stressed the simple contrast between the many and the few, the *élite* and the mob. At one end of the scale were the 'coarse, dull, contracted multitude', who existed chiefly to serve and minister to the middle ranks of society and the upper classes. Trollope's poor have a language of their own – a very stilted language – but little independent life; in so far as they have aspirations of their own, they make themselves ridiculous, as does Mr Bunce in *Phineas Finn*. Bagehot believed that 'the character of the poor is an unfit topic for continuous art' and attacked Dickens's poor people because they were 'poor talkers and poor livers, and in all ways poor people to read about.... Mean manners and mean vices are unfit for prolonged delineation; the everyday pressure of narrow necessities is too petty a pain and too anxious a reality to be dwelt upon.'

A lack of deep sympathy with the poor and a failure to perceive the continued existence of a social problem of poverty are common to both Trollope and Bagehot. Neither of them knew much of the poor, except the servant and retainer class, or cared for 'the enthusiasm of humanity'; both believed that any transfer of political power to the poor would mean 'the supremacy of ignorance over instruction and of numbers over knowledge'. It was Bagehot who coined the perfect Trollopian phrase that 'a fulcrum and a position in the world ... is quite necessary to comfort in England'.

Trollope was the more successful of the two writers in passing from a simple contrast between the many and the few to a more detailed exploration of the connexions, the gradations, the boundaries, and the no-man's-lands which separated them. Between the 'multitude' and the select group of the socially secure there were the lower ranks of the middle classes, almost as ridiculous as the poor; in attempting to meddle with politics, they did not seek the rainbow's end but rather got cluttered up in their drawing-room parlours. Like Mr Tappitt in *Rachel Ray*, they were trapped into a series of perpetual scrapes and finally had to console themselves that political activity 'is just what gentle folks is fit for when they're past their regular work'. It was only a few members of the middle classes who managed to rise honestly above the level of their station and to mix freely with the squirearchy in a world of politics, where not too many questions were asked, provided that one was a gentleman. Although the classes were not separated by high walls of caste, to be accepted as a gentleman was by no means easy, as Trollope himself found out.

While the world described by both Bagehot and Trollope seems at first sight to be surprisingly static, it contained within itself seeds of change which compelled both writers to qualify their picture of a society divided between the many and the few. But it was changes in the distribution of wealth rather than changes in legislation or social and political theory which were challenging the existing basis of the constitution. There was a distant but clearly apprehended danger of a new working-class hegemony, of an attempt to build a paradise for the poor; but there was a more immediate danger of government being undermined by plutocracy. Bagehot defended the deference structure of English society because it saved the country not only from the rule of the mob but also from the rule of wealth, 'the religion of gold'; but he saw clearly that in the 1860s the kingdom of wealth was daily extending its boundaries with alarming rapidity and challenging traditional social structure. 'Every day our companies, our railways, our debentures and our shares, tend more and more to multiply these *surroundings* of the aristocracy and in time they will hide it.'

Trollope went further along the path of criticism than the author of *Lombard Street*. For Trollope the world of wealth was completely dissociated from both the world of land and the world of industry; it was concerned not with the creation of valuable real capital in the form of machinery or buildings but with senseless speculation, dangerous bubbles, and 'the infamous trade of stock-jobbing'. In its intrusions into politics it destroyed old values without suggesting new ones; it subtly insinuated itself into the old aristocracy as well as into the new business community. In all Trollope's novels the stock-pusher – often a Jew – is a conventional villain, leading the simple and the frail down the slippery slopes of temptation. The slopes are considered so slippery that Trollope often takes as his text, both in the *Autobiography* and in many of the novels, the phrase *facilis descensus Averni* ('Easy is the descent into Hell'). Many men, like Alaric Tudor in *The Three Clerks*, could persuade themselves that they were rising in the world through speculation when all the time they were on the verge of destruction. 'What if a man be going down, down to Tophet, and yet think all the while he is scaling the walls of heaven?'

This was, indeed, a pertinent question in mid-Victorian England. The social bases of the constitutional stability of the age of Palmerston often appeared to be undermined by dangerous patches of shifting sands. The expansion of the world of wealth was making it difficult to distinguish between fortune-hunting and real industry, between social aspiration and legitimate self-help, even between 'gentlemen' and 'cads'.

All Trollope's themes revolve around the ease of individual advancement in a fluid society and the much greater ease of individual disaster. Integrity appears as a rare gift rather than as a common denominator of action. *The Way We Live Now*, which is usually considered apart from the rest of his novels, is a bitter attack on the social shams of his day. Influenced by Delane, who was writing along the same lines in *The Times*, Trollope spared no one, rich or poor, aristocrat or bourgeois, landlord or financier. What Michael Sadleir calls 'the clash between conventional poise and secret catastrophe' is always stressed as a universal phenomenon.

Society revolves around Melmotte, a financial magnate who becomes a social potentate and a political aspirant merely because he is rich and can make others rich too. Yet, even at the height of his power, in his day of glory, when he recognized that he must either 'domineer over dukes or else go to the wall', there was doubt as to whether he was an enormous swindler or a Napoleon of wealth, the titan not only of England but also the whole world. 'As the great man was praised, so also was he abused. As he was a demigod to some, so was ne a fiend to others.' Until the whole tremendous structure of illusion crashed, almost the whole of society, young and old, seemed to cry aloud that 'there was but one virtue in the world, commercial enterprise – and that Melmotte was its prophet'.

The bitter satire of this remarkable novel shows how keenly Trollope, for all the blanket of dullness in many of his other novels, felt the sense of danger in his own society. Like Bagehot, he believed that 'the first duty of society is the preservation of society', but he could never bring himself to appreciate Bagehot's optimistic opinion that the expansion of the world of wealth was up to a point worth while, even though it let in 'a dirty crowd of little men', because it prevented England from becoming 'sleepy'. Unlike Bagehot, he cared little for the analogy between science and politics and the glib consolation that 'the rough and vulgar structure of English commerce is the secret of its life; for it contains "the propensity to variation", which, in the social as in the animal kingdom, is the principle of progress.' For Trollope it was the impact of society and politics on personality and on personal notions of self-interest which was of fundamental importance, and not a general law of social progress. He could find little consolation in a Darwinian notion of the survival of the fittest or of the unfolding evolution of society as a whole.

There was a second pertinent question in mid-Victorian England which was as important as the first. How could individual advancement in society – advancement of any kind – be reconciled with the maintenance of a necessary social balance between groups and classes? How could the creed of self-help fit into a society where the landed interest still dominated the social scene and where most Conservatives preferred the effortless grace of the 'gentleman' to the rugged individualism of the striving businessman?

Palmerston believed – and his belief was in line with the orthodoxy of the age – that we have shown the example of a nation in which every class of society accepts with cheerfulness that lot which Providence has assigned to it, while at the same time each individual of each class is constantly trying to raise himself in the social scale – not by injustice and wrong, not by violence and illegality – but by persevering good conduct, and by the steady and energetic exertion of the moral and intellectual faculties with which his Creator has endowed him.

Samuel Smiles, as we shall see, could have spoken no more persuasively. Trollope, although he showed the pitfalls and dilemmas which checked an automatically beneficent operation of individual exertion and believed that comfort was a summit to attain rather than a plateau to dwell in, accepted the general principle. So did Bagehot, specifically, in his literary essays on Sterne and Thackeray, where he distinguished between social systems founded upon caste and those founded upon equality. The English system of 'removable inequality', in which many people were inferior to and worse off than others but in which each might hope *in theory* to be on a level with the highest below the throne, was superior to both. Indeed, the English system allowed each individual 'reasonably and without sanguine impracticability' to gain one step in social elevation and to be at least on a level, after a period of striving, with those who had originally been slightly above him.

One of the advantages of the system, it was generally claimed, was that it provided through its 'mild social discipline ... a wise and temperate substitute for those harsh police laws and perpetual interference with the freedom of private action generally enforced throughout the continent and nowhere more so than in the revolutionized countries.' Coercion, which Bagehot had approved of in the Paris of 1851, was unnecessary in England, and social conflict was avoided.

Such appreciations of the peculiar excellencies of the English social system attempted to reconcile self-help and social order. They were often specious, and were only plausible so long as there was continued economic progress and social peace. They were as effectively undermined by the passing of the second Reform Bill in 1867 and by the industrial and agricultural 'depression' of the seventies as was the Palmerstonian constitution itself.

Robert Lowe's speeches, which were successful on the eve of 1867 in providing a mid-century reconciliation, were, in fact, the swan song of mid-Victorianism. He was following the authentic voices of his age – Smiles, Trollope, and Bagehot – when he pointed out that a large measure of parliamentary reform would be unnecessary if every workingman eight-pound householder abstained from the consumption of twenty quarts of beer a year and acquired the ten-pound property suffrage by effective, but not excessive, self-help. Indeed, the rise in prices, by reducing the value of the ten-pound house, was permitting a widening of the social base of the constitution without even a minimum of self-help being necessary.

These arguments of Lowe were swept away in a welter of political excitement which transformed the whole basis of the constitution. By 1872 not a brick of the Palmerston house was left standing. Palmerston's death had produced 'a change not in one point but in a thousand points . . . a change not of particular details but of pervading spirit'; and the danger of the future appeared to lie not only in constitutional upheaval but in the complete overthrow of the dignity and deference structure of society. The change in the economic atmosphere after 1873 and the collision of classes in the last quarter of the century merely served as the final acts of a play which had begun in an earlier decade.

3

Within the framework of the half-reformed constitution there were two problems which Trollope explored more realistically and profoundly than did Bagehot – the problem of electioneering and the problem of civil service reform.

Like Bagehot, Trollope was conscious of the honour of becoming a member of Parliament, of belonging to the inner circle of the political *élite*; but he realized that elections were a somewhat unsatisfactory means of getting into Parliament, because they were sordid and corrupt exercises in bribery, cajolery, and violence rather than rational verdicts of the local will.

If society really was constituted as both he and Bagehot believed, the would-be member of Parliament had to lower himself at election times in order to raise himself when the election was over. The way to the Palace of Westminster led through the pigsty. From his own actual experiences, as well as from his meditations on society, Trollope acquired a lively and provocative picture of the place of elections in politics.

In his *Autobiography* he wrote that he had always thought that to sit in the British Parliament should be the highest object and ambition for every educated Englishman.

I do not by this mean to suggest that every educated Englishman should set before himself a seat in Parliament as a probable or even a possible career; but that the man in Parliament has reached a higher position than the man out – that to serve one's country without pay is the grandest work that a man can do – that of all studies the study of politics is the one in which a man may make himself most useful to his fellow-creatures – and that of all lives, public political life is capable of the greatest efforts.

In his interesting commentary on Trollope, Michael Sadleir refuses to take this remark seriously and for no apparent reason calls it 'a quaint declaration'. In fact, it was in keeping with the whole of Trollope's attitude towards politics and society. He had never found in the public service of the Post Office, which employed him, that prestige which membership of the House of Commons gave. He realized, despite all his success as a public servant, that, in Bagehot's famous phrase, 'a clerk in the public service is "nobody"; and you could not make a common Englishman see why he should be anybody.'

Bagehot himself tried on four occasions to get into Parliament, but constituencies as different as Manchester, Bridgwater, and London University rejected him. His defeats were not surprising. He had little sympathy with the 'enthusiasms' of the Liberal party, for which he stood. 'I hate the Liberal enthusiasts,' he once told a friend. 'I feel inclined to say, "Go home, Sir, and take a dose of salts, and see if it won't clean it all out of you." Nature did not mean me for a popular candidate.' Only when he had failed did he convince himself that, although the member of Parliament gained social position, a modicum of power, and a smattering of inside knowledge, he had to pay the heavy price of listening to very dull debates and cutting down his ideas to the dead commonplaces of the electoral mind. Trollope also had to undergo an election defeat before he persuaded himself that writing political novels was more exciting than sitting in the Commons.

He has left a fascinating account of his experiences. Seeking the social prestige and the political distinction of the House of Commons, he decided in 1867 at the age of fifty-two to enter Parliament. 'I had an almost insane desire to sit there,' he wrote; in fact, when he failed to secure nomination for a safe seat in Essex, he actually went to the very corrupt borough of Beverley, in Yorkshire, a year later to try out his fortune. He had no illusions about the dangers and difficulties of the enterprise; indeed, a friend there began by telling him not only that he would not get elected but also that he would lose a vast sum of money in the process of trying. 'You will spend a thousand pounds and lose the election. Then you will petition and spend another thousand pounds. There will be a commission, and the borough will be disfranchised. For a beginner such as you are, that would be a great success.' Trollope did not flinch. 'In the teeth of this, from a man who knew all about it, I persisted in going to Beverley.'

Beverley, with 12,000 inhabitants and just over 2,500 electors, was by no means unique among small English boroughs, where corrupt practices long survived the Reform Bill of 1832; but it had a long-standing record of corruption which was made public for all to see after the famous 1868 election. There had been election petitions challenging the announced result in 1837, 1857 and 1859. In 1868 a further petition was presented, and the High Court judge who examined it found that over a hundred persons had been guilty of corrupt practices. The most influential manipulator of a highly corrupt electorate was a local draper who acted as Conservative agent.

The Conservative member of Parliament from 1857 to 1868 was Sir Henry Edwards, chairman of the Beverley Waggon Company, and a powerful political boss who worked through local politics as well as at general elections. The only hope of the Liberals was to acquire what was aptly called 'rolling stock'.

A royal commission thoroughly examining the state of Beverley in the summer of 1869 brought to light this traditional structure of corruption. One witness even produced an account book for the 1807 election which showed that, of 1,010 electors who voted for one of the candidates, only 78 had received no money. These and similar revelations led to the disfranchisement of the borough in 1870. Trollope's friend had been right.

Trollope himself described the fourteen days of his canvassing in Beverley as 'the most wretched fortnight of my manhood'. 'In the first place,' he declared, 'I was subject to a bitter tyranny from grinding vulgar tyrants. They were doing what they could, or said that they were doing so, to secure me a seat in Parliament and I was to be in their hands at any rate for the period of my candidature.... From morning to evening every day I was taken round the lanes and by-ways of that uninteresting town, canvassing every voter, exposed to the rain, up to my knees in slush, and utterly unable to assume that air of triumphant joy with which a jolly successful candidate should be invested.... But perhaps my strongest sense of discomfort arose from the conviction that my political ideas were all leather and prunella to the men whose votes I was soliciting. They cared nothing for my doctrines, and could not even be made to understand that I should have any.'

On the two issues concerning which his most radical supporters felt most strongly – the ballot and the Permissive Drink Bill – Trollope disagreed violently with them. But it was not issues which decided the election but bribes.

It had come to pass that political cleanliness was odious to the citizens. There was something grand in the scorn with which a leading Liberal turned up his nose at me when I told him that there should be no bribery, no treating, not even a pot of beer on our side! It was a matter for study to perceive how at Beverley politics were appreciated because they might subserve electoral purposes, and how little it was understood that electoral purposes, which are in themselves a nuisance, should be endured, in order that they may subserve politics.

Electioneering provided a favourable opportunity and a provocation for petty violence of every kind; it also provided a unique opportunity for making money or drinking free beer and eating free food. As at Sudbury, which had been completely disfranchised in 1844, the party spirit which prevailed there was not affected by the local or national political situation but by 'a contest of the parties amongst themselves as to which shall make most money at elections'. 'The use of the borough,' said Trollope, 'seems to be realized and approved in the borough in general. The inhabitants have taught themselves to think that it was for such purposes that boroughs were intended.'

From Trollope's account it is clear that he shared, as a result of personal experience, Bagehot's reluctance to transfer political power from Parliament to the constituencies, from the men who knew to the men who did not know. He went further than Bagehot, however, in showing that constituents were not only potentially dangerous as manipulators of puppet members in a democracy but also actively corrupt agents in an undemocratic system. The electorate was far more wicked than the candidates. Only the glory of the goal made the contestants' struggle worth while.

Even before he contested Beverley, Trollope had described parliamentary elections in his novels. *Rachel Ray*, for instance, written in 1862, described an election in the small borough of Baslehurst, where the expected cost of campaigning, petitioning, and scrutiny amounted to over six thousand pounds. Voting behaviour depended upon custom and the supply of drinks and gifts rather than upon political propaganda or persuasion. When the Conservative candidate was a little worried about his bad speaking, his agent told him: 'It don't matter. It's only done for the show of the thing and to fill up the day. If Gladstone were here he wouldn't talk a vote out of them one way or the other, nor yet the devil himself.' The result, indeed, appeared to be a foregone conclusion before the poll. 'It was all known and fairly understood as though the matter was past a doubt.'

The description of the election in Baslehurst was merely a

foretaste of what Trollope would do when he had added personal experience of an election to acute observation from outside. For in *Ralph the Heir* written in 1870-71, Trollope took his revenge on Beverley. *Ralph the Heir* contains the best election episodes in English fiction, more convincing than Dickens's picture of Eatanswill, and introduces us to one of the most sympathetic candidates who ever presented himself to a corrupt electorate – Sir Thomas Underwood.

Sir Thomas had been in Parliament before and had held minor office; he wished to get back again, even though he knew the difficulties involved. 'I dare say I am a fool for my pains. It will cost me some money that I oughtn't to spend. If I get in, I don't know that I can do any good or that it can do me any good.' But he clung on despite illness, violence, and ultimate unseating by petition. As in Beverley, the end of the story was the disfranchisement of the borough.

The account of the campaign is fascinating. The constituency of Percycross had been fortunate to survive even the Reform Bill of 1832. It had in its Tory agent, Trigger, a consummate political manipulator who dealt in votes as easily as pioneers dealt in oil. Underwood came to loathe Trigger, but he had to depend upon him, particularly in keeping in touch with the local network of business interests, represented by the mustard-maker, the paper manufacturers, and two boot factors. When Sir Thomas declared himself in favour of purity of election, one of his most influential supporters was shocked into sickness.

The idea of purity of election at Percycross made him feel very sick. It was an idea which he hated with his whole heart. There was to him something absolutely mean and ignoble in the idea of a man coming forward to represent a borough in Parliament without paying the regular fees. . . . It might be all very well in Manchester and such-like disagreeable places. But that candidates should come down to Percycross and talk about purity there, was a thing abominable to him.

Blessed with such supporters, Sir Thomas began to feel a curious but understandable sympathy for the very raw and ingenuous Radical candidate, Ontario Moggs, who disassociated himself completely from his Whig colleague and stood for the advanced doctrines of purity and the rights of labour. Moggs also soon realized that there were far too many men in Percycross 'who hate the very name of purity and who know nothing of the Rights of Labour'.

Ralph the Heir recapitulated the gloomy experiences of Beverley, and in a sense all Trollope's other political writings were substitutes for political action, 'his compensation for disappointment'. If he could not air his political views in the House of Commons, he could air them in his novels; but it was not the defeat of Beverley which turned him to the election as a literary theme. What the defeat at Beverley did was to quicken his insight and to goad his pen. Just as the election in *Ralph the Heir* is more vividly described and more corrupt in its character than the election described in *Rachel Ray*, so *Phineas Redux*, written in 1870, is more bitter in its tone than *Phineas Finn*, written in 1868.

There is one other picture of an election in Trollope which is of great interest – that in *The Way We Live Now*, written in 1874–5. In his other novels Trollope discussed conditions in small constituencies, the backwaters of old England. In *The Way We Live Now*, however, the election he describes is that in Westminster, a popular metropolitan constituency – a constituency which before the Reform Bill had returned John Stuart Mill to Parliament. It has been suggested by some historians that Percycross and Baslehurst were unrepresentative constituencies even before 1867, that they were lingering survivals rather than characteristic examples, and that the so-called 'popular constituencies' were theatres of very different political behaviour. In his picture of a Westminster election employing the ballot for the first time, Trollope does admit that electoral choice was more complicated and more obscure than in the older constituencies, but he does not admit that it was any more rational.

Melmotte himself, who was very anxious to become a member of Parliament, found it difficult to decide whether he would enter Parliament as a Conservative or as a Liberal. His financial interests turned him into a Conservative, and his committee consisted, 'needless to say,' of peers, bankers, and publicans, 'with all that absence of class prejudice for which the party has become famous since the ballot was introduced among us.' The ballot, however, introduced an unknown element into the political equation. Before 1872 there had been open voting at the hustings; now there was secret filling-in of election forms. 'Men who heretofore had known, or thought that they knew, how elections would go, who counted up promises, told of professed enemies, and weighed the doubtful ones, now confessed themselves to be in the dark.' But, if there was a newness of method, there was no spectacular battle of new issues. Melmotte 'had very little to say when he attempted to explain the political principles on which he intended to act. After a little he confined himself to remarks on the personal attacks made on him by the other side, and even in doing that he was reiterative rather than diffusive.' His opponent, Mr Alf, was a newspaperman, part editor, part owner, who was willing to spend ten thousand pounds on the election and bear ten thousand pounds in possible costs of libel. He, too, was ready to forget about issues and to fight the battle with the full help of the press on the question of Melmotte's financial integrity and reputation. The more material he produced, however, in his newspaper, the more opinion moved in favour of Melmotte.

It was supposed that the working classes were in favour of him, partly from their love of a man who spends a great deal of money, partly from the belief that he was being ill-used – partly, no doubt, from that occult sympathy, which is felt for crime, when the crime committed is injurious to the upper classes. Masses of men will almost feel that a certain amount of injustice ought to be inflicted on their betters, so as to make things even, and will persuade themselves that a criminal should be declared to be innocent, because the crime committed has had a tendency to oppress the rich and pull down the mighty from their seats.

The final election of Melmotte with a majority of about a thousand was a triumph of prejudice rather than reason; but, however it had been secured, it produced incomparable dividends.

It was very much to be Member for Westminster. So much had

at any rate been achieved by him who had begun the world without a shilling and without a friend – almost without education! Much as he loved money, and much as he loved the spending of money, and much as he had made and much as he had spent, no triumph of his life had been so great to him as this. Brought into the world in a gutter, without father or mother, with no good thing ever done for him, he was now a member of the British Parliament, and member for one of the first cities in the empire. Ignorant as he was, he understood the magnitude of the achievement. . . . If they sent him to penal servitude for life, they would have to say that they had so treated the Member for Westminster.

Melmotte's election pushes to the final point of bitter satire Trollope's conviction that the way to glory lay through the darkest regions of prejudice and misunderstanding. *The Way We Live Now*, like his other political novels, reflected his experiences, but it also reflected the constitutional theories of Bagehot. *The English Constitution* appeared just when Trollope's series of political novels was beginning. It was probably seen by Trollope at an early stage, for it first appeared between 1865 and 1867 as a series of articles in the *Fortnightly*, a review which Trollope had helped to launch in 1865.

Trollope's novels bring to life through illustrative examples Bagehot's notions of responsible power. They are concerned with the niceties of party and the perils of coalition, with the maintenance of majorities in a period when 'majorities were collected God knows how, and voted God knows why', and with the conventions of dissolution. But they are concerned, too, with problems which Trollope could explore more sensitively than Bagehot, the nineteenth-century equivalent of the problems of Bacon's *Essays*, which Trollope read carefully from cover to cover. Character and circumstances are explored in all their subtle interrelations. The attempts of men like Phineas Finn, Palliser, and Monk to keep their ethical standards above the level of those of purely professional politicians are properly praised, but the defects in the general pattern of politics are not obscured. To Trollope the greatest tragedy of all was that men should want to get seats in Parliament merely to protect their interests as directors of city companies. This was political prostitution of the worst sort and a sign that public life was not all that it ought to be, even after the sordid business of fighting elections was concluded. Parliament deserved better than this and quickly made its new members aware of its standards. Melmotte's degradation was carried to its crowning point when he made a fool of himself in his speech in the House of Commons.

4

The second problem which Trollope discussed more fully than Bagehot was that of civil service reform. The background of the unreformed civil service was systematically examined by Charles Dickens in his novel *Little Dorrit*, which appeared in 1857 shortly after the end of the Crimean War. The first title of *Little Dorrit* was *Nobody's Fault*; the picture which is painted in it of Barnacles and the Circumlocution Office reveals the failure not of individuals but of a system. It demonstrated the necessity for far-reaching reform. Reform was designed to substitute the principle of competitive choice for the principle of patronage, to open up government to new influences, to make it suit the needs of middle-class aspirants as well as gentlemen.

This problem had been discussed during the Crimean War by bodies like the Administrative Reform Association, which Dickens supported; but, several years before that, the demand for retrenchment by Radical groups had forced the government to appoint commissions of inquiry into particular departments. Eleven reports had been drawn up by 1853. They were supplemented in that year by the general report of Sir Charles Trevelyan and Sir Stafford Northcote, commissioned by Gladstone. After stressing the growing importance of the permanent civil service for the country 'in view of the great and increasing accumulation of public business', the report attacked the methods of selection and the great divergences in procedure in the existing departments. It recommended the establishment of a central board composed of independent men, headed by a privy councillor, to conduct periodical examinations and drew a sharp distinction within the service between 'intellectual' work and merely 'mechanical' clerkship.

Although the aim of the report was to secure a more efficient civil service, this last distinction which it drew was far from democratic in character. Its sharpness was strongly emphasized by Dr Jowett, professor of Greek at Oxford and later Master of Balliol, and many of the public school headmasters, who had recently been experimenting with new examinations in schools and universities; their purpose was to strengthen and multiply the ties between the upper classes and the holders of administrative power. 'The tendency of the measure will, I am confident,' wrote Trevelyan, 'be decidedly aristocratic, but it will be so in a good sense by securing for the public service those who are, in a true sense, worthy. At present a mixed multitude is sent up, a large proportion of whom, owing to the operation of political and personal patronage, are of an inferior rank of society . . . the idle, and useless, the fool of the family, the consumptive, the hypochondriac, those who have a tendency to insanity are the sort of young men commonly "provided for" in a public office.' In short, the reformers did not wish to throw open the civil service to the middle classes but rather to the new educational *élite* of the public schools and universities. Whitehall was not to be surrendered to Manchester, but to Oxford. Jobbery was to go, and education was to become the test; but stratification was to remain. 'Our people are few compared with the multitudes likely to be arrayed against it,' wrote Trevelyan to Delane, 'and we must prepare for the trial by cultivating to the utmost the superior morality and intelligence which comprise our real strength. It is proposed to invite the flower of our youth to the aid of the public service.'

The method – competitive examination – had its moral as well as its intellectual side. It was considered to be far more effective than patronage, which merely provided the higher aristocracy with a sort of foundling hospital for their waifs and strays, 'their sons, legitimate and illegitimate'. It would make the most able young men willing to compete for the prizes offered and in consequence, in the phrase of John Stuart Mill, act as 'a great and salutary moral revolution'.

There were obvious difficulties before an examination system could be established. Some critics complained that it would be difficult to find capable and impartial examiners, and Mill had to reply pragmatically that, if they had been found in the universities, there was no reason why they could not be found for the civil service, 'supposing that there is a sincere desire to find them.' Even if this were so, there remained Macaulay's fear that the examiners would be paid too much and that 'the whole thing' would be turned into 'a job', a new and more sinister form of patronage than the old.

In 1855 the government took the first tentative step by order in council to make the competitive examination work. Limited competition among selected candidates was introduced rather than open competition among all comers, and the final responsibility for appointment rested with the heads of departments. A civil service commission was set up, empowered to arrange with the heads of departments responsible the conditions of entry and to prescribe the subjects of examination. It was not until 1870, when the civil service had become much more complex and far more was demanded of it, that the principle of examination and differentiation was carried further towards its logical conclusion.

Trollope was a civil servant, and, like the head of his department, Sir Rowland Hill – it must have been one of the few points on which they agreed – he did not like competitive examinations; indeed, he thought with Macaulay that they might increase rather than diminish the danger of jobbery. He was very sceptical about dons dividing 'the adult British male world into classes and sub-classes' and poured scorn on his Cambridge don, Mr Jobbles, who knew how to get through five thousand oral examinations in every five hours with due assistance. The whole notion of 'government on principles of the strictest purity' seemed as unreal in Whitehall as it was in Baslehurst. As Sir James Stephen, one of the greatest civil servants of the day, claimed, it was completely utopian. 'It is unknown,' he said, 'to the great commercial and municipal corporations among us. In every age, and land, and calling, a large share of success has hitherto always been awarded to the possessors of interest, of connexion, of favour, and of what we call good luck.... The world we live in is not, I think, half moralized enough for the acceptance of such a scheme of stern morality as this.'

The reader of *The Way We Live Now* could hardly fail to agree with this assessment of mid-nineteenth-century manners. There was a struggle for 'purity', for higher institutional morality, rather than a confident trust in its existence. The issue was clear: public probity was as essential to the civil service as was Smiles's code of hard work to the world of business. While he was preaching the virtues of self-help to manufacturers and artisans, the public schools and universities were laying the foundations of a new institutional morality for the reformed public service. But the new institutional morality was based on the old code of the 'gentleman'.

Trollope stood back from the change and viewed it with scepticism. He was sensitive, as we have seen, to the social boundaries which surrounded the gentleman, and he could point out that the Queen herself had feared that competitive examinations would 'fill the public offices with low people without the breeding or feelings of gentlemen'. Trollope liked gentlemen who had been taught how to be gentlemen, and he liked gentlemen to remain intrenched in the civil service.

The Three Clerks describes with superb satire the difficulties of young gentlemen trying to cope with the sort of traps laid for them by Mr Jobbles.

A man has before him a string of questions, and he looks painfully down them, from question to question, searching for some allusion to that special knowledge which he has within him. He too often finds that no such allusion is made. It appears that the Jobbles of the occasion has exactly known the blank spots of his mind and fitted them all. He has perhaps crammed himself with the winds and tides, and there is no more reference to those stormy subjects than if Luna were extinct; but he has, unfortunately, been loose about his botany, and question after question would appear to him to have been dictated by Sir Joseph Paxton or the Head

Gardener at Kew. And then to his own blank face and puzzled look is opposed the fast scribbling of some botanic candidate, fast as though reams of folio could hardly contain all the knowledge which he is able to pour forth.

This is a very gloomy picture of an examination. It shows the reaction of a sensitive Victorian observer, determined to be a gentleman, to the moral milieu of the competitive examination, to the dismal scene of blank faces and scribbling pens, and to the uninspired pedantry of the civil service allies of the college dons, administrative pedants like Sir Gregory Hardlines. Palmerston shared most of Trollope's prejudices, and Lord John Russell could not be convinced even by the eloquence of Gladstone that civil service reform was necessary. It is significant that the Peelites, with their great interest in effective administration, rather than the Whigs, with their sense of family connexion, were the keenest supporters of civil service reform.

Behind the fears of Trollope – and also of Bagehot, when he very sketchily touched on the question of the civil service – was the distrust of a bureaucracy, recruited and modelled perhaps on Prussian lines. 'The leaning towards bureaucracy' had to be resisted. Trollope, who intensely disliked experts and feared the influence even of 'expert' professional 'castes' outside the civil service, shared Bagehot's opinion that bureaucracy tended to undergovernment in point of quality and overgovernment in point of quantity. Men selected for training as bureaucrats would come to think of the routine of business not as a means but as an end – 'to imagine the elaborate machinery of which they form a part, and from which they derive their dignity, to be a grand and achieved result, not a working and changeable instrument.'

The question of the civil service led back, indeed, to the central problem of all government. 'Politics are made in time and place – institutions are shifting things to be tried and adjusted to the shifting conditions of a movable world.' There were tendencies towards administrative uniformity and centralization in the 1860s, but few people were prepared to follow the Benthamite Chadwick or the essayist Matthew Arnold in believing that a powerful civil service could manage

England's destinies. 'Every Englishman is proud of his country,' wrote W. R. Greg in 1855. 'No Englishman is proud of his Administration.'

5

Trollope and Bagehot's approach to politics cannot be given a party label. Neither of them was a Tory, clinging tenaciously to the traditions of the past. Trollope called himself an 'advanced Conservative-Liberal', for both he and his generation like political hyphens more than we profess to do today. Bagehot claimed that he was 'between size in politics'; he was liberal enough to welcome the fundamental 'march of improvement' of the nineteenth century, yet conservative enough to believe that reforms should produce greater stability and not generate accelerating demands for further change. He believed in driving neither so slow as to miss the train nor so fast as to meet with an accident.

The political conditions of the middle years of the century allowed Trollope and Bagehot to maintain a position of intellectual detachment which they would have found extremely difficult to hold ten years earlier or fifteen years later. Bagehot, who had been an 'enthusiastic worshipper of Cobden' in 1846, could settle down in the 1850s to admire Sir George Cornewall Lewis, whose chief attraction was that 'his mind was like a registering machine with a patent index'. Trollope 'did not give a straw' for the Great Exhibition of 1851 and characteristically mocked himself in mocking the spirit of the times: 'God send that we all meet in 1851 under the shadow of some huge, newly-invented machine. I mean to exhibit four three-volume novels – all failures – which I look upon as a great proof of industry.'

The very 'dullness' of mid-Victorian England was what both of them loved, for never were two men more at home in their age. 'Dull' Englishmen provided 'good' self-government. 'What we opprobiously call stupidity, though not an enlivening quality in common society, is Nature's favourite resource for preserving steadiness of conduct and consistency of opinion,' wrote Bagehot. Trollope proved that it could have an enlivening quality if it were given fictional form. It was English as nothing else was: 'Dullness is our line, as cleverness is that of the French. Woe to the English people if they ever forget that.'

The dullness was accompanied by a consensus about major political issues. 'The spirit of the country is quiet, but reasonable,' wrote Bagehot, 'indisposed to sweeping innovations, and equally indisposed to keeping in the old Tory way, everything which is because it is. The moderate members of both parties represent this spirit very fairly. At a recent election a poor voter is reported to have said that both candidates were very nice gentlemen, but that for his part he could not see much difference between them; and this is the simple truth.' Palliser put it in much the same words in *Phineas Redux*:

When some small measure of reform has thoroughly commended itself to the country, so thoroughly that all men know that the country will have it – then the question arises whether its details shall be arranged by the political party which calls itself Liberal or by that which is termed Conservative. The men are so near to each other in all their convictions and theories of life that nothing is left to them but personal competition for the doing of the thing that is to be done.

Both Trollope and Bagehot lived long enough to see the consensus disintegrate as a result of the death of Palmerston, the second Reform Bill of 1867, and the Ballot Act of 1872; but they did not live long enough to witness the cleaning-up of the electoral system, the emergence of a national press, or the growth of powerful party organizations which redesigned political machinery and forced new issues into the open. Bagehot died in 1877 and Trollope in 1882; neither was happy about the changed conditions of affairs in the last few years of their lives. Trollope saw his own reputation dwindle away, while Bagehot, contented enough in his private life, became increasingly alarmed about the prospects of the nation: 'Our old system of parliamentary choice will be completely destroyed, for it is already half gone.'

The faithfulness of both writers to the self-satisfied world of the fifties and sixties is their chief title to consistency. Both were observers rather than actors – clever, at times cynical, observers – and they lead us without difficulty into the heart of mid-Victorian society. If we are to understand that society fully, we must move from the area of observation to that of action and abandon our looking glasses for walking sticks. We must turn from Bagehot and Trollope to the makers of mid-Victorian values, to those who did not scruple to preach values to the select few or to the multitude and sometimes – though very rarely – to both. Neither Trollope nor Bagehot ever preached; they left this task to men like Samuel Smiles and Thomas Hughes, whose efforts illuminate the patches of change in the middle years of the century.

CHAPTER FIVE

Samuel Smiles and the Gospel of Work

As steady application to work is the healthiest training for every individual, so is it the best discipline of a state. Honourable industry travels the same road with duty; and Providence has closely linked both with happiness. The gods, says the poet, have placed labour and toil on the way leading to the Elysian fields.

SAMUEL SMILES

I

Every society has its propagandists who try to persuade their fellow-citizens to develop a special kind of social character which will best serve the needs of the day. In mid-Victorian England one of the most important propagandists was Samuel Smiles, described by the editor of the *Autobiography* as 'the authorized and pious chronicler of the men who founded the industrial greatness of England'. Smiles set out, as he said in the Preface to his most famous book, *Self-Help*, to

re-inculcate those old-fashioned but wholesome lessons – which cannot perhaps be too often urged – that youth must work in order to enjoy – that nothing creditable can be accomplished without application and diligence – that the student must not be daunted by difficulties, but conquer them by patience and perseverance, and that, above all, he must seek elevation of character without which capacity is worthless and worldly success is nought.

It is interesting to learn that the lessons were considered 'old-fashioned' in the middle of the nineteenth century, for many people have claimed that the Victorians were the first to proclaim the 'gospel of work', or at least the first to set it out systematically in texts and stories. The sense of gospel may have been new, but the admonition and even the apocalyptic enthusiasm were old. William Hutton had already proclaimed the importance of work in eighteenth-century Birmingham; the new Poor Law of 1834 had consecrated it; William and Robert Chambers, the sponsors of *The Miscellany of Instructive and Amusing Tracts*, had popularized it in little didactic tales like 'The Three Ways of Living: Below, Up to, and Beyond One's Means' or 'A Tale of Life Assurance'. Above all, Thomas Carlyle had made work the cornerstone of his philosophy. 'An endless significance lies in Work,' he affirmed; 'properly speaking all true work is Religion.' Where Carlyle thundered, Samuel Smiles warned and pleaded. What Carlyle prophesied, Smiles turned into homilies. And behind both the prophecies and the homilies was what Smiles considered his deepest source, the proverbs of Solomon.

Smiles owed much to Carlyle's influence. He began *Thrift* with Carlyle's motto, 'Not what I have, but what I do is my kingdom'. He felt the splendour of all 'the quantity of dull and forgotten work that lies silent under my feet in this world and escorts and attends me, and supports and keeps me alive.' Where Carlyle meditated on the abbot Samson, Smiles told his stories – true stories of men like Josiah Wedgwood, William Lee, James Brindley, and George Stephenson. He saw that the everyday work of applied science had its romance, and he found his heroes among the engineers, the inventors, and the enterprisers.

He told his tales to eager listeners who were waiting for a message. The material for *Self-Help* was first presented to about a hundred young workingmen in Leeds who entirely on their own initiative had set up an evening school for 'mutual improvement'. Smiles addressed them on more than one occasion, 'citing examples of what other men had done, as illustrations of what each might, in a greater or less degree, do for himself'. The lectures were so popular that Smiles sought a wider audience, and, although in book form they were turned down by Routledge because of publishing difficulties during the Crimean War, they were printed as *Self-Help* by John Murray four years later.

The book was a remarkable success. Twenty thousand copies were sold in the first year; fifty-five thousand by the end of five years; a hundred and fifty thousand by 1889; and over a quarter of a million by 1905. These sales far exceeded those of the great nineteenth-century novels. What was more remarkable, however, was the book's popularity when translated into other languages. It appeared in Dutch and French, Danish and German, Italian and Japanese, Arabic and Turkish, and 'several of the native languages of India'. As it went round the world, the gospel of work was spread just as efficiently and as fervently as any of the other great nineteenth-century missionary enterprises. The seed sometimes fell on stony ground, but it often took root in peculiar places. Like the lessons of the Crystal Palace, the lessons of this gospel were designed for all men; they boldly asserted that not genius but 'the energetic use of simple means and ordinary qualities' was the real transforming agent in society. The fame of Smiles had travelled far since he first taught his classroom lessons to the group of Leeds workingmen in a dingy hall, which had once been used as a temporary cholera hospital. Cholera itself could have travelled no faster.

The speed of transmission was determined as much by the circumstances of the time as by the eloquence of the words or the power of the stories Smiles employed. The creed of *Self-Help* presupposed a more mobile society than had existed even a hundred years before. In the eighteenth century, when writers like Hannah More were writing tracts for the poor or even for the middle classes, they assumed a relatively static society in which it was cruelty, not kindness, to educate a child beyond his station. 'The poor are always with us.' They should remain content with the positions in life to which God had called them. Distinctions of rank and fortune were not dangerous but beneficial; they were sanctioned by Christianity and, along with religion, laid the foundations of the social order. Smiles was writing for a more dynamic society, which was searching for social and economic levers and trusting in material progress. The poor man's remedy lay in his own hands. If he were only hard-working, thrifty, and determined, he could do anything. 'God helps those who help themselves. Go thou and do likewise.'

On both sides of the Atlantic in the middle years of the nineteenth century there was a great wave of 'success' literature, designed to provide its readers not only with a message but with a practical guide to the problems of city life and the right tactics for 'getting on'. *Success in Life*, a book published by Nelson and Sons in London in 1852, anticipated the creed of self-help in all its details, and the anonymous author admitted that 'the original idea of this volume was suggested by an American publication.' Later on, Horatio Alger (1832–99) found fifty million readers for his stories of success. Smiles must be considered in relation to this general movement of feeling and aspiration, although he was far more solid than Alger and more profound in what he had to say. There were no fairy godmothers or fairy godfathers in Smiles assisting the thrifty hero to find money and success, as there were in many of Alger's stories. Nor was there an unlimited belief in success itself. He was always at great pains to point out that he did not like success stories for their own sake. Good work, honestly done, character sustained, and independence secured were more important than worldly success. As his biography pointed out if he had been merely interested in worldly success itself, he would have produced a 'factory of biography' rather than a series of carefully chosen homilies.

2

Smiles's own life is of great interest in relation to his work, even though he himself was reluctant to write his autobiography and believed that 'my books, such as they are, must speak for themselves, without any biographic introduction.' It was the appearance of Trollope's biography which made a friend write to Mrs Smiles, 'Tell your husband to go and do likewise.' The autobiography was never completed, however, and did not appear until after Smiles's death.

Smiles was born in Scotland, in the same town as John Knox. He was 'fonder of frolic than of learning' when a young man and was not even thrifty. 'I thought,' he said, 'that the principal use of money was to be spent.' He even forced open his money box with a table knife in order to collect the few pennies he had bothered to save. His later life was an exercise in self-discipline; before he moulded others, he set out to mould himself. This is perhaps the most important thing about him as a person. In 1885, when he was seventy-three, he reviewed the circumstances of his life and the many achievements he had secured. 'Does this mean that I lead a happy life or does it mean that I have led a happy life?' he asked. But he did not answer his own question. He complained rather that there were many things still left to do and took refuge in Carlyle's aphorism that 'perseverance is the hinge of all the virtues'. 'I wish I had the power to retouch my life,' he said, 'as the artist retouches his picture. But I cannot do so. My life must stand or fall by what I have done, not by what I have dreamt.' It is a revealing comment.

What he had done filled a large volume of several hundred pages. He had begun as a doctor, publishing his first book, *Physical Education*, in 1836, but he had soon turned from medicine to journalism and from Scotland to England. For twenty years, from 1838 to 1858, he lived in Leeds, the smoky capital of Yorkshire industry. He was an active participant in Radical politics in the hungry forties, advocating an extension of the suffrage, the repeal of the Corn Laws, and improved education of the working classes. These political experiences left their mark on the rest of his life and provide the background of his later social philosophy. Unlike Alger or most of the other 'success' writers, he turned to self-help and thrift only when he saw the inadequacy of collective striving in an atmosphere of ignorance and poverty. Although he said little of politics in the later years of his life and had no sympathy with socialism or even with organic constitutional reform, he had known politics from the inside and had found political formulas inadequate. He had seen the artisans of Leeds – and even the Leeds manufacturers – 'groping after some grand principle which they thought would lead them to fresh life, and liberty and happiness,' but they were groping in the dark, and the flickers of light, like Owenite socialism, were merely will-o'-the-wisps.

Samuel Smiles and the Gospel of Work

Smiles gave his famous talk to the Leeds workingmen in the middle of the forties, not in the middle of the fifties. He told his audience categorically that it was a fallacy that self-help

is to be regarded merely as a means of gaining a higher position in society than that which you now hold.... The education of the working classes is to be regarded, in its highest aspect, not as a means of raising up a few clever and talented men into a higher rank of life, but of elevating and improving the whole class – of raising the entire condition of the working man. The grand object aimed at should be to make the great mass of the people virtuous, intelligent, well-informed, and well-conducted; and to open up to them new sources of pleasure and happiness. Knowledge is of itself one of the highest enjoyments.

In short, the creed of self-help grew out of radicalism and was not designed as an antidote to it. 'It may be – nay, it will inevitably happen –' he remarked in 1845, 'that education will teach those who suffer how to remove the causes of their sufferings; and it may also make them dissatisfied with an inferiority of social privilege. This, however, is one of the necessary conditions of human progress. If a man be degraded, he must be dissatisfied – discontented, if you will, with that condition of degradation – before he can make the necessary effort to rise out of it. It is the opprobrium of some of the most wretched and suffering classes in our land, that they are *contented* with their condition. Theirs is the satisfaction of the blind who have never known light.'

Although Smiles reiterated this point frequently during the rest of his life and used it in self-defence against many of his critics, he never went any further. Indeed, he became less and less concerned with public causes and more and more concerned with writing and business, particularly after the revolutions of 1848. In 1845 he had become secretary of the Leeds and Thirsk Railway, and in 1857 he produced his first popular book, *The Life of George Stephenson*, the railway pioneer, which gave him the opportunity of linking his business and his literary interests. From 1857 onward his future as a writer was secure, and, when he persuaded his company to take on a shorthand writer to save him the laborious task of writing his own letters and minutes, he freed his mind and stored up his energies for an active literary career. *Stephenson*, which was read with 'real profit and pleasure' by George Eliot, was followed two years later by *Self-Help*. In 1862 there followed the *Lives of the Engineers*, a powerful panegyric of the aristocracy of Victorian technical enterprise. Tangye of the Birmingham Engineering Works gave a copy of this book to all his apprentices, the Queen gave one to Prince Louis of Hesse when he married Princess Alice, and Gladstone found time to read it, 'in little fragments at midnight hours each night, as a composing draught'. Gladstone saw as clearly as Smiles that 'the character of our engineers is a most signal and marked expression of British character'. He even referred to Smiles in a public speech at Manchester.

Industrial Biography was followed by *The Huguenots* and *Character*. By this time Smiles had taught himself what character meant. Although he had a stroke in 1871, which paralysed his right hand and robbed him of his memory for proper names, he taught himself how to write and how to remember again. For every later book he wrote, including *Thrift*, he rejected two or three offers made to him, including offers made by wealthy sponsors who were anxious to have him write public panegyrics of their business careers. Smiles rightly pointed out to some of his detractors that 'perhaps if I had written about millionaires, I might have been more successful myself'.

Smiles lived on through a silent old age and did not die until 1905, by which time the temper of the age had completely changed and there was more interest in paradox than in common sense. His last manuscript, *Conduct*, was turned down by his publisher in 1898. Two other projected books on race and matrimony never got past the note-collecting phase. In persistent work and in his quest for common sense, Smiles had repressed much which might have made his life more colourful; but he himself, after all, was the first to admit that it was his works rather than his adventures which deserved to be remembered. There could be nothing more colourful than letters he received from Bohemia or Croatia praising his writings or the Arabic inscriptions on the walls of the khedive's palace in Egypt which were taken not from the Koran but from *Self-Help*. The French and the Spaniards were more sceptical. Smiles himself tells the story of a Frenchman paying tribute to the artist who invented ruffles, and Sir John Sinclair 'shrewdly remarking that some merit was also due to the man who invented the shirt'. Shirts, preferably cotton shirts, and not ruffles were essential to an Anglo-Saxon nineteenth-century philosophy.

3

The most important of Smiles's writings are *Self-Help* (1859), *Character* (1871), *Thrift* (1875), and *Duty* (1887). They are best studied as a whole, not merely because they follow the same method of organization and argument – 'anecdotal illustrations of life and character' – but because they develop a common theme. Indeed, in his Preface to *Thrift* Smiles wrote that it was intended as a sequel to *Self-Help* and *Character*. It might have appeared, he added, as an introduction to those volumes, for 'Thrift is the basis of Self-Help and the foundation of much that is excellent in character.'

Smiles took none of his ideals for granted. He realized from observation as well as experience that there might well be a war between men's natural temperaments and the social character they were seeking to acquire. 'Prodigality is much more natural to men than thrift. . . . Economy is not a natural instinct, but the growth of experience, example, and foresight. Self-help was more difficult to live up to as a guiding principle than a dependence on the good will of others or reliance on convenient political panaceas, what Carlyle called 'Morrison's Pills', cures for all complaints.

Some call for Caesars, others for Nationality, and others for Acts of Parliament. . . . Whatever is done *for* men and classes to a certain extent takes away the stimulus and necessity of doing for themselves. . . . No laws, however stringent, can make the idle industrious, the thriftless provident, or the drunken sober. Such reforms can only be effected by means of individual action, economy, and self-denial, by better habits rather than by greater rights.

It was a point which had been made to Smiles in an interesting letter from Cobden, written in 1853.

Depend upon it, there is a spice of despotism at the bottom of all this intervention by combined bodies in the concerns of individuals. . . . I think we shall not get right till there is a revolt against all such organizations, whether on one side or another, in the interests of *Liberty* – PERSONAL LIBERTY.

The 'better habits' to which Smiles referred were frequently lacking. Smiles was no triumphant panegyrist of an Augustan age. 'The deterioration of the standard of public men, of public morality, and of political principles is undeniable.' Scamped work, gambling, fraud, intemperance, dishonest advertisement, and sharp practices dominated the business field he portrayed. Smiles's catalogue of social virtues is best considered alongside his catalogue of social sins, just as his social philosophy is best considered against the background of the forties as well as the fifties. His list of virtues did not spring from some peculiar source of moral smugness. It reflected the needs of a society in which, despite striking industrial achievements, there were still great areas of waste and inefficiency. The Victorians were not in possession of a secure moral order which enabled them to tame nature and to harness the machine; rather they needed such an order if they were to achieve that rate of economic growth which they themselves demanded.

Smiles understood how far from realization was his dream of self-reliant men in a developing society. 'We often hear that "Knowledge is Power",' he wrote, 'but we never hear that Ignorance is Power. And yet Ignorance has always had more power in the world than Knowledge. Ignorance dominates because Knowledge, as yet, has obtained access only to the minds of the few.' He wanted knowledge to be diffused among the minds of the many, for better education would abate drunkenness, improvidence, and crime. By itself, however, it would not go far enough. Duty and character would be needed to direct it towards general social improvement. Smiles saw the whole of life as a school in which lessons were taught and values expounded. But it was a school where the scholars acted rather than read and paid for their mistakes not with punishment but with wasted opportunity.

Smiles emphasized self-set standards as the props of society. 'National progress is the sum of individual industry, energy, and uprightness as national decay is of individual idleness, selfishness, and vice. What we are accustomed to decry as great social evils will, for the most part, be found to be but the outgrowth of man's own perverted life.' Social improvement could come about only by and through individuals, through deeds, not through words. 'Men cannot be raised in masses, as the mountains were in the early geological states of the world. They must be dealt with as units; for it is only by the elevation of individuals that the elevation of the masses can be effectively secured.'

This scepticism about political action did not imply that Smiles was a complete believer in *laissez faire*. He began by justifying the resentment of the self-made man against too much interference in the conduct of his business affairs, but he went on to advocate certain limited forms of state intervention with as much enthusiasm as the Benthamite Chadwick. Too much has been made of the mid-Victorian belief in *laissez faire*; the concept was always challenged, particularly by writers like Carlyle, and even those economists – mainly 'vulgar economists' – who popularized it found themselves compelled to introduce a whole range of exceptions and qualifications. The Benthamites in particular were attracted by the possibility of employing the machinery of the state to regulate some of the obvious social disharmonies of the middle years of the century.

For Smiles, as for Chadwick, complete *laissez faire* was too simple an answer. Both of them had seen in their own lifetimes some of the worst effects of standing back and letting things be. Both were far too industrious and pertinacious to identify *laissez faire* with *dolce far niente*. Physical disease rather than social waste opened their eyes to the shortcomings of a *laissez faire* society. 'The sanitary idea,' as contemporaries called it, the quest for an efficient system of public health, stirred them rather than dissatisfaction with economic individualism. 'Before the age of railroads and sanitary reforms, the pastoral life of the Arcadians was a beautiful myth. The Blue Book men have exploded it for ever.' The failure to respond to the advice of the 'Blue Book men' sprang from the powerful driving force of inertia, which slackened effort and delayed attention. 'When typhus or cholera breaks out,' Smiles exclaimed, 'they tell us that Nobody is to blame. That terrible Nobody! How much he has to answer for. More mischief is done by Nobody than by all the world besides. Nobody adulterates our food. Nobody poisons us with bad drink.... Nobody leaves towns undrained. Nobody fills jails, penitentiaries, and convict stations. Nobody makes poachers, thieves, and drunkards. Nobody has a theory too – a dreadful theory. It is embodied in two words: *laissez faire* – let alone. When people are poisoned with plaster of Paris mixed with flour, "let alone" is the remedy.... Let those who can, find out when they are cheated: *caveat emptor*. When people live in foul dwellings, let them alone, let wretchedness do its work; do not interfere with death.'

The discovery of this malevolent and invisible 'Nobody' revealed a hidden figure of evil at the heart of the social world. Yet at the same time it was still generally believed that a benevolent and equally invisible hand was directing individual action, along lines suggested by Adam Smith, to produce social gain. Smiles was never troubled, as were many of his successors, about the possible identity of these two invisible powers. He felt no doubts about their respective spheres of influence. They were hostile powers at perpetual war with each other, the one ensuring economic progress, the other producing social chaos. Fortunately, despite all the black spots in Victorian society, England was on the right side. Smiles believed in the persistent Victorian contrast between Anglo-Saxon countries like England and the United States and Latin countries like Spain. The difference lay not in climate but in social organization. 'A Spaniard will blush to work; he will not blush to beg.' There was Protestantism as well as radicalism behind such a judgement and also pride. 'The spirit of self-help, as exhibited in the energetic action of the individual, has in all times been a marked feature of the English character, and furnishes the true measure of our power as a nation.' If Nobody could only be defeated within, Anybody could be challenged without.

There was one certain way of failing to defeat Nobody – reliance on socialism. Smiles met Owenites in smoky Leeds and was not impressed. He objected to Owen's 'spinning jenny of a universe', too far removed from life to deserve serious attention. He met the poet Ebenezer Elliott, the Corn Law rhymer, in 1847 and agreed with him that competition was 'the great social law of God'. 'What is a Communist?' Elliott had asked in one of his poems:

> One who hath yearnings
> For equal division of unequal earnings:
> Idler, or burglar, or both, he is willing
> To fork out his penny, and pocket your shilling.

Smiles heartily agreed. 'The metaphysics of socialism,' he wrote, 'were comprised in an axiom that character is formed *for*, not *by*, the individual; and that society may so arrange "circumstances" as to produce whatever character it pleases.' The only character Smiles wished to see was self-made character. He would rather be 'a pagan suckled in a creed outworn' than be a socialist.

Yet it was significant that Smiles, who worshipped self-help and individual enterprise and abhorred waste of economic resources on military expenditure, could not resist the magic of organized discipline, even military discipline. He never went so far as the popular versifier and author of *Proverbial Philosophy*, Martin Tupper, who urged Englishmen: 'Up, make ready your rifles!' promising that

> ... with a nation of riflemen ready,
> Nobody'll come – because no one will dare!

But he did write:

Wonderful is the magic of drill! Drill means discipline, training, education. ... These soldiers – who are ready to march steadily against vollied fire, against belching cannon – or to beat their heads against bristling bayonets ... were once tailors, shoemakers, mechanics, weavers, and ploughmen; with mouths gaping, shoulders stooping, feet straggling, arms and hands like great fins hanging by their sides; but now their gait is firm and martial, their figures are erect, and they march along to the sound of music, with a tread that makes the earth shake.

Even after the French danger was past and the Crimean War was over, room was found in his gallery of service for the soldier as well as the engineer, and obedience, submission, discipline, and courage were extolled. Smiles might have quoted Carlyle; instead, he chose his words from Ruskin:

Out of fiery and uncouth material, it is only soldiers' discipline which can bring the full force of power. Men who, under other circumstances, would have shrunk into lethargy or dissipation are redeemed into noble life by a service which at once summons and directs their energies.

Smiles went further. Impressed by the Volunteer Movement by which civilians trained for national service, he headed one of his chapters with Whyte-Melville's phrase, 'the highest of us is but a sentry at his post'.

One dare scarcely hint, in these days, at the necessity for compulsory conscription; and yet, were the people at large compelled to pass through the discipline of the army, the country would be stronger, the people would be soberer, and thrift would become much more habitual than it is at present.

4

It was in his analysis of thrift that Smiles outlined the essentials of his theory of society. Individual savings provided the foundation of the national accumulation of capital, and the national accumulation of capital was essential to continued economic growth. But thrift was more than an economic necessity; it was in itself a praiseworthy social objective. 'Thrift produces capital; and capital is the conserved result of labour. The capitalist is merely a man who does not spend all that is earned by work. He is a man prepared to forgo present satisfaction for the hope of future reward.' Smiles agreed with John Stuart Mill that 'the principal industrial excellence of the

English people [lay] in their capacity of present exertion for a distant object'. Enjoyment was subordinated to prudent foresight and self-denial. Smiles made no distinction between big and small capitalists or between small savers and large investors, nor did he worry himself, as Mill did, with the uncomfortable thought that 'the majority of Englishmen have no life but in their work and that alone stands between them and *ennui*'. He thought the thrifty man was the good man as well as the wise man, and he was particularly anxious to encourage the working classes to find their ideal social type among the provident men and women with bank accounts. The workingman could become a capitalist by adding prudence to industry. 'Little things' added up. Marginal income – that little bit wasted on gambling or drink – could guarantee individual security. He discussed in detail seven possible ways of augmenting savings of one penny a day. On a slightly more ambitious calculation 'a glass of beer a day is equal to forty-five shillings a year. This sum will insure a man's life for a hundred and thirty pounds, payable at death. Or placed in a savings bank, it would amount to a hundred pounds in twenty years.'

Such savings would guarantee a man's independence. It was the moral rather than the economic aspect of savings which Smiles stressed. The little capital a man has saved up 'is always a source of power. He is no longer the sport of time and fate. He can boldly look the world in the face.... He can dictate his own terms. He can neither be bought nor sold. He can look forward to an old age of comfort and happiness.'

Savings were thus the fruit of individual responsibility, or rather self-abnegation, and provided insurance against the hazards of the working life and the cares of sickness and old age. It was the duty of the prudent individual to allow for such emergencies. The state was in no sense responsible for the social contingencies of working-class living.

In his approach to this problem, Smiles showed none of the twentieth-century concern for the maintenance of full employment and social security. He considered that periods of full employment – 'prosperous times' – were very often the least prosperous of all times.

In prosperous times, mills are working full time; men, women, and children are paid high wages; warehouses are emptied and filled. ... Everybody seems to be becoming richer and more prosperous. But we do not think whether the men and women are becoming wiser, better trained, less self-indulgent, more religiously disposed. ... If this apparent prosperity be closely examined it will be found that expenditure is increasing in all directions. There are demands for higher wages; and the higher wages, when obtained, are spent as soon as earned. Intemperate habits are formed, and once formed, the habit of intemperance continues. ... When a population is thoughtless and improvident, no kind of material prosperity will benefit them. Unless they exercise forethought and economy, they will alternately be in a state of 'hunger and burst'. When trade falls off, as it usually does after exceptional prosperity, they will not be comforted by the thought of what they *might* have saved, had it ever occurred to them that the 'prosperous times' might not have proved permanent.

There was no natural tendency to full employment, even in the so-called mid-Victorian boom years, and there was considerable short-term unemployment after the financial crises of 1857 and 1866. But Smiles showed little interest in the economic causes of waves of prosperity and depression and accepted them with far fewer qualms than he accepted epidemics of disease. 'Trade has invariably its cycle of good and bad years, like the lean and fat kine in Pharaoh's dream – its bursts of prosperity followed by glut, panic, and distress.' He was concerned solely with the 'moral' effects of cyclical fluctuations. It was part of his gospel of work not only that bouts of prosperity were often founded on over-speculation, but that the easy gains of a period of real prosperity, characterized by flourishing industry and trade, were also demoralizing if they served merely to increase individual waste and improvidence.

He blamed some English workmen not for want of industry so much as for want of foresight and compared the conspicuous spending of some working-class families with the prudent care for the future of professional people. He quoted Chadwick's remarks on the Lancashire cotton famine during the American Civil War: 'Families trooped into relief rooms in the most abject condition, whose previous aggregate wages exceeded the income of many curates.' Wage statistics were collected from Blackburn, Middlesbrough, Newcastle, Edinburgh, and Sunderland. They are an interesting collection less on account of their reliability than because of the light they throw on the nature of current controversy. At Middlesbrough rail-rollers earned a rate of pay equal to that of lieutenant-colonels in the Foot Guards; plate-rollers, equal to that of majors of Foot; and roughers, equal to that of lieutenants and adjutants. At Blackburn a perturbed employer complained that he could not afford lamb, salmon, young ducks, and green peas until after his hands 'had been consuming these delicacies of the season for some three or four weeks.' No doubt the diet of the same hands varied considerably, with potatoes and porridge providing the staple food in lean times; but, if only the men had exercised a little more restraint, they might have been eating bacon and beans the whole year round.

Smiles did not connect thrift and avarice, even though he always tended in his private life to a certain austerity of consumption. He claimed that he hated the miser, the screw, and the scrub. He was no Scrooge. Of the eight Keynesian motives for refraining from spending – precaution, foresight, calculation, improvement, independence, enterprise, pride, and avarice – he recognized the first six and spelled them in letters of gold and rejected with scorn the last two. 'Thrift is not in any way connected with avarice, usury, greed, or selfishness. It is in fact the very reverse of these disgusting dispositions.' If it were applied universally among the working classes, it would raise their whole social position, not reduce their enjoyment or narrow their horizon. Smiles went back again to the dingy room in Leeds where he had addressed his first audience.

Those who do society's work – who produce, under the direction of the most intelligent of their number, the wealth of the nation – are entitled to a much higher place than they have yet assumed. We believe in a 'good time coming' for working men and women – when an atmosphere of intelligence shall pervade them, when they will prove themselves as enlightened, polite, and independent as the other classes in society.

It is important to stress that in his writing Smiles's main

appeal was a direct one to the working classes through the medium of the Sunday-school prize and the guidebook of the self-taught man. He had a warm-hearted admiration for the labourer as much as for the artisan, but what he distrusted was their lack of self-dependence. 'Their pay nights were often a Saturnalia of riot and disorder,' he wrote of the railway navvies who helped George Stephenson. Smiles believed that such scenes almost irretrievably damaged the reputation of working-men, while organizations like the cooperative movement enhanced it. When the working classes recognized the values which he attempted to inculcate, he showed every sympathy with them.

The creed of the humble man shines through all Smiles's writing. In *Life and Labour* he divided great men into different categories according to their social origins. The resulting table is more amusing than edifying, but it was designed to be taken very seriously. In the 'Nobles and Squires' column he placed Galileo, Mirabeau, and Wellington; in the 'Middle Class' column he placed Newton, Shakespeare, and Carlyle; in the 'Working Class' column he placed Columbus, Copernicus, and Marshal Ney, as well as more familiar figures like Brindley, Stephenson, and Arkwright. He admitted that the line which separated the middle from the aristocratic classes was difficult to draw, but he did not identify the working class with an industrial proletariat, brought into existence by the rise of steam power. The working class was identified with 'all toilers of hand and brain'. Humble they might be, but they were the real makers of the future; from the start they had the advantage over the aristocracy that they tended to produce great inventors rather than great soldiers, a far more useful result despite the appeal of military service. It was with great approval that Smiles quoted the words of his friend Arthur Helps, the civil servant, who taught him the advantages of using shorthand: 'Deduct all that men of the humbler classes have done for England in the way of inventions only, and see where she would have been but for them.'

For those workers who did not rise, Smiles stressed the value of sound corporate institutions like cooperative societies and savings banks, which gave a ticket to independence. He praised 'good' trade unionists, who encouraged individual temperance and mutual assistance and bitterly attacked employers who were opposed to the introduction of savings banks on the grounds that the workmen might use their savings to finance strikes.

Above all, he advocated a greater sympathy among classes. 'Want of sympathy pervades all classes—the poor, the working, the middle, and the upper classes. There are many social gaps between them, which cannot yet be crossed.' An increase in sympathy could not come about by charity – by 'giving money, blankets, coals, and such like to the poor'; it could come about only by increased working-class independence and by mutual understanding of common interests. 'Thus only can the breath of society be sweetened and purified.'

5

Yet if Smiles was talking primarily to those artisans and workmen who were capable of appreciating the magic of self-help, his message was a general one. The gospel of work was as important for the businessman as it was for the working-man. He, too, had to work or to perish.

All life is a struggle. Amongst workmen, competition is a struggle to advance towards high wages. Amongst masters, to make the highest profits ... Stop competition, and you stop the struggle of individualism. ... Under competition, the lazy man is put under the necessity of exerting himself; and if he will not exert himself, he must fall behind. If he do not work, neither shall he eat. ... There is enough for all, but do your own share of work you must.

Smiles reacted strongly against lingering mercantilist conceptions of the utility of luxury and the evil of thrift, the superiority of idleness and the inferiority of work. He had a puritan conception of the fortress wall separating work from play, although he recognized the need for recreation and was too good a businessman himself to omit from his illustrative anecdotes occasional spicy unmoral tales. He told of Sheridan and Lamartine, both 'heroes of debt', the latter running through half a dozen fortunes while boldly proclaiming that 'he hated arithmetic, that negative of every noble thought.' Smiles naturally found this approach extremely unsatisfactory. Instead of finding 'heroic virtue' in conspicuous spending, he saw only 'the seedy side of debt'. 'A man has no business to live in a style which his income cannot support, or to mortgage his earnings of next week in order to live luxuriously today.' Nor had he any right to spend his time daydreaming when he might be working.

The unhappy youth who committed suicide a few years since because he had been 'born to be a man and condemned to be a grocer' proved by the very act that his soul was not equal to the dignity of grocery. ... In human society, social rights necessitate their own observance. When the sense of responsibility is blunted, society goes to ruin.

Smiles stressed that the arguments he was using were not new and that they had to be reiterated even in a business context. The competitive struggle in mid-Victorian England was far more effective than 'the vortex of extravagant fashion' in determining men's attitudes; and, as Mill pointed out, there was an 'extreme incapacity of the people for personal enjoyment' which made hard work and capital accumulation possible. But the lure of social ideals older than capitalism led many nineteenth-century businessmen, and even more frequently their sons and grandsons, if not into heroic debt, at least into a relative idleness in the country. It was difficult to resist the attractions of a graceful and effortless country gentlemen's society. In the battle between the self-made man and the gentleman, the self-made man won in England only if he became a gentleman himself, or tried to turn his son into one.

Smiles hated all such forms of snobbery, particularly when they tempted his new heroes of self-help. He wanted his self-made man to remember how he had risen, not to forget it, and to relate his mature attitudes to the process by which he had acquired them.

The parvenus are of the people, belong to them, and spring from them. Indeed, they are the people themselves. In recognizing the great parvenu spirit of this age we merely recognize what, in other words, is designated as the dignity of labour, the rights of industry, the power of intellect.

The parvenu became a gentleman not by aping his 'betters' but by remaining true to himself. 'The true gentleman' was not the creature of inherited privilege but the person who was polite, civil, tolerant, and forbearing. He might be of any rank or class, peasant or noble. Any other definition of a gentleman was grounded in snobbery.

Smiles would have none of Trollope's subtle dividing lines between different sections in society; the same rules applied to all, and by the same tests they could be judged. All real gentlemen 'at once identify each other. They look each other in the eye and grasp each other's hands. They know each other instinctively. They appreciate each other's merits.' They would no more think of using their power for private reasons than of allowing themselves to forget strict self-control; outer conduct and inward disposition were always perfectly correlated.

Such a picture was based not on observation but on a rooted belief in a moral code, on the world of *ought*, not on the world of *is*. It was to Thackeray, who had brilliantly satirized 'the diabolical invention of gentility', that Smiles turned to discover his final advice:

> Come wealth or want, come good or ill:
>   Let young and old accept their part,
> And bow before the Awful Will,
>   And bear it with an honest heart.
> Who misses or who wins the prize –
>   Go, lose or conquer as you can,
> But if you fail, or if you rise,
>   Be each, pray God, a gentleman.

6

The relevance of Smiles's advice to the circumstances in which his readers found themselves considerably declined during the last quarter of the nineteenth century, and his popularity waned. The industrial system was becoming less competitive and far more impersonal, and social mobility was beginning to depend more on education than on perseverance and initiative in adult life. As a result, the heroes of Samuel Smiles ceased to command the same prestige as they had done twenty years before.

Some critics attacked Smiles for turning self-reliance, which was undoubtedly a virtue, into a ruthless will to success, irrespective of social cost. They found virtue in failure, if the failure had been the product of striving against great odds:

> Behold the leader of a vanquished cause
> His arms extended on the bitter cross.

Other critics, who were beginning to defy the whole body of mid-Victorian orthodox economics, disputed much that Smiles had said about the levers of economic progress. A. F. Mummery and J. A. Hobson, for instance, in the *Physiology of Industry* (1889) claimed that excessive saving was responsible for the underemployment of capital and labour in periods of bad trade. Thrift was conceived of not as a virtue but as a vice, or at least as a check upon healthy development. Orthodoxy was still powerful enough to refuse to allow Hobson to deliver political economy lectures for the London University Extension Board on the ground that his book was 'equivalent in rationality to an attempt to prove the flatness of the earth'. The arguments seemed a little less silly after the economic system itself had toppled over the edge of world war and world depression. The stage was then set for books like R. H. Tawney's *The Acquisitive Society* (1921), which challenged the social presuppositions of the age of Smiles, and J. M. Keynes's *General Theory of Employment, Interest and Money* (1936), which provided a new economic synthesis.

Since the time of Smiles the social framework has changed almost beyond recognition, and it requires an effort to see the relevance of his idea of social character to the particular circumstances of his times. But most of his critics, then and now, were somewhat unfair to him. To those who accused him of sneering at failure, he could reply quite rightly that his analysis of success was not designed to justify ruthless selfishness. To those who criticized his economics, he could reply that he was merely relating the gospel of work – a necessary gospel at all times – to the particular circumstances of an expanding economy, a competitive economic system, and an atmosphere of social peace. In quite different economic circumstances, in the twentieth century, it is still true that the attitude of our society to work is the most crucial issue it has to face, since the fate of every society depends in the long run on the productivity of its workers. The engineers of a planned economy in twentieth-century England have not so far been able to manufacture the social complements of their economic techniques. In the nineteenth century Smiles was successful in this difficult quest.

He was successful because, for the most part, he let his little stories speak for themselves rather than attempted to dress them up in the garments of a unifying philosophy. The lack of such a philosophy makes some of his books little more than collections of fragmentary anecdotes and quotations, yet at the same time it makes it possible for different readers to interpret Smiles in different ways. Each man, indeed, can discover in himself his own Samuel Smiles.

One of the most unexpected admirers of Smiles was Robert Blatchford, the socialist pioneer of Merrie England, who wrote a most interesting essay about *Self-Help* which appeared when Smiles's popularity was at its lowest ebb, particularly among socialists. Blatchford admitted that many socialists spoke of Smiles as 'an arch-Philistine' and of his books as 'the apotheosis of respectability, gigmanity, and selfish grab'; but he himself, writing as a socialist, found Smiles 'a most charming and honest writer' and *Self-Help* 'one of the most delightful and invigorating books it has been my happy fortune to meet with'. He pointed out that Smiles had never claimed that the acquisition of wealth was a proof of moral worth. Rather he had argued that 'the glitter of riches often serves only to draw attention to the worthlessness of their possessor as the light of the glow-worm reveals the grub'. 'Far better and more respectable,' Smiles had said, 'is the good poor man than the bad rich one – better the humble silent man than the agreeable well-appointed rogue who keeps his gig. A well-balanced and well-stored mind, a life full of useful purpose, whatever the position occupied with it may be, is of far greater importance than average worldly respectability.'

The 'nimble and picturesque' style of *Self-Help* appealed to Blatchford, as did the gospel of work itself. 'Its perusal has often forced me to industry, for very shame.' Indeed, the stories in *Self-Help* would shame any sluggard into action and inspire any fainéant with hope and courage. 'The sayings of the heroes quoted ring in the ear like the blare of trumpets, the firm but glowing sentences of the author stir one's blood like the throb of drums.' Above all, Smiles judged men not by precepts but by practice. He paid little attention to titles, honours, and wealth but rather to the usefulness of creative achievement.

Blatchford's praise was echoed by other writers like the rationalist Grant Allen, who certainly did not share what is commonly thought to be a Smilesian philosophy. In a little book published in 1884, called *Biographies of Working Men*, Allen admitted his debt to Smiles and made explicit what Blatchford had found implicit in Smiles's writings.

It is the object of this volume to set forth the lives of working men, who through industry, perseverance, and high principle have raised themselves by their own exertions from humble beginnings. Raised themselves! Yes; but to what? Not merely, let us hope, to wealth and position, nor merely to worldly respect and high office, but to some conspicuous field of real usefulness to their fellow men.

But Allen admitted that self-help was no social panacea.

So long as our present social arrangements exist . . . the vast mass of men will necessarily remain workers to the last, [and] no attempt to raise individual working men above their own class into the professional or mercantile classes can ever greatly benefit the working masses as a whole.

It was right and proper for able men to rise, but it was also right and proper to provide for politicians to legislate for social improvement as well. In other words, Allen, like Blatchford, saw self-help and socialism not as incompatible but as in some sense complementary. Other socialists in the last years of the nineteenth century were prepared to go even further and to produce a theory not of complementarity but of reconciliation, though it was left to George Bernard Shaw and Oscar Wilde to claim that only socialism could provide a proper foundation for full-blooded individualism. Such a paradox would have shocked Smiles in the same way that he was shocked by Robert Owen's 'sophistries', but it would have seemed a truism to Blatchford.

For Smiles's individualism depended not upon the liberated aesthete or the life-force but upon each man building his own character, 'the crown and glory of life'. Such character was usually acquired in the workshop and home rather than in the school. 'The best culture is not obtained from teachers when at school or college, so much as by our own diligent self-education when we have become men.' None the less, Smiles recognized that there were some teachers in England, like Dr Arnold of Rugby, who taught their pupils to rely upon themselves and to develop their powers by their own active efforts.

To understand how within the schoolroom a parallel process of character formation was developed, it is necessary to turn from Smiles to Arnold and to those writers like Thomas Hughes who most actively advertised Arnold's achievements. The transition is not difficult, for Arnold is frequently mentioned in the pages of *Self-Help*; and, after all, Arnold himself once said that he would rather send a boy to Van Diemen's Land, where he would have to work for his bread, 'than send him to Oxford to live in luxury, without any desire in his mind to avail himself of his advantages.'

CHAPTER SIX

Thomas Hughes and the Public Schools

Every pupil was made to feel that there was work for him to do – that his happiness as well as his duty lay in doing that work well. Hence an indescribable zest was communicated to a young man's feeling about life; ... and a deep and ardent attachment sprang up towards him who had taught him thus to value life and his own self, and his work and mission in this world.

BONAMY PRICE ON THOMAS ARNOLD OF RUGBY

I

A Czech reviewer and admirer of Samuel Smiles wrote in his review of *Self-Help* that 'nations are gathered out of nurseries, and they who hold the leading strings of children may even exercise a greater power than those who hold the reins of government.' In examining the influences brought to bear upon the mid-Victorians, the school is of central importance, particularly the public school, which did much to set the attitudes and determine the values of the leaders of society.

The public boarding school is a highly distinctive English educational institution; indeed, it has been claimed bombastically but with no deliberate attempt at exaggeration that 'if a composite history of all the public schools is ever written it will be, in reality, the history of England, since the British Empire has been in the main built up by the founders of the schools and the pupils who gained their knowledge and had their characters moulded in those institutions.'

Such a claim could hardly have been true in the very early nineteenth century, for, although there were nine ancient schools in the country which stood out above the rest, preparing boys for the universities of Oxford and Cambridge and associating boarding-school life with classical education, they were not dominant in the process of the training of national leaders. Neither Macaulay nor Tennyson, Newman nor Disraeli, received their education in such establishments. Robert Lowe, who did, was always unhappy while at Winchester and subjected it in later life to scathing criticism.

The schools had obvious weaknesses and were ripe for reform. Their endowments were often misapplied, their organization inefficient, their discipline loose and uneasy. In most of the schools, boys set the tone rather than masters. 'Deference to public opinion', as it was called, frequently meant the rule of the bully, and 'boy nature' revealed itself either in intermittent 'epidemics of turbulence' or in persistent noncooperation. The 'keen sense of honour' and 'patriotic feeling' in some of the schools were the result rather of rigid custom among the boys than of influence by the masters. The customs were often not only rigid but indefensible. At Westminster, for instance, there was an old rule that no boy below the sixth form might walk in school. If a boy wanted to move, he had to run. 'The idler and the bully had no fears,' the historian of the school has written, 'while wit and industry fought an uphill battle against neglect and dislike.' As we read in *Tom Brown's School Days*, 'there are no such bigoted holders by established forms and customs, be they never so foolish or meaningless, as English schoolboys.'

In attempting to abolish old customs or to make them harmless, masters frequently had to resort to dubious methods themselves. At Eton, where the maximum amount of independence was granted to the schoolboy, the famous John Keate (headmaster from 1809 to 1834) used to make point-blank charges of lying to his boys, quite at random. 'You're hardened in falsehood,' he told them; yet he expected a certain amount of lying to go on as 'a mark of proper respect'. At Rugby, before Thomas Arnold arrived as headmaster in 1829, the school was in the grip of an icy discipline; one of the masters jovially remarked to him that 'the boys were the excrescences of pond life'. For the most part, the boys slept in communal beds holding six, although some parents paid special fees each term for single or double beds. Even the grimmest discipline could not have controlled a school in such conditions, and headmasters were frequently overburdened with the cares of office. So bad were conditions at Harrow when C. J. Vaughan arrived in 1844 that he was told not to throw himself away on the school. When Stuart Adolphus Pears first arrived at Repton in 1852, 'he was for a moment overwhelmed by the desolate prospect. He sat at a table with his head upon his hands, in the attitude of a man appalled at the magnitude of the task he had set himself.'

By 1852, however, the position was changing as a result of influences from inside the schools rather than from outside, particularly from the influence of men like Thomas Arnold of Rugby. While the radical opponents of the public schools, who disliked endowed and socially stratified education, failed in their efforts at reform from without, there was a convincing attempt to reform the old public school from within. Their essential characteristics were retained, but many of their abuses were overcome. New schools were established in keeping with the dominant ideas of the age, and old and new schools together provided a reconciliation of necessity and tradition. While Arnold was important in the reconciliation, it would probably have been accomplished without him. A society of the type of mid-Victorian England had much at stake in the schools question; the answer it reached bore all the marks of what has been called 'the mid-Victorian compromise'.

The old public schools had been founded at different times for different purposes and with different schemes of organization. They all depended, however, upon endowments for their effective maintenance. The new public schools which emerged in the middle of the nineteenth century were anxious to manufacture traditions comparable with the best of those of the older foundations. Taken together, both types of school began to be considered not only as places of learning but as national institutions, so that on the eve of the Public Schools Act of 1868, which ended a decade of investigation and controversy, Leslie Stephen could write that 'neither the British jury, nor the House of Lords, nor the Church of England, nay scarcely the monarchy itself, seems so deeply enshrined in the bosoms of our countrymen as our public schools'.

The importance of the public school in English nineteenth-century social history was twofold. First, it produced 'gentlemen', types as distinct as Samuel Smiles's heroes of self-help. 'It is not necessary,' wrote Thomas Arnold of Rugby, one of the nine old public schools, 'that this should be a school for three hundred, or even one hundred, boys, but it *is* necessary that it should be a school of Christian gentlemen.' The type required careful nurture. Boys are not gentlemen by nature, nor do they naturally become so, and there is no reason to believe that they are by nature Christian. In Arnold's phrase, 'they are not susceptible of Christian principles in their full development and practice; and I suspect that a low standard of morals in many respects must be tolerated among them, as it was on a larger scale, in which I consider the boyhood of the human race.' Arnold was no Rousseau. 'Here in the nakedness of boy-nature,' he wrote on another occasion, 'one is quite able to understand how there could not be found so many as even ten righteous in a whole city.' Yet he looked beyond imperfect boyhood to a more perfect manhood. The school was to be the training ground for character. 'Our work here would be absolutely unbearable,' he said in one of his sermons, 'if we did not bear in mind that we should look forward as well as backward – if we did not remember that the victory of fallen man lies not in innocence but in tried virtue.'

Only the community of a public school under the direction of a powerful headmaster and the care of 'public spirited and liberal' assistant masters could prepare boys for active life and act as a powerful agent in society. Preparation foreshadowed performance. The character-forming role of the school was considered more important than its strictly intellectual task. Like Carlyle and Smiles, Arnold believed in the gospel of work and the formation of character through trial. Work was a sacred duty, and, under the direction of Arnold, Rugby became, in Carlyle's phrase, 'a temple of industrious peace'. The diligent plodder was as cherished as the erratic genius. Arnold was typical of his age when he condemned 'mere intellectual acuteness, divested as it is, in too many cases, of all that is comprehensive and great and good, [as] more revolting than the most helpless imbecility, seeming to me almost like the spirit of Mephistopheles'. Academic successes or failures were less important than moral or religious principles. 'If there be one thing on earth which is truly admirable, it is to see God's wisdom blessing an inferiority of natural powers, where they have been honestly, truly, and zealously cultivated.' In speaking of a pupil whose character had triumphed over his lack of ability, Arnold once said that he would stand to that man 'hat in hand'.

This exhortation of character was not accompanied by any denigration of outstanding ability, which Arnold and the best public schools did much to encourage; but it was the formation of character which was the central purpose of the whole theory of education in the many new public schools which were created in the 1850s and 1860s. The stress laid on the principle suggests that during this period character was a scarcer endowment than ability and that it had not been fostered previously in the older public schools, where boys were allowed simply to be boys. The emphasis on character was only challenged effectively later in the century when ability rather than character became the scarce good, and the public schools were turning out, in A. C. Benson's phrase, 'well-groomed, well-mannered, rational, manly boys, all taking the same view of things, all doing the same things,' conformists to a code rather than highly developed or distinctive personalities. The standardization of character had sapped individuality. By that time the opponents of the public school, as much as its defenders, were arguing in entirely different terms from the controversialists of the middle century.

The second way in which the public school was of central importance was in its mixing of representatives of old families with the sons of the new middle classes. This social amalgam cemented old and new ruling groups, which had previously remained apart. The working classes were for the most part excluded from the schools as they still are in the twentieth century, but the great social divide of the 1840s between landlords and businessmen was bridged. The public school, consequently, provided for the gradual fusion of classes and their drawing upon a common store of values. 'There was nowhere in the country so complete an absence of servility to mere rank, position, or riches,' wrote Charles Dickens; while Matthew Arnold, the son of Dr Arnold of Rugby, told Arminius with pride, in one of the letters in *Friendship's Garland*, that

it is only in England that this beneficial salutary inter-mixture of classes takes place. Look at the bottle-merchant's son, and the Plantagenet being brought up side by side. None of your absurd separations and seventy-two quarterings here. Very likely young Bottles will end by being a lord himself.

Yet, if Matthew Arnold could point to the unique distinction of the public school, he could be gently ironical about its limitations. In one of his conversations with Arminius he complained in conventional liberal terms of the frightful gap between the poor and 'the educated and intelligent class'. 'Your educated and intelligent classes,' sneered Arminius, 'where are they? I should like to see them.' The deficiency of the schools reflected the weakness of all aristocracies – an insensitivity to ideas. They were more successful, however, in giving to their boys those qualities which birth and rearing were least likely to give them – 'the notion of a sort of republican fellowship, the practice of a plain life in common, the habit of self-help'. These qualities were just as important for the sons of the aristocracy and the upper middle classes as were 'sweetness and light' for the philistine lower middle classes.

In mixing classes together, the public schools did something to sustain that 'practice of a plain life in common' which acted as a counter to aristocratic display and middle-class comfort. The living was sometimes so austere that writers could complain that the inmates of a workhouse or a jail were better fed and lodged than the scholars of Eton. Neither the old nor the new public schools pampered birth or wealth; what both did, at their best, was to introduce their pupils to an ideal of responsible service. This ideal had little to do with technical expertise or originality of ideas; it enhanced the prestige of the professions and the civil service but failed to enliven the world of business or to illuminate the world of learning. In time it lent a characteristic flavour to the new ideal of empire.

The obvious limitations of such an ideal were clearly apparent before the end of the century, when middle and upper classes were cementing a new conservative alliance against labour, but in the middle years of the century its limitations mattered little when compared with its immediate efficacy. If Mr Creakle's school at Blackheath, described in Dickens's *David Copperfield*, had been all that the middle classes were looking for, or if unreformed Eton had been the model institution for the aristocracy, Victorian society would never have discovered any balance or Victorian government any persistent responsible direction. In the making of the balance and the formation of character necessary to sustain it, the public school was a key institution, and changes in the public schools were responsible in some measure at least for the adaptation of old institutions to meet new needs.

The idea of the school influenced the idea of the nation, sometimes very directly. As Sir Joshua Fitch said of Thomas Arnold:

It would appear that he had formed an ideal of a Christian State organized on some such mould as his own school at Rugby, with a chief magistrate, energetic, God-fearing, and wise, with the clergy and aristocracy a sort of sixth-form, exercising large influence in the repression of evil and encouragement of good, and a whole community not necessarily holding one set of opinions, but willing to share the same worship and to work together as the servants of the same divine master.

2

Thomas Arnold was by no means the first reformer of the public schools, but he was above all others responsible for spreading the gospel of reform and inspiring other headmasters to follow his example. He died in 1842, nearly twenty years before the Public Schools Inquiry Commission, set up in 1861, exposed the grave defects of school organization and teaching in some of the nine oldest schools in the country. His influence bore fruit in the middle years of the century more than in his lifetime, and the commissioners paid tribute to 'the personal influence and exertions of Dr Arnold and other great school masters.' Many of Arnold's pupils secured positions in other schools and in turn produced their own disciples, so that there was a natural continuity in the reform movement. C. J. Vaughan, for instance, the headmaster of Harrow from 1844 to 1859, was a pupil of Arnold, 'able and willing to carry out the Arnold system of education.' When Pears, one of Vaughan's housemasters, became a reforming headmaster at Repton in 1845, his most helpful colleague, Messiter, was a product of Rugby School. He had been captain of football under Arnold and shared the same philosophy of education.

Both Vaughan and Pears were men with missions, and both refused to be daunted by the difficulties of their tasks. Pears, for example, did not sit with his head in his hands for long. Like Arnold, he applied himself with vigour to the task of training Christian gentlemen. Like Arnold, he was a born ruler. 'His authority in no wise depended upon the outward paraphernalia at one time considered inseparable from the dignity of a Headmaster'; it sprang from within.

The same point was frequently made about Arnold. One of the best accounts of his headmastership is given in an article on him in the *Dictionary of National Biography*, written by Theodore Walrond, the head boy of the school when Arnold died. Walrond stressed that part of Arnold's hold over boys was explained by his 'extraordinary sense of the reality of the invisible world'. In an age when Christian values were the central values of society and all deep individual problems were related to Christian morals, Arnold's sense of spiritual insight was of fundamental importance.

If Arnold's influence was transmitted through former pupils and former colleagues in other public schools, it was transmitted to a far wider public through two written testimonials – Dean Stanley's *Life and Correspondence of Thomas Arnold,* written in 1844, and Thomas Hughes's *Tom Brown's School Days*, which first appeared in 1858.

The simplified picture of the headmaster as a strong, just, and fearless captain which was drawn in the pages of *Tom*

Brown's School Days was more influential than the complicated original, for such a bold but obvious picture was essential to the development of the public school as a national institution. The fact that Thomas Hughes, who was a Radical as well as an old Rugbeian, presented a favourable – indeed, an enthusiastic – verdict on the public schools was as important in establishing their position as the fact that twenty years previously the liberal Arnold, who might have been supposed likely to join in the attack on schools like Eton or on the narrowness of the classical curriculum in the old schools, was the one who took the most active part in their defence. Hughes did more than any other writer to acquaint the non-public school boy, 'the simple reader' as well as 'the gentle reader', as he addressed them in his *envoi*, with the conditions of life and teaching at Rugby. The first edition of his book, which appeared early in 1858, was followed by a second edition in July, a third in September, a fourth in October, and a fifth in November. By the beginning of January 1859 eleven thousand copies had been sold. *Tom Brown's School Days* has continued to sell ever since in British and foreign editions. One American reader was so impressed by it, for instance, that in 1860 he presented a large velvet flag to the schoolhouse at Rugby as a token of his esteem.

Hughes wrote his novel when he was preoccupied with the question of the education of his own son, aged eight, who was just about to go to school. Because he had been at Rugby under Arnold, he felt none of the difficulties which Mr Tulliver felt in *The Mill on the Floss*. 'It's an uncommon puzzling thing to know what school to pick.' Hughes was clear that Rugby alone was the proper destination, not only because it was a good old school, but because Arnold had been there, 'the tall, gallant form, the kindling eye, the voice, now soft as the low notes of a flute, now clear and stirring as the call of a light infantry bugle'. The novel recaptured all Hughes's boyish enthusiasm. If we can occasionally be permitted some doubts about the authenticity or at any rate the completeness of the author's picture of Arnold, we can be permitted no doubts that Tom Hughes himself was the real, though highly idealized

Tom Brown, a grown-up Tom Brown, who had loved his school days so much that to some extent he remained a boy all his life. There is an eager anticipation of life in the novel, not a mere nostalgia for the past, and, as Charles Kingsley wrote soon after the book came out, 'from everyone, from the fine lady on her throne, to the red-coat on his cock-horse, and the school boy on his form . . . I have heard but one word, and that is, that it is the jolliest book they ever read.'

It needed a jolly book to popularize the public school with the middle-class and later on with the working-class reading public, just as it needed a serious biography by Dean Stanley to provide a convincing assessment of the public school for Christian intellectuals. National institutions need to be defended at different levels; even those claims which are vindicated in controversy need to be buttressed by good-humoured popular acquiescence. Thomas Hughes, whose work influenced not only all later fiction about public schools but also the daily round of the schools themselves, was and remains one of the most powerful advocates of the system. His lack of subtlety was an advantage; his colourful melodramatics have won more admiration than the whole of Arnold's sermons put together or those carefully compiled histories of particular schools which lovingly and meticulously trace each change in the timetable and plot the laying of each new brick in the buildings.

The picture of the school in *Tom Brown's School Days* is a very simple one indeed. Rugby is the background against which Tom discovers himself and builds his character. His experiences there are worth while recapitulating. He comes from the sturdy family of Browns, 'who are scattered over the whole Empire, on which the sun never sets, and whose general diffusion I take to be the chief cause of that empire's stability'. His father, a small squire, tells him before he goes to Rugby to stick to the truth and to keep a brave and kind heart and meditates to himself that the reason why he had sent him there was not to produce a good scholar – 'I don't care a straw for Greek particles; no more does his mother' – but to turn out 'a brave, helpful, truth-telling Englishman, and a gentleman, and a Christian. . . . That's all I want.'

Truth-telling, bravery, and even the manners of a gentleman are acquired at Rugby only after innumerable trials and adventures, but the process of acquisition begins as soon as Tom passes the school gates and begins 'already to be proud of being a Rugby boy'. After he has heard the Doctor's first sermon, he starts to be proud of being one of Arnold's boys as well. He makes a serious resolve 'to stand by and follow the Doctor, ... feeling that it was only cowardice (the incarnation of all other sins in such a boy's mind) which hindered him from doing so with all his heart.'

Some of the older boys prefer 'the good old ways', the battle of wits with the masters, to the Doctor's morality; but Tom, helped by other boys as much as his teachers, begins to realize that the battle against evil where the stakes are life and death is the decisive struggle. The sense of battle remains dominant. 'After all, what would life be without fighting? ... From the cradle to the grave, fighting, rightly understood, is the business, the real highest, honestest business of every son of man.' Tom grows out of the struggles both mental and physical. He 'was becoming a new boy, though with frequent tumbles in the dirt and perpetual hard battles with himself, and was daily growing in manfulness and thoughtfulness, as every high-couraged and well-principled boy must, when he finds himself for the first time consciously at grips with self and the devil.'

The crisis of the story develops around Tom's use of cribs to help him in his Latin translation. Arthur, one of the boys in his class, who acts as his externalized conscience, tells him to abandon them and to rely upon himself. East, his great friend, the voice of 'nature', reminds him that relations with masters are 'a trial of skill – like a match at football or a battle. ... We're natural enemies in school [boys and masters] – that's the fact.' The crib was a fair weapon, not a means of fraud; to dispense with it would be to cut at the root of all school morality. 'You'll take away all mutual help, brotherly love, or, in the vulgar tongue, giving construes, which I hope to be one of our highest virtues.' Tom is pulled between two moralities: that of his schoolfellows and that of the Doctor. But his conscience is on the Doctor's side. Arthur prevails over East. Tom is prepared for the harder school of life, where such choices must constantly be made:

> Once to every man and nation comes the moment to decide,
> In the strife of truth with falsehood, for the good or evil side.

Pleasing the Doctor means scrapping the crib, searching the depths of his young soul, visiting 'the great grim man himself', and becoming 'a hero-worshipper, who would have satisfied the soul of Thomas Carlyle himself'.

The story ends with the visit of a bigger and wiser Tom to Arnold's tomb. He has realized that beyond the hero-worship of the headmaster is 'the worship of Him who is the King and Lord of heroes', just as beyond the School is Life. And, though the Doctor dies, Tom's life of action begins:

> Death keeps watch beside the portal,
> But 'tis life that dwells beyond.

For Hughes it was to be a life of action. For Arnold's more intellectual pupils, like Clough and Stanley, Arnold's death placed them 'on a little island of memory, and all who share in that memory must hold together as long as life lasts'.

3

How far is Hughes's account of Rugby and of Arnold's work there an accurate one, and does it afford a fair assessment of the virtues and weaknesses of the mid-Victorian public school?

Hughes himself was never a member of the small inner circle at Rugby, which included Stanley and Clough, brilliant boys bound to the Doctor by close spiritual and intellectual ties. He was a more ordinary boy, although a natural leader. He was captain both of Bigside at football and of the cricket eleven and not unnaturally had 'very little time to give inferior industries, such, for instance, as the cultivation of Greek Iambics or Latin Alcaics'. His interest in school stopped short at the bounds of scholarship, nor did he measure the success of the school in scholastic terms. In *Tom Brown's School Days*, Gray, the winner of a scholarship to Balliol, is, as *The Times* pointed out in its first review, a silent character. 'I'd sooner win two School house-matches running than get the Balliol Scholarship any day,' exclaims Brookes, the captain of Bigside, while East evidently thought the half-day holiday which Gray secured for the school was more important than the academic triumph itself.

Hughes, with his boyish love of fighting and his muscular brand of Christianity, which he derived from Charles Kingsley rather than from Thomas Arnold, clearly considered games more important than the Doctor did. 'A struggling half hour of Rugby football is worth a year of common life,' he said. Tom tells one of the masters that cricket is more than a game; 'it is an institution', while Arthur, whom Tom has saved from too much reading, adds that it is 'the birthright of British boys, old and young, as *habeas corpus* and trial by jury are of British men'. 'The discipline and reliance on one another, which it teaches, are so valuable,' replies the master. 'It ought to be such an unselfish game. It merges the individual in the eleven; he doesn't play that he may win but that his side may.'

This appraisal of cricket was characteristic of the new 'public school', which turned games into an instrument of character-building instead of a mere exercise or amusement. It is significant that in the 1850s and 1860s the rules of many games were codified. The Rugby rules were formulated as early as 1846, but Repton was more typical in consolidating its rules a generation later. The Queensberry Rules were formulated in 1867. *Wisden* dates from 1864. There was an interplay between what happened nationally and what happened in the schools. For example, Rugby school rules gave way to national rugby union rules in 1871. Inter-school matches canalized school loyalties and enthusiasms, while even at Eton turbulent games on the river were giving place to fierce contests for places in the rowing eight. Games became something more than mere games; they became institutions, both absorbing the energies of growing boys living in a boys' world and preparing for real-life situations by inculcating 'games values' and team spirit – values as important to the gentleman as were competitive values to Smiles's businessman or skilled labourer.

Hughes foresaw this aspect of school development more clearly than Arnold, who himself liked physical exercise and used occasionally to wander down to the playing fields and in a somewhat detached way observe the battle of the teams. Arnold did nothing, however, to place games on an equality with work, nor did his successors at Rugby. He would have disapproved of the late-nineteenth-century fetish of games on the grounds that it vulgarized intellectual labour, that it substituted self-indulgence for self-denial, and that it placed those boys in positions of command and influence who were frequently most unfit to exercise authority. Arnold, with his love of classical parallels, spurned the example of Sparta and saw in cultivated athleticism 'brutality of soul', not embryonic team spirit.

Although Hughes exaggerated in reading back a cult of games into his days at Rugby, he did not exaggerate the trend in many of the new and some of the old public schools. The team spirit was easier to nurture on the playing field and its lessons more simple both to understand and to preach than intellectual eminence or individuality of spiritual experience, and the masters in many of the public schools were content to rest satisfied with it. Its limitations were lost in an excess of sentimentalism and piety for 'the dear old school house – the best house and the best school in England'. Loyalty took the place of any lucid appreciation of the ends for which the team spirit was to be applied. Cotton, who had been a pupil of Arnold, deliberately used organized games in the new school at Marlborough (1851–70) to discipline a rebellious mob of schoolboys and build up a disciplined community. It is interesting that in his novel Hughes mentioned Cotton, then an assistant at Rugby, with high praise; at Marlborough belief in games was crystallized into a code, quite consciously and deliberately.

There is little suggestion in Hughes, or in the schools which turned to his pages for their standards, of the intellectual purpose of the school, a purpose which was close to Arnold's heart. The reader is given the impression – the jolliest of all impressions – that it is the chief business of a public school to produce healthy animals, to supply them with pleasant companions and with faithful friends, and to teach them the rudiments of character.

This impression is very different from that given by Arnold's critics, many of whom accused him of turning boys into men before their time – indeed, of forgetting that 'there should exist for a certain time, between childhood and manhood, the natural production known as a boy.' It is different too from the impression given in Stanley's *Life of Dr Arnold*, the second of the two influential studies of Rugby, though the two books are best seen as complementary rather than antagonistic. With full documentary materials at his disposal and with the memory of a close personal friendship with Arnold, Stanley could penetrate the headmaster's mind and survey his purposes far more effectively than Hughes. With a healthy awe and a bold zest for life, Hughes could recall the 'informal' organization of the life of the boys at Rugby, which Stanley admitted himself he had never known at all. Indeed, when he read *Tom Brown's School Days*, he found it 'an absolute revelation', opening up 'a world of which, though so near to me, I was utterly ignorant'.

Stanley knew a different side of Arnold. He was one of the small group of Rugby boys who went on to Oxford University stamped with a gravity and deep seriousness of purpose in life which were not to be found in most other young public school boys. To their enemies Arnold's serious 'disciples' were 'prigs'; to themselves they were dedicated men, bound to their headmaster with what Stanley described as 'idolatrous affection'. Stanley's picture of Arnold was coloured by his own reverence, and, powerful though it is, it only becomes complete when supplemented by Hughes's more homely description. If Stanley saw what happened in Arnold's mind, Hughes saw what happened in many of his pupils' minds, in the minds of all the Tom Browns who made up 'the masses' of the school.

Stanley brought out more clearly than Hughes Arnold's high-minded pursuit of his purpose within his chosen field. In accepting his headmastership, Arnold believed that his employment provided him with opportunities which no other calling presented. To those who complained what a pity it was that a man fit to be a statesman should be employed in teaching schoolboys, he retaliated with a modest but firm insistence on the importance of the school as a training ground of character. He did not consider his headmastership as a prelude to a different task or a passport to promotion but as a full-time vocation, offering its own rewards. Sure of his mission, Arnold never warped it by letting the affairs of the school slip out of their proper perspective. He always insisted on the 'great work of government' as 'the highest earthly desire of the ripened mind'. He governed his school with as deep a sense of responsibility as statesmen govern a country. Indeed, as one of his masters is made to say in *Tom Brown's School Days*, 'perhaps ours is the only little corner of the British Empire which is thoroughly, wisely, and strongly ruled just now'.

But, as Stanley saw, his government was not absolute, and his choice of policy was characteristically English and characteristically Victorian. 'If the King of Prussia were as sincere a lover of liberty as I am,' Arnold wrote in 1829, 'he would give his people a constitution – for my desire is to teach my boys to govern themselves – a far better thing than to govern them well myself.' As much as possible should be done by the boys, and as little as possible for them. He realized that the public school was a national institution, not only because it was rooted in the past, but also because it depended upon a high degree of self-government by the boys. He refused to rule as a tyrant or a jailer, preferring to delegate authority to the thirty oldest, strongest, and cleverest boys in the sixth form. Such delegation insured a regular government among the boys themselves and avoided the evils of anarchy, in other words, of the lawless tyranny of physical strength. From 1829 onward he and the senior boys met from time to time, almost as equals, to consider ways of improving the school. He even caused a flag to be flown close to his study – a signal that any boy could come to him for a talk. His sixth form was his pride. 'When I have confidence in the Sixth,' he exclaimed in one of his farewell addresses, 'there is no post in England which I would exchange for this, but if they do not support me I must go.'

In relying upon the sixth form, Arnold was not following a

new course of action. He was rather adapting for his own purposes a traditional feature of the public school system – the
substantial degree of independence of the older boys. Conventions were turned into ideals with surprising success. It was one
of the boys who wrote in the *Rugby School Miscellany* in 1843
that

the Sixth Form was an aristocracy of talent and worth, created
neither by birth, interest, nor physical strength. It was a happy
thought, and spoke the observant mind in him who first set boys
to govern boys, and who turned those who should themselves have
been the ringleaders in any disturbance into an organized and responsible nobility, with power, privileges, and a character of their
own to preserve.

Hughes enables us to understand as clearly as Stanley the
methods by which Arnold converted an old feature into a new
institution. There was little of the real revolutionary in Arnold;
he set out not to undermine old ways but to Christianize them,
to pour new wine into old bottles. 'You need not fear my
reforming furiously,' he wrote to a friend just after his appointment. It is true that he raised fees very sharply and exercised a strict control over conditions of entry; but he was
always careful to retain customs and institutions which bound
the school with the past, unless their retention was positively
harmful to good morals and discipline. He venerated 'the historical associations and beauty' not only of Rugby but of his
own school, Winchester, and indeed of the public school system as a whole. Although he had a deep distrust of Toryism, he
expressed a Liberal–Conservative opinion characteristic of the
middle years of the century when he said, 'Another system
may be better in itself, but I am placed in this system, and am
bound to try what I can make of it.'

What he made of it depended partly on his choice of assistant masters but mainly on the strength of his own will. His
masters, who were expected, like the boys, to be 'Christians
and Gentlemen', were persuaded that their positions offered 'a
noble field of duty' and that they could only be secured by
men who were willing 'to enter into the spirit of our system,
heart and hand'. Arnold was an unquestioned leader, creating

an impression of unhasting and unresting diligence. Like all the great men of his age, he admired energy and activity. At the end of a day's work he would sometimes say that he felt that he could dictate to twenty secretaries at once. Such energy could have driven a bigger institution than a school, but to Arnold even a school was too big to make perfect. 'I came to Rugby,' he said, 'full of plans for School reform; but I soon found that the reform of a public school was a much more difficult thing than I had imagined.' 'I dread to hear this called a religious school,' he added on another occasion. 'I know how much there is to be done before it can really be called so.'

Arnold's modesty needs to be confronted with Hughes's pride. Tom Brown's reformation was itself a sign that the bad old ways inside Rugby were coming to an end and that, although there were pockets of resistance, Arnold's battle against the combination of aggressive boys and complacent 'public opinion' was proving successful. The change of tone can be traced in his sermons as headmaster. In the first few years after he came to the school he concerned himself with the contrast between the evils of school opinion and the purity of the moral law of Christianity; in the last few years he was more exhortatory. Particular faults were forgotten, and general values were stressed.

His methods were in keeping with the reformation of manners which characterized mid-Victorian England as a whole. He insisted upon truth as fervently as Tennyson. A boy's word was taken as his bond, and in consequence a general feeling grew up that it was a shame to tell Arnold a lie, for he always believed it. There could be no more eloquent evidence of the change of attitudes within a school.

The impact of the change at Rugby was felt both in the universities and in other schools, although Eton was not 'sensibly affected', in Gladstone's phrase, 'by any influence extraneous to the place itself'. It had been said in one of Arnold's testimonials before he was appointed to Rugby that, if he were elected, 'he would change the face of education all through the public schools of England'. The prophecy was fulfilled, although – or perhaps because – he made few changes in methods or organization. His influence came through his simplicity of purpose and the force of his personality. Without improvements in tone and atmosphere, it is doubtful whether the public schools would have survived the critical examination of the 1860s. Arnold purged them of their obvious abuses while retaining their essential characteristics. 'My love for any place or person, or institution, is exactly the measure of my desire to reform them,' he had written to Stanley. The reform made other people love the places and institutions all the better too.

4

The investigation of the 1860s began with a literary controversy in the periodicals of the first year of the decade and the setting-up of a commission of inquiry by George Cornewall Lewis, Palmerston's Home Secretary, a year later. The government justified its increasing interest in the welfare of the schools. It had already examined the universities in the 1850s; now it turned to the schools on the ground that they were no longer monastic establishments or private corporations but 'the great seminaries of learning in this land. . . . Their welfare and progress concerns in the highest degree the Empire itself.' But the members of the commission were for the most part friends of the public schools. The chairman, Lord Clarendon, who was more critical than most of the members, was the son of an Etonian and the father of a Harrovian, while Sir Stafford Northcote, who had been concerned with civil service reform, was also a well-known defender of the public school system.

The commission published its report in the spring of 1864 after a thorough and painstaking examination of conditions in the nine old public schools – Eton, Harrow, Winchester, Shrewsbury, Westminster, St Paul's, Merchant Taylors', Charterhouse, and Rugby. Reforms were suggested both in administration and in curriculum, but there was no criticism of the main features of the system. Competitive examinations were welcomed, and the need for securing capable recruits for the civil service was underlined, but at the same time the schools were praised for cultivating the essential English qualities –

'their capacity to govern others and to control themselves, their aptitude for combining freedom with order, their public spirit, their vigour and manliness of character, their strong but not slavish respect for public opinion, their love of healthy sports and exercise'.

The commissioners recognized that the genius of one school differed much from that of another and that it was desirable that the masters of every school 'should be perfectly familiar with its system of discipline and teaching, its unwritten customs, and all that stamps it with a character of its own, as well as that they should be animated by a warm attachment to it'. Loyalty to the school was itself an essential element in character-building. The schools as a whole had been

the chief nurseries of our statesmen; in them, and in schools modelled after them, men of all the various classes that make up English society, destined for every profession and career, have been brought up on a feeling of social equality, and have contracted the most enduring friendships, and some of the ruling habits, of their lives; and they have had perhaps the largest share in moulding the character of an English gentleman.

It was not until 1868 that a Public Schools Act was passed to follow up the proposals of the commission. An executive commission, appointed by Parliament, was created to insure a new system for securing governing bodies for the public schools and to prepare new statutes. Some Conservatives fought hard against any reform, claiming that the schools were 'products of Time and of Nature', not to be upset by a utilitarian generation; some Liberals urged a root-and-branch reform and considered the bill 'one of the most delusive and reactionary measures ever put before the country'. But it passed, as it was bound to pass once the commissioners had stated the issues in terms congenial to the ruling opinion of the time.

Like all English national institutions, the public school depended upon the support not of extremists but of liberal conservatives. One Tory critic had maintained that 'it is as little easy to found a school like an Eton, a Harrow, or a Rugby as it would be to call into existence a nation'. But the nine old public schools were already being supplemented by many new ones. Cheltenham, Marlborough, Rossall, and Radley had all been founded between 1840 and 1850; Wellington followed in 1853; and in one single year – 1862 – Clifton, Malvern, and Haileybury were all established. The new upper middle classes launched on the wave of mid-Victorian prosperity were demanding new schools for their large numbers of children, new schools as much like the old ones – the reformed old ones – as possible. At the same time improvements in transport were making it possible for children to be sent far away from their homes. The public school system was nationalizing education as well as stratifying it, and parents were quick to realize that 'all good schools have a tendency to become expensive, almost in proportion to their goodness'.

It was not only the interests of parents which were at stake. The drive for civil service reform depended upon a plentiful supply of able and healthy young men from the public schools and universities. Reform in the public schools and reform in the civil service had always been closely associated; in both competitive examination played its part, but in both the ideal of the gentleman remained predominant. Reform of the school, it was believed, would lead to reform of the service, and reform of the service would lead to reform of the school. As Sir Stafford Northcote put it, and his opinion was echoed by most headmasters, 'There is nothing which would so promote the system of education as the throwing open of the Civil Service to competitive examination.'

The new public schools and universities could be relied upon to supply character as well as ability. Jowett, the master of Balliol, could boast that university experience 'abundantly showed that in more than nineteen cases out of twenty, men of attainments are also men of character', while Northcote and Trevelyan corroborated the point from the civil service side. The young men selected by open competition, it was maintained, would be more likely to be 'gentlemen' than those who were appointed by patronage.

Open competition would thus be safe because it would be geared to the public school and university system. Proficiency in the subjects set in the examination would, as Professor

Thompson pointed out, 'afford a sufficient test of the social rank of the candidate' or, at any rate, prove that he had been brought into contact with influences conducive to the sentiments of a gentleman. In an age when the shadow of democracy was already looming on the horizon, men like Vaughan, Jowett, and Trevelyan realized the need for a plentiful supply of informed gentlemen. It would be dangerous, argued Trevelyan if, 'when the irresistible tendency of the times is to bring into activity the political power of the lower classes of society', the 'higher orders' were to relax into intellectual sloth. 'We must be diligent in our own education,' wrote Sir J. T. Coleridge, the old Etonian Lord Chief Justice. 'It will not do to rest on traditions or on ancient privileges; if we will lead, we must make our selves fit to be leaders; if even we will float with the current, and not be overwhelmed by it, we must, by discipline and training, learn to throw out our intellectual powers with the strongest and best trained. ... While all around us, the underwood of the forest is making vigorous shoots, our own growth must not stand still, lest haply we should be overgrown and stifled.'

5

The consciousness of a changing social balance fascinated and alarmed most of the thinkers of the middle years of the century. The defenders of the public schools were deliberately supporting the claims of institutions from which the masses of the population were excluded. How did they conceive of the relationship between the privileged classes and the rest, and how far did they create attitudes at school which conditioned the answers of adult men to this question?

In terms of school standards the answer was plain: the ideal of the gentleman involved a sense of social duty as well as good form. Arnold was at great pains to insist upon this aspect of the educated man. He would preach his sermons both in the school chapel and in the little mission which grew up around the new railway junction. He would appear before the local Mechanics' Institute as well as before his own sixth form. He would visit the homes of the poor as well as the classrooms of the boys.

He even cooperated in working-class journalism, and, as early as 1831, letters which he wrote to the *Sheffield Courant* 'were read with great interest by the mechanics and people of that class' in one of England's busiest industrial cities.

Arnold's attitude toward the poor was neither condescending nor patronizing. 'Feeling keenly what seemed to him at once the wrong and the mischief done by the too-wide separation between the higher and lower orders,' wrote Stanley, 'he wished to visit them as neighbours, without always seeming bent on relieving or instructing them,' and could not bear to use language which to anyone in a higher station would have been thought an interference. If at times he drew a distinction between the 'good poor' and the rest, he was merely behaving like all his contemporaries; but for the most part he was far ahead of most social workers. Poor people were sometimes embarrassed by his treating them on equal terms and did not know quite how to deal with him. 'He used to come in to my house,' said an old woman who lived near his home in Westmorland, 'and talk to me as if I were a lady.' There was nothing patronizing about such an encounter, but it could hardly be called an equal one. Indeed, it was difficult to discover a true equality of classes in the England of the early nineteenth century, for the very words 'lady' and 'gentleman' were barriers, not avenues, to real understanding.

Mid-Victorian deference could not be broken down from above, even when a genuine attempt was made; it needed a great democratic upsurge from below to sweep away the barriers. Arnold was no unqualified believer in a theory of democracy, but he did not attempt to break the first democratic waves. It was only later in the century, as the democratic tide advanced, that some of the public schools began to take an increasingly anti-democratic stand. It is true that some of their pupils turned into rebels rather than conformists and allied themselves with democratic movements, but the average boys became increasingly complacent and proud. The 'old school tie' became the gentleman, the man inside it the dummy, and by that time the voice of the ventriloquist was very different from the voice of Thomas Arnold.

It is dangerous to generalize too glibly; and certainly in the middle years of the century, when stratification was being talked of most openly, there was no complete standardization of product. The career of Thomas Hughes himself reveals just how much and how little the public school of his day succeeded in fitting an able but not outstanding boy into a mould. The approach of the real Tom Brown to the social questions of his day is as deserving of attention as the approach of the sanctified Arnold.

Hughes was 'formed' by his family and by Rugby. His father was a squire with 'true popular sympathies', but a true Tory as well, insisting on 'strict obedience and deference' from his servants. His headmaster was an equally important voice of authority. During the important years from ten to eighteen he had been placed under the spell of Rugby and Arnold and for half a century had 'never ceased to thank God for it'.

At Oxford he became a Radical – 'the noble side of democracy was carrying me away' – and in 1848, the year of revolutions, when Smiles was prudently turning from politics to self-help, Hughes joined F. D. Maurice and the Christian Socialists. To the dogmas of capitalist competition he opposed the ethics of the cooperative team. A lawyer by profession, he devoted most of his time to 'causes', particularly cooperation and the Working Men's College Movement. But, if he was a Radical, he was not a rebel. Rugby guided him in his social work among the London workingmen even more than it had guided him in his studies at Oxford. Little in demand as a lecturer, he was in great demand as an athlete and a pugilist. 'Round shoulders, narrow chests, stiff limbs,' he told the students at the London College, 'are as bad as defective grammar and arithmetic.' The science of fisticuffs was a necessary prelude to the science of government, in London as much as at Rugby.

In the 1850s and 1860s Hughes became a more militant Christian and a less dogmatic socialist, but he did not abandon his belief in workingmen. In 1859, when he joined the Volunteer Movement, he raised a corps of two companies from the Working Men's College. During the American Civil War he was a staunch supporter of the North: 'If the North is beaten, it will be a misfortune such as has not come upon the world since Christendom arose.' Right and wrong were as clearly defined in American politics as they had been by Arnold at Rugby: 'I think the free-soilers were as much in the right, and the pro-slavery party as much in the wrong, as parties composed of human beings are ever likely to be.' This was the sort of decision for which Rugby had prepared him. As James Russell Lowell, who became one of Hughes's regular correspondents and mentors, had put it in 1859:

> We know we've got a cause, John,
> That's honest, right, and true;
> We thought t'would win applause, John,
> If nowhere else, from you.

The American Civil War, which reinforced the lessons of Rugby, drew Hughes closer to the English working classes, who discovered a new conscience and vitality during the conflict.

Even before the war Hughes had been interested in trade unions, the growing voluntary organizations of workingmen, which were to become a national institution as intrenched as the public schools. In 1860, at a meeting of the Social Science Association, he defended the representative character of the new unions and their regulative possibilities in the world of labour. They could become guarantors of social peace as well as agents of national productive power. Hughes's support of the unions and of the cause of the North brought him into close touch with the leaders of the London Trades Council, who were largely responsible for pushing his candidature for Parliament in 1865 and assuring his victory at the top of the poll at Lambeth. Tom Brown had become a working-class leader. 'Hughes has the art of ingratiating himself into the favour of the artisans,' wrote one of his opponents; 'a leader of the people he undoubtedly is.'

The people he led were not socialists, but they were resentful of their incomplete citizenship. They demanded the right to vote and the protection of their unions. 'Labour is here at the door, asking respectfully that it may be opened.' Hughes was already trying to open the door from the other side. As a member of Parliament and later of the Royal Commission on Trade Unions in 1867, he was a vigorous advocate of social and political rights for workingmen. During the commission he was in constant touch with Robert Applegarth, the trade-union leader, and, when the work was concluded, he was a signatory to the minority report, which expressed the union's point of view. 'Under a system which professes the right or rather the duty of all men peacefully to pursue their own interest for themselves, unionism appears to us the exact correlative of competition.' The legal reforms he suggested became the basis of the new trade-union code of the 1870s.

Hughes's association with the royal commission was the high-water mark of his political career. Between 1870 and 1875 he ceased to be the champion of the unions and no longer went wholeheartedly with them in the pursuit of their claims. At the general election of 1874 he was at the bottom of the poll in Marylebone, and, when he accepted a place on Disraeli's new and unpopular royal commission to examine trade union law, he was regarded as a traitor to the union cause. It was only when Disraeli had recognized the strength of the unions in 1875 and, indeed, had gone much further than Hughes was prepared to go that the unionists paid tribute to Hughes's work in the past. By that time Hughes felt misgivings about union power and recognized that the social mood of the country had changed. 'Their future is practically in the hands of the work-people themselves . . . and it is for them to show that they can rise to the new situations and prove themselves patriotic and true Englishmen who can put their country before their class.' Rugby had done its work. 'It is quite natural that a new generation should turn to new admirers, and I certainly am neither sad nor sorry that it should be so.'

The passing of the Reform Bill of 1867 had created a new world in which Hughes had a minor part to play. Full political citizenship for the urban working classes separated them from Hughes instead of drawing them closer to him. And so he turned back from the greater community to the smaller, and pitched his hopes in a pioneer community in the great new world overseas. He planned a settlement in Tennessee, where grown-up Tom Browns could prove that they were not anachronisms and could work with their hands to create a new society. England was no longer big enough or adventurous enough to provide a home for Brown or East: 'The spirit of our highest culture and the spirit of our trade do not agree together. The ideas and habits which those who have most profited by them bring away from our public schools do not fit them to become successful traders.' Nor could they be union leaders. Colonists they might become if they had a cause which was big enough. It is significant that Hughes was responding to a challenge which had fascinated Arnold many years before. 'If we are alive fifteen years hence,' Arnold had written in 1829, 'I think I would go with you gladly to Swan River [in Australia], if they will make me a schoolmaster there, and lay my bones in the land of kangaroos and oppossums. . . . No missionarizing is half so beneficial as to try to pour sound and healthy blood into a young civilized society.'

Hughes called his colony in distant Tennessee 'Rugby' and gave it a church in the heart of the community to stand like Rugby Chapel in the midst of his old school. If it had no Bigside, it had a tennis club, and its monthly magazine was called the *Rugbeian*. When Hughes went out to visit the settlement for the first time in 1880, he was greeted there by five exiled Englishmen, all former public school boys, from Eton, Harrow, Wellington, and Rugby. But there was no Thomas Arnold in Tennessee, and the colony failed. Only the dream remained – the old recurring dream of Rugby, England, which haunted Hughes until the end of his life – so that his last book, published in 1894, two years before his death, was dedicated jointly to Rugby and the Working Men's College.

The word 'haunted' is misleading. Hughes was too eager, too active, too optimistic to be troubled by ghosts. He was rather 'a grown-up school boy in a large playground', as staunch and true to his school values as he had been fifty years before. Stock product he never was. Beyond the values and behind the carefully formed character was the irrepressible temperament, the cheerful disposition, that neither public school nor political hurly-burly could transform. When Lowell left him after their first meeting in 1870, he wrote: 'I was really saddened to part with him – it was saying good-bye to sunshine.' The sun always shone. It was the natural Tom Hughes and not the transformed Tom Brown who uttered the most convincing *cri de cœur*:

I love vagabonds, only I prefer poor to rich ones. Couriers and ladies-maids, imperials and travelling carriages, are an abomination unto me; I cannot get away with them. But for dirty Jack, and every good fellow who, in the words of the capital French song, moves about,

> *'Comme le limaçon,*
> *Portant tout son bagage,*
> *Ses meubles; sa maison'*

on his own back, why, good luck to them, and many a merry roadside adventure, and steaming supper in the chimney corners of roadside inns, Swiss châlets, Hottentot kraals, or wherever else they like to go.

No institution, not even a reformed public school, could standardize a boy like that.

CHAPTER SEVEN

Robert Applegarth and the Trade Unions

We shall be faithless to our fellow working men if we omit to record our honest conviction that this much to be desired condition must be preceded by the equally universal spread of the principles of economy and sobriety, which would be accelerated by our meeting for business in public halls or private rooms, where, by the establishment of libraries and listening to the voice of the lecturer on all subjects connected with our interests, we and our sons shall become respectful and respected, and make rapid progress in the onward march of reform.

RULES OF THE AMALGAMATED
SOCITEY OF CARPENTERS AND
JOINERS (1869)

I

Thomas Hughes established his position as an active friend of the trade unions during the great building dispute of 1859–60. When the carpenters, masons, and bricklayers went on strike in London to defend the right of combination and to press for the nine-hour working day, Hughes leaped to their defence, wrote articles on their behalf, and helped to secure a settlement. In the course of the strike he came to know Robert Applegarth, the secretary of the Amalgamated Society of Carpenters and Joiners, with whom he remained on friendly terms for the rest of his life. Public school boy and trade unionist met and found much in common with each other. After all, both had a highly developed sense of order and community. As the building unionists told the Central Master Builders' Association in 1860 – 'that our society shall be governed by laws, and that the members shall be requested to conform to those laws is but natural, and we believe that such is the case in all corporations and every club among the upper classes in Pall Mall and St James's.'

Robert Applegarth was an outstanding specimen of the new labour leader of the middle years of the century; in the words of the manufacturer and politician, A. J. Mundella, he was 'an ornament to his class, and I know some of the best men in the country are proud to call him their friend.' His career and outlook illuminate intelligent working-class attitudes – the attitudes of a new artisan *élite*, for whom the trade union was as basic an institution as the public school was for Hughes. Unlike the public school, however, the trade union was considered by many orthodox spokesmen of the age as a tyrannical and seditious organization. Not even the prudent tactics and the obvious public spirit of Applegarth could convince all his contemporaries, or even the most influential among them. The public school reflected national values; the trade union often seemed to subvert them. Yet the union, like the school, was gradually establishing itself as a characteristically English institution, and in 1875, after more than a decade of agitation, it secured what appeared to be a full and comprehensive charter from Parliament. The new franchise of 1867, based on the urban working-class vote, had turned the artisans into full citizens; within ten years, with the full recognition of trade-union rights, the seeds of social as well as political democracy had also been sown.

The active political and trade-union life of Applegarth spans the exciting years between widespread social fear of the unions – fear which reached the point of terror in 1866 and 1867 – and genuine recognition. It gains in importance, moreover, because it was not a narrow life devoted to a particular cause or a single battle. Applegarth saw the trade union merely as one instrument of working class emancipation; cooperation, full participation in politics, and a greatly extended educational system were equally important elements in working-class progress. Such progress alone could transform society. 'To teach workmen the practical lesson of self-reliance, to provide during the term of prosperity for the hour of need, is one of our great objects; but the highest duty of trade unionists is to teach "man's duty to man".' Trade unionists would be judged not only by the care they devoted to their own interests but by the willingness with which they contributed to 'the well-being of the whole human family'.

The events of Applegarth's life fall into place only if they are related to the greater pattern of which they were a part. Applegarth was both an actor with a leading part in the social history of the period and a symbol. His actions speak for themselves, but, to grasp their full significance, they must be studied against the social background of his age.

2

He was born in Hull in 1834, the son of a sailor who went whaling in the southern seas and rose to be the captain of a brig. Although the young Applegarth became a carpenter, not a mariner, he always remained something of a wanderer. He was never bound by the confines of a workshop or even the coasts of England; he was a worker of the world as well as a Yorkshireman.

Fired by descriptions he had heard of life in America, he left Sheffield, the bustling industrial community where he had learned his carpentry, for New York and Chicago. When he landed in New York in December 1854 he had only half-a-crown in his pocket, but he soon met a fellow-worker from Sheffield who welcomed him in homely fashion to his new country. Within three years he had raised sufficient money to be able to invite his wife to join him. If Mrs Applegarth had not been too ill to go, there would have been no place for Applegarth in the English working-class story. His undoubted enterprise and persistent energy would have carved out for him a more than comfortable niche in the open society of the United States. He might have become a very successful businessman. Even in England, after his trade-union career ended, he was sufficiently forceful to become a small employer, proprietor of a firm of engineering manufacturers. However far he diverged from the views of Samuel Smiles, he can in fact be regarded as a distinguished minor example of the triumph of self-help.

In *Who's Who* he characteristically gave his recreations as 'work, more work, and still more again'.

His American experiences taught him, first, that working-class problems were international in character and, second, that democracy could exist as a reality as well as a dream. They also taught him what slavery meant. He did not rest content with reading the novels of Harriet Beecher Stowe; he went down the Mississippi himself to see a slave market and actually collected one of the slave-dealers' receipts, which he later presented to the National Liberal Club in London. He became a strong supporter of Negro emancipation and met Frederick Douglass, the freed slave and orator of the liberationist cause.

Such experiences broadened Applegarth's horizons. They helped him to appreciate the issues of the American Civil War, which broke out a few years after his return to England. During that struggle most, though not all, English workers who had never been to America rallied to Lincoln and the support of the North. To them the contest needed no explanation: freedom was contending with slavery. 'They saw the one great issue,' wrote one of their admirers, Richard Hutton, later the editor of the *Spectator*, 'and left out of consideration all the comparatively unimportant issues, to which our professional classes attach such undue weight.' They were less insular in their enthusiasms than the middle classes or many sections of the aristocracy. 'They have a livelier sympathy with the popular feelings and the lives of other nations than the classes now most influential in politics,' continued Hutton. 'This may be based upon their mobility. If the working man does not prosper in England this year, he may prosper next year in the United States, or Canada, or Australia.... This is a condition of things which tends to liberate him from the more selfish prejudices of place and time.' Applegarth translated the language of one continent into the language of another and eventually became as vigorous an advocate of understanding between the workers of different countries in Europe as he had been of understanding between the workers of Europe and the United States.

His American journey did not separate him from his English fellow-workers but rather drew him closer to them, for there was a general feeling when he went there that the United States was a workingman's paradise, a natural escape route from the hardships of life in England. Applegarth saw working-class visits to America as a form of tramping, shifting temporarily from one job to another, while the Amalgamated Society of Carpenters and Joiners, of which he became secretary, praised emigration 'as a prudent means of getting on in the world' and America as the natural destination of the surplus of a growing English population. The escape route lost some of its significance as the century progressed, but even during the cotton famine of 1861 operatives paid visits to America, in an effort to better themselves, with an ease and carelessness that astonished commentators. One writer described the widespread habit of Scottish miners visiting the Pennsylvanian coal mines for a few months each summer. When social mobility was impeded in England, it appeared to be still possible across the Atlantic. For Applegarth belief in social mobility was not a matter of theory but a segment of his own experience.

Yet it was not America but England which turned Applegarth into a democract or a radical. Once in the late sixties his bitter Sheffield opponent, Roebuck, asked him if he had learned his radicalism in America, to which he replied with characteristic pungency: 'No, I learnt it from the *People's Paper* by Ernest Jones and *Papers for the People* by John Arthur Roebuck.' The Chartist tradition more than the American tradition lay behind his social philosophy, but it was a Chartism tempered to the new mood of the middle years of the century and to the new middle-class–working-class understanding which he himself did much to foster. Indeed, one of his oustanding gifts as a working-class leader was, as the Webbs have pointed out, 'instinctively to make use of those arguments which were best fitted to overcome the prejudices and disarm the criticism of middle-class opponents'.

He was always willing to take part in deputations which conferred with national statesmen like Palmerston and Gladstone and to address middle-class societies, such as the Social Science Association and even the Statistical Society. The first of these bodies quickened the conscience of social reformers;

the second presented the facts of the contemporary situation. For every such encounter Applegarth had ready advice. That a distinguished Liberal statesman should misrepresent union organization was too much, he told Gladstone to his face in 1864; 'for gentlemen to read essays', he told the statisticians, 'and for workmen to agitate' were not enough. Only by discussion between the two groups could 'much good' result.

Such a discussion – a discussion on more or less equal terms – demanded the creation and consolidation of independent working-class organizations. Applegarth was important not because he was the workingman follower of a middle-class movement but because he remained a real workingman, seeing the world through the eyes of a workingman:

> Toiling hands alone are builders
> Of a Nation's wealth and fame.

He did not turn the artisan or the labourer into a metaphysical abstraction or an ideal type, as some so-called workingmen's 'friends' from other ranks of society did – 'friends' described by one pamphleteer as 'Crushers, Spouters, and Codlins'. 'The fashion among a certain class of politicians,' Applegarth once said, 'is to treat the working man as a peg on which to hang any pet theory or crochet they may happen to have, or as a stepping-stone on which to walk in the direction of their own interests. Such persons dress up a dummy in their own fashion as a tailor dresses his block figure and call it "the working man". For this model man they are prepared to legislate, talk, write goody-goody style of books for his edification, tell him what he ought and ought not to do, in fact to do everything for him except one, to treat him as a rational thinking being.'

There is something characteristically English about Applegarth's picture of the 'rational thinking' workingman and his assessment of working-class objectives, yet for a time he was closely associated with the group of militant socialists who founded the First International in 1864. The original programme was one which a Gladstone or a Bright might have accepted with a good conscience – but it soon became extremist. Applegarth nonetheless attended many of its meetings and was chairman of its General Council in 1868 when it met at Brussels. In 1869 he was prominent at the conference at Basel which reiterated its belief in the nationalization of land. Even when the International was breaking up, Applegarth remained faithful to its programme long after most of the English leaders – 'out and out opportunists', Marx angrily called them – had withdrawn. During the Franco–German War of 1870–1, some of the Paris *communards* were actually piloted out of the city with the help of his passport. Applegarth stressed the interests of workers everywhere in proletarian peace, and it is not surprising that Longuet, Marx's grandson, was willing as late as 1913 to describe Applegarth as an 'old and respected warrior in the great international army'.

Applegarth's support of a programme of left-wing socialism must be examined in the light of his experience in America, the background of Chartist and Labour politics, the state of affairs in the building trades after the London lock-out and strikes of 1859-62, and, above all, his own warm and sympathetic temperament. Like most English labour leaders of his time, he was more interested in working-class causes than in theories of 'scientific politics'. Indeed, just because he was an indefatigable supporter of causes, he was able in one year – 1870 – to cooperate with Joseph Chamberlain in the National Education League, to win the support of Marx, and to achieve the tacit approval of Queen Victoria. The Queen recognized his right to be considered 'our Trusty and Well-beloved' by making him the first working-class member of a royal commission, that on contagious diseases. Contagious diseases became as important to Applegarth as the nationalization of the means of production; there was a fine catholicity about his political preoccupations.

Yet, while he might urge the necessity for international working-class solidarity and talk of the capitalist evils that oppressed the workers in all countries, he was anxious to distinguish even at Basel, in 1869, between the relatively fortunate lot of trade unionists in England and their tyrannical exploitation overseas. 'Fortunately we in England have no need to creep into holes and corners lest a policeman should see us, but can meet in open daylight and organize ourselves, and treat of any questions which affect us without fear.' He was proud of his country, and he was not ashamed of his English political tactics. Although another English delegate at the conference, Eccarius, warned those present that the 'political love-making' of 1867 between the middle and working classes could not go on in Britain forever, Applegarth knew that he himself had been responsible for some at least of the original advances. By his subsequent actions he proved that the courtship was by no means over.

In one last personal way Applegarth conformed to English type. He turned in later life from city to country, from the delights of the public meeting to the sports and pleasures of garden and estate. In 1890 he went to live in Epsom, a rural area and race-course centre outside London – he was then fifty-six years old – and taught himself to ride. Occasionally he followed the hounds, and it was he who protected the rights of the public on Epsom Common against the attempted encroachments of the oligarchic Grand Stand Association. In 1898 he became still more of a countryman. He moved to a small estate at Bexley in Kent, kept poultry – even introducing a new type of hen, the Favorelle – diverted a small stream through his garden, and built a handsome rustic bridge. Although he abandoned this estate and went to live in Brighton, the fact that he chose at all to 'return to the land' is of great significance. Just as middle-class manufacturers were able to buy farms on the strength of mill chimneys, so even trade-union leaders could acquire land and become smallholders, at any rate if they showed Applegarth's indomitable spirit of self-help.

But Bexley was one of the last chapters in Applegarth's life-story. Before Bexley there were Sheffield and Manchester and London – busy Sheffield, smoky Manchester, and gas-lit London; above all, that corner of mid-Victorian London managed by a little group of full-time trade-union secretaries, which the Webbs called the 'Junta'.

3

Applegarth became a 'Junta' leader in 1862, when he was appointed general secretary of the recently founded Amalgamated Society of Carpenters and Joiners. Between 1858 and 1862 he had served his union apprenticeship in a small localized Sheffield craft union, which attracted his support soon after his return from the United States. In Sheffield Applegarth soon demonstrated his gifts of leadership. He persuaded the members of his little union, not without opposition, to change its place of meeting from an inn to a reading-room. He had little use for the traditional association between the bar and the union which existed in most of the highly localized carpenters' organizations. He believed that the foundations of a healthy unionism could be established only in a proper moral atmosphere. This was not because he was a convert to middle-class morality, but because he believed that there was a real working-class conflict between temperance and improvement. Like the Flint Glass Makers, he considered that it was more important to get intelligence than to get alcohol: 'it is sweeter and more lasting'. Already in America he had started a mutual improvement society; back in England, on 17 May 1858, he became a union member, and on 1 June he acquired his Sheffield free library ticket. Again he was setting a fashion which other trade unionists learned how to follow. As Patrick Kenney wrote two years later: 'On 20 September 1860 I left off buying beer and took to buying books to improve my mind.' Behind such decisions rang the voice of necessity, not the voice of convention. When Applegarth persuaded his local union to join the newly established Amalgamated Society of Carpenters and Joiners in 1860, he must have been proud that the society laid stress on the fact that its members aspired to 'become respectful and respected'. Not all the little unions in Sheffield reached such heights of ambition; that they did not was a threat to the future of unionism as a whole.

The setting-up of the Amalgamated Society of Carpenters and Joiners was an important event in the history of the trade-union movement. Already, nine years before, the Amalgamated Society of Engineers, though a natural product of the past, had set what was called a new model. Its aim was exclusive and protective, and though its organization was based on strong central control from London, it did not attempt to dictate local trade-union 'custom and practice'. It did not win over all types of skilled engineering craftsmen, but within its limits it brought together into a compact bargaining body the majority of skilled fitters and turners in London and Lancashire. The carpenters, more dispersed than the engineers, took longer to organize, both locally and nationally, and their deficiencies were plainly revealed during the London builders' strikes. The old General Union of Carpenters and Joiners, founded in 1827, was less effective in practice than the new amalgamated union, and it was with a mixture of awe and gratitude that the builders accepted three successive weekly donations of a thousand pounds from the engineers while their strike was in progress. The canny William Allan, general secretary of the engineers, helped the carpenters to adapt the rules of his society to their own trade. From the start the A.S.C.J. was modelled on the A.S.E.; Applegarth himself deliberately used the word 'model'.

By the end of 1860 the new union had twenty branches and 618 members, but there were only two branches outside London. It was not until 1862, when Applegarth himself left Sheffield to become secretary of the union in place of a man who had just embezzled some of the funds, that it really became a national organization, and one which prospered. Although it never won the allegiance of all the local carpenters' unions and remained smaller in total membership than the older General Union of Carpenters and Joiners, it increased the scale of its operations until in 1870 it had over ten thousand members and over two hundred and thirty branches. The effects of Applegarth's leadership are clear from a perusal of the society's *Reports*. By 1865 Applegarth could boast that 'in the most remote parts of the country, as well as in the principal seats of industry, the name of our Society is fast becoming a household word'.

Building an effective craft union, financially sound and economically powerful, was Applegarth's main objective. It was a labour of love and faith rather than a lucrative employment. Applegarth was never paid more than £2 10s. a week, and when he was first appointed he only received £1 10s. His private residence in Lambeth also had to serve as the meeting place for the executive council of the union. It was indicative of Applegarth's desire for self-help as well as for union advancement that out of his small initial salary he paid fees to a writing master in order to improve his penmanship. Throughout his career as secretary he never neglected his own improvement or his general duties as a politically conscious citizen, but he put the union first.

The union which he created bore no resemblance to the small secret societies which dominated the old skilled trades of Sheffield. Its primary object was to act for trade purposes; that is to say, to organize the labour market and to enable carpenters and joiners to engage in collective bargaining. Applegarth was very efficient in the conference room. As secretary of his little union in Sheffield he had once appeared before the formidable John Brown, the great Sheffield steel master, who had himself risen in the world from the son of a Sheffield slater to an adventurous captain of industry.

'You're from the trade union,' said Brown curtly.

'Yes,' admitted Applegarth.

'Well, I shall cut you short,' said Brown.

'Please don't,' replied Applegarth. 'I'm only five foot two, and that's short enough.'

Like Roebuck in physique if not in temperament, he was a small man with a big voice, and on this occasion he too was a David facing Goliath. But he was less petulant than Roebuck; he could honestly claim that he never 'had a wrong word with an employer in my life, either as a workman or as a representative of working men'. He could be as powerful in influencing workers as he was firm but disarming in dealing with employers, and he did much to persuade the workers that the most effective form of collective bargaining was not always the most noisy and seldom the most violent.

But the union he built up had important secondary purposes as well. It set out to raise funds for the mutual support of members in the case of sickness and accidents; for superannuation; for meeting the funeral expenses of members and their wives; for replacing tools lost by fire, water, or theft; and for assisting members out of work. Social security benefits, provided at a time when the state paid no attention to social needs, were so great a boon to the workers that even the opponents of the trade unions could not directly challenge such mutual aid. They rather insisted on drawing a difference between the friendly society activities of the unions and their regulative trade activities, claiming that the necessary funds for the two types of activity should be kept apart. Applegarth refused to separate them. When questioned on this point by the Royal Commission on Trade Unions in 1867, he resolutely refused to distinguish between different forms of union action. 'I am afraid there has been so much said about the social aspects of our societies,' he remarked, 'that is their benevolent purposes, that the main purposes for which they are established have been somewhat lost sight of, and therefore I take this opportunity of stating that pure and simple ours is a trade society, and as such I wish it to be regarded, although we have a number of excellent benefits in connexion with it.' Applegarth believed that members supported his society, 'and all such societies as ours, the better on account of the many benefits they gave the members'; but it was not true to say that some people joined for benevolent purposes and some for trade purposes. 'The fact is that they join it as a whole.'

The sound management of union funds both in the branches and in the central office in London was a responsible and essential task if the union were to become a permanent organization, yet it was not easy to pursue it. Applegarth insisted that the members should all be 'men of good moral character, steady habits, and good workers'. He was able to boast to the royal commission that the union 'as a rule consists of the superior class of workmen' who were capable of paying the relatively high subscription of a shilling a week; like the engineers and others, 'many of our members hold positions of responsibility as foremen and managers, which renders it necessary that they should be men of good character and steady habits, and however much we regret to leave a man behind who is not up to our mark, we do it '.

The local branches, which had to consist of at least seven workers with at least five years' experience in their trade, were free to conduct their own business along their own lines, and this allowed for substantial autonomy in tactics in relation to determining hours, wages, and strikes. At the same time Applegarth urged that the centralized funds of the union were to be used prudently and not to be dissipated through financial incompetence or neglect. Yet it would be a mistake to believe that Applegarth was interested merely in the accumulation of large central funds or that he was opposed to all forms of strike action. 'Never surrender the right to strike,' he told his union, 'but be careful how you use a doubled-edged weapon.' Immediately after his own local Sheffield union joined the A.S.C.J. in 1862, there was a short successful strike which led directly to the employers' recognition of a code of working rules. Applegarth did not believe in indiscriminate or hasty strikes, but he admitted with no regrets to the commission of 1867 that the number of short strikes had increased, not diminished, in the previous four years. What he insisted upon was that the workers involved in a dispute should look to outside opinion as well as to their own judgement in determining the rightness of their course of action. Strikes should not be a secret weapon but a final sanction of union power. He agreed with another of his trade union colleagues, George Odger, the secretary of a small union but a key figure in London working-class politics, that 'strikes in the social world are like wars in the political world; both are crimes unless justified by absolute necessity'.

By advocating moderation, Applegarth won considerable respect from people who were not in any way connected with the trade-union movement. Above all, he persuaded them that a sharp distinction could be drawn between the new national amalgamated unions and the old secret union clubs, which had their roots in the distant past. It was an important distinction to clarify, for the critics of trade unionism often assessed the movement as a whole in terms of its worst manifestations rather than its best, while its enemies concentrated on obvious abuses and publicized them with considerable skill. Respectable though Applegarth and his close friends among the London trade-union leaders were, they did not find it easy to make their unions respectable. For every enlightened employer, like Mundella, who became member of Parliament for Sheffield in 1868, there were several who viewed trade unions as pernicious institutions, created and led not by good men but by 'designing and idle men for their own purposes'. Much as Applegarth, Allan, and Odger might wear gold watch chains in their waistcoats and look like chosen representatives of the 'bourgeoisie', they were often visited with the sins of the cloak-and-dagger unionists in the dark recesses of great industrial cities.

The distinction became of crucial importance in 1866 and 1867, when events in Applegarth's adopted home of Sheffield provoked anger and alarm among the middle classes and caught the attention of all sections of the press. Cloak-and-dagger unionism, often based upon crude intimidation of members to make them pay their dues, and violent threats to non-members to make them join the union, had already received some publicity in 1854, 1857, and 1859, when there were shootings and murders, and in 1861, when an attempt was made to blow up a small workshop. In October 1866 national attention was focused on the explosion of a can of gunpowder in a house belonging to a workman who had just seceded from the local Saw Grinders' Union.

The Sheffield police were unable to trace the culprit, and there was demand for a national investigation. At a time when many critics of the unions were claiming that trade unionism was little better than a criminal conspiracy, the government responded to the clamour – and to the genuine desire for a full inquiry both by employers and by enlightened unionists like Applegarth – by appointing a royal commission. It was this body's task to examine not only the background of the Sheffield outrages but the whole position of trade unions in society.

Before the commission met, the chief constable of Sheffield

had discovered that William Broadhead, a saw-grinder, landlord of a local inn, and treasurer of the Associated Trades of
Sheffield, to which Applegarth had once belonged, was
behind the group of strong-arm men who intimidated non-
unionists. He had been clever enough to avert any suspicion
by heading a subscription list for increasing the reward
promised to an informer, but, when his secret was revealed,
he and a group of other unionists confessed in July 1867
to a whole series of acts of violence. The cause of unionism was threatened by these disclosures and similar evidence
from Manchester, particularly when Broadhead made it clear
that he believed that trade unions, like guilds or local town
councils, were entitled to apply what sanctions they chose. The
London Trades Council and the executive of the Amalgamated
Society of Engineers, which sent a joint deputation to Sheffield
to investigate the case, attacked intimidation and 'the abominable practice of rattening' – the temporary removal of the
tools of a workman whose subscription was in arrears – 'which
is calculated to demoralize those who are concerned in it, and
to bring disgrace on all trade combinations'. They pointed out,
however, the unhealthy conditions in the grinding trade, the
narrowness of the horizons of the local leaders, and the high
risks they took. There was an obvious contrast between these
conditions and this leadership and conditions and leadership
in the engineering and carpentry trades.

The opponents of the trade unions were in no mood, however, to accept qualifications, and in 1867 the trade unions
faced a real crisis – the turning-point in their national history.
The urgency of the crisis was enhanced when, in the same year
that Broadhead made his confession, a decision in the Court of
Queen's Bench (*Hornby* v. *Close*) declared that, though trade
unions were not forbidden by the law, they were nevertheless
associations 'in restraint of trade' and consequently could not
be allowed to sue for the recovery of funds appropriated by
dishonest officials. As one writer put it, trade unionism became,
'if not criminal, at any rate something like betting or gambling, public nuisances and criminal publications – things condemned and suppressed by the law'. This legal decision, along

with the public outcry against the outrages and the appointment of a commission which seemed to some workers like the
beginning of an inquisition, provided a decisive challenge to
the unions. It was vitally important that at that moment of
crisis the unions could rely upon leaders of the calibre of
Applegarth, who could point to years of responsible management of the amalgamated unions and who had already won the
good will of non-working-class sympathizers like Thomas
Hughes. It was to Hughes that Applegarth appealed immediately after the Sheffield outrages, asking him to write a letter to
the *Spectator* defending the trade organizations. Applegarth
did not fear an impartial investigation. 'By all means let there
be a Commission of Inquiry,' he wrote, 'and if a searching
investigation leads to the discovery of an ulcer in our system,
however small it may be, let the knife go to the very core.'
He believed that it would be shown conclusively that the
trade unions were not the cause of all the disputes and heart-
burnings which alarmed the middle classes. 'The causes of
these things are a thousandfold [and are all] parts of one
stupendous whole.'

4

Applegarth had pressed for the appointment of two experienced trade unionists to the commission, but Walpole, the Conservative Home Secretary, refused on the grounds that he was
anxious to avoid all partisan interests and that he wished the
commission to act as a quasi-judicial body. As constituted, it
comprised a band of distinguished individuals, not all of them
unfriendly to the unions. Two of the outstanding members
were Hughes and Roebuck. Their opinions were as sharply
opposed as any two men's opinions could be. Hughes was
strongly supported by Frederick Harrison, the young positivist
philosopher and barrister and a great friend of the unions,
while Roebuck was supported by Lord Elcho, who had been
bitterly opposed to him during the Crimean War. By this time
Roebuck had moved almost entirely from the Radical position
and Chartist sympathies of his youth and had become the most
virulent opponent of the trade unions.

Divergence of opinion showed itself among the members of the commission from the very first meeting and in all the questions put to the witnesses who had been summoned. On Applegarth's suggestion the witnesses were granted a bill of indemnity so that they could testify without fear, but the sort of questions asked them was mixed and sometimes hostile in character. As each member had the right of asking questions, the witnesses continually found themselves subjected after their first examinations to a cross-examination put by some commissioner anxious to criticize the value of their evidence and to demonstrate its weakness when it happened to contradict his own views. Roebuck, in particular, profited from this procedure to harrass union sympathizers whenever he could.

The most important union witness was Applegarth, who attended the meetings of the commission as a representative of the London trade union leadership, the Association of Organized Trades; he soon became the star of the proceedings. His integrity was unquestionable. Once, in his absence, when a witness had cast aspersions on his veracity, one of the commissioners promptly retorted, 'I do not suppose that any man who has sat at this table and heard Mr Applegarth can doubt, for one moment, a single word he has stated.'

Applegarth's evidence ranged widely over the experience of his own union and also over the whole field of trade union organization and problems. He told the commissioners about the history of his own union and the methods it employed, offering the written rules of his society for their perusal. He explained why the society opposed piecework, what was its attitude to foreign competition, how it enforced its rules, and what its members thought about strikes. His language was forceful and persuasive.

Piecework was opposed because it led to the introduction of bad material and of overlong working hours; in consequence homes and leisure were neglected. 'We believe that it deters men from pursuing education and other matters which they really should attend to.'

Roebuck pressed him on this point and asked him whether he had ever directed his mind to the piecework of a sculptor like Praxiteles creating a statue of Venus. 'You, as I understand, would interfere and say "No, you must work on the same terms as Thomas Smith, and not work by the piece."'

Applegarth replied with considerable shrewdness, 'I do not admit that that is a fair application of principle. We are not all Arkwrights, Brunels, or Stephensons. Men of such extraordinary talent soon become other than working men. We have to make rules and regulations which will apply to workmen generally.' Even if Applegarth had never heard of Praxiteles previously, he did not forget him. In the report of the Amalgamated Society of Carpenters in 1868 he said that the union was 'tired of that system of individualism which gives Praxiteles his due and Arkwright, Brunel, and Stephenson "full scope for the exercise of their extraordinary skill," but leaves the thousands less skilful to scramble through a selfish world as best they can'. The union acted as a harmonizing and uplifting influence, raising 'the less fortunate to their proper position'.

On the subject of foreign competition Applegarth refused to take up that protectionist position which was so bitterly assailed by orthodox economists. He showed similar moderation in countering charges of 'union tyranny'. Admitting frankly that some of the smaller unions engaged in rattening, he went on to add that, while he detested the practice, 'he could yet understand it'. Roebuck asked him why a non-unionist was not entitled to make his own private bargain with an employer and why the employer could not make his own private bargain with the men. Applegarth replied that the union helped both the employers and the men.

'How should you like me to interfere with you as you interfere with those men?'

'If you were a member of my society, and you, in conjunction with the majority, decided that I must conform to certain regulations, I should be bound to do so; but if we are all to be left to do as we like, the sooner we dissolve our society the better.'

'Is not that bringing the opinion of the majority in all cases to govern mankind?'

'Undoubtedly, and I see no reason against it.'

'Then you think that the minority should have no voice?'

'Undoubtedly, let them have a voice, and if they have right on their side, let them agitate till they convince the majority they are right.'

'But who is to decide whether they have right on their side?'

'The same remark may be applied to the question of the suffrage, about which I suppose we shall have to go on agitating until we get what we wish.'

Once again Applegarth had worked his position round to the point where it was difficult for Roebuck, the former Benthamite upholder of the greatest happiness of the greatest number and the supporter of an extension of the suffrage, to make any effective reply.

The whole case against 'union tyranny' was finally exploded after Frederick Harrison, the positivist friend of the unions, asked two leading questions to which Applegarth made simple one-word replies.

'The restriction upon your freedom of labour which your society imposes amounts to this, that the members of the society will voluntarily consent to work under certain conditions so long as they receive certain benefits?'

'Certainly.'

'And if they choose to work under different conditions they must forego those benefits and leave the society?'

'Yes.'

Finally, on the question of strikes, Applegarth did not attempt to minimize their beneficial value on certain occasions or to deny that the number of small strikes had actually increased during the previous four years. But he did claim that some of the strikes were caused by the employers rather than by the men and that it was true in general that 'employers, by their overbearing and tyrannical conduct, compel workmen to combine for their mutual protection'. He held up the ideal of cooperation between masters and men and supported the beginnings of a system of voluntary understanding, which eventually was to become the guiding principle of British industrial relations. 'We are doing all we can to extend it; we believe that nothing can be more advantageous than for the masters and men to meet and agree upon certain conditions, and we think that it should be a matter left to themselves.'

Summing up, Applegarth claimed that the excellence of his union consisted in the fact that it was a general organization extending throughout the kingdom and that it was an absolute impossibility for any one branch to become bankrupt. The fortunate assisted the less fortunate at the end of every year, and in mutual help the carpenters and joiners were bound to one another. Only by such working-class solidarity was it possible to guarantee real national progress.

It is sometimes claimed that the trade-union leaders of the middle of the century were uninterested in social as distinct from political and civil rights, but Applegarth looked beyond the machinery of collective bargaining and the apparatus of mutual insurance to certain basic social rights which it was the task of working-class organizations to vindicate. 'I would have a man do a fair day's work for a fair day's wage. .... I believe that every man who is willing to toil for his bread is entitled to sufficient to feed, clothe, and educate his family, and to lay by something to keep him in his old age, so that he shall not need to work after sixty or fifty-five years of age.' The same basic philosophy had been expressed in the first report of the A.S.C.J. in 1861:

Where a man, who is willing to work for the bread of life, is seen wending his way through the streets and returning unsuccessful, you see a walking evidence of the necessity for such societies as this to provide him that bread of which political economy deprives him, until the future develops a state of society in which it will not be possible for such an anomaly to exist.

Applegarth lived long enough – until 1925 – to see the beginnings of an English welfare state dedicated to the achievement of these objectives; but in 1867 the state was still a 'night watchman state' concerned essentially with the protection of property. The main preoccupation of the unions themselves was with the protection of their own property and the recognition of their rights to dispose of it as they wished. The majority of the commission, while prepared to hear Applegarth with respect, were strongly swayed by the counter-evidence of the Central Association of Master Builders. They accepted the existence of trade unions as a *fait accompli*, but they wished registration to be limited to those unions which had no rules to control the number of apprentices, to prevent the use of machinery, to stop men doing piecework, and to maintain a closed shop; they also wished to forbid unions to assist other unions in trade disputes. Orthodox political economy took little account of union solidarity, 'the associative spirit, strongly implanted in man', or the theory of social rights implicit in Applegarth's organization. The majority were expressing the view, natural to employers in an age of an expanding competitive economy, that the unions were restrictive bodies impeding the efforts of the most hard-working employers, keeping up the costs of production, threatening property through violent strikes and picketing, and diminishing the power of Britain to produce staple commodities better and more cheaply than its commercial rivals. The year 1867 was the occasion not only of the Sheffield outrages and the second Reform Bill but also of the Paris Universal Exhibition, which, it was alleged, exhibited the increasing advantages that Continental competitors were deriving from the fetters imposed on British industry by the unions.

A minority of three of the commissioners – Hughes, Harrison, and Lichfield – supported the arguments put forward by Applegarth and published a report of their own, which became the basis of subsequent legislation. They pointed to Applegarth's statistics and evidence to prove their point that the expansion of the new amalgamated trade unions was not 'the spasmodic growth of a temporary movement, but the progress of a stable institution. The degree of completeness to which the organization has attained, and the scale on which the operations are conducted, quite equal that of a first-rate mercantile enterprise.' No contemporary note of praise could have been more firmly sounded. There was no connexion between trade unions like those of Applegarth and Allan and the Sheffield societies.

Outrages of the Sheffield kind, however lamentable, are proof of an unhappily low state of intelligence, and of an unsettled industrial condition; but the riots of the rough population have but very little bearing on the claims of such societies as the *Amalgamated Engineers* or the *Amalgamated Carpenters* to a legal position and to the protection of their property. ... We cannot suppose that the officials of the Engineers, or the Carpenters, or the Printers ... look on the acts of illegality and violence with any less feeling of abhorrence than we do ourselves.

The moral was obvious.

In proportion as the unions acquire extent in area, regularity, and publicity in their transactions, and become properly constituted associations, they gain in character and usefulness. In proportion as they are irregular in organization, and approach the form of the old secret trades union, without 'benefits', they preserve some criminal features of the surreptitious unions under the old law.

The minority report served as the basis for the trade-union legislation of the Liberal government in 1871. Applegarth, along with his colleagues, refused to accept any of the recommendations of the majority report and remarked that, if this was the price trade unions had to pay for protection, 'they will prefer to go unprotected to Doomsday. ... Not even for legal recognition will they attempt to smother one of the highest motives by which men can be actuated – that of desiring to assist others less fortunate than themselves.' The 1871 act conceded the demands of the unionists for adequate legal status: no union could be regarded as criminal because it was 'in restraint of trade', any unions whose rules were not criminal could be registered; registration gave protection to funds. All these privileges were granted without the unions having to become incorporated. But there was one new and very serious complication. The Liberal government passed a criminal law amendment act at the same time which declared that picketing and all allied activity was illegal.

This second act, which was originally phrased as part of the first, meant that the trade unions lost their most effective practical sanction at the same time as they secured their legal recognition. From previous experience of interpretations of 'molestation', 'intimidation', and 'obstruction' in the courts, the unions knew how much more difficult it would be to organize effective strike machinery in the future under the new legislation. As one trade-union manifesto put it, 'Instead of the spirit of fairness, the same class bitterness and prejudices as of old characterize the passing of this measure, which for unjustness and one-sidedness exceeds the old law which it supersedes.'

Trade unionists of all types rallied against the new bill. The London leadership of the large Amalgamated Trade Unions for the first time associated with the provincial union leadership of the miners, metalworkers, and textile employees. George Howell, the bricklayer, became secretary of the Trades Union Congress, which had its roots not in London but in the provinces, and four years of lobbying began, which only ended with the passing of the Conspiracy and Protection of Property Act of 1875. By this measure peaceful picketing was legalized, and no act carried out in combination was to be a punishable offence in the future unless it would have been considered so when committed by an individual. It seemed that the burden of the criminal laws specially relating to labour had finally been lifted and that 'every legal grievance' of which they had complained had been removed.

The trade-union legislation of the 1870s brings to a close the mid-Victorian period in the history of labour. The acts could never have been passed if Applegarth and his friends had not exhibited remarkable qualities of organization and tactical skill. If they had not been passed, there could have been no burst of new unionism among unskilled workers later on in the century and no subsequent alliance between trade unions and Labour party to insure the emergence of the working classes as an effective force. The political developments of the last quarter of the century, which have been considered crucial by most historians, had their roots in the middle period of the century. Yet between the passing of the legislation and the great bursts of new unionism from 1889 to 1892 there was deep depression. The unemployment of those years and the sectional battles between trade unionists cut a deep divide between mid and late Victorian England.

5

It is doubtful whether the legislation of 1871 and 1875 would have been carried so easily, or at all, had it not been for the extension of the suffrage to the urban artisan in 1867. Applegarth was just as active in the fight for the vote as he was in the parallel fight for union recognition. He had always refused to separate economics from politics, even though some of his trade unionist colleagues, like Allan, warned him that 'fools rush in where angels fear to tread'. When he became secretary of the A.S.C.J. in 1862, he made it clear from the start that he intended to instruct his society to use political action.

The action which he himself took was, as always, varied in character. He enjoyed equally leading delegations to see cabinet ministers and organizing mass rallies. He was as eager to attend a meeting of the International in Switzerland as to take part in a pioneer conference on trade-union rights called by the Glasgow Trades Council in 1864. Although he avoided too close a cooperation with those militant provincial trade-union leaders who were associated with industries less skilled and exclusive than his own, he welcomed the rise of agricultural labour and wished to see the farm worker take his place in the community as a full citizen. One of his great delights was meeting and corresponding with foreign workers or visitors; for instance, he was one of the 1864 committee which welcomed Garibaldi to London as a popular hero when the cheers were so lusty that it was difficult to believe that the English had ever acquired the reputation for being 'a cold, calculating, phlegmatic, and undemonstrative race'.

The most important of all the political associations of the 1860s with which the working classes could completely identify themselves grew out of Garibaldi's visit. A public meeting called by the Working Men's Garibaldi Committee to protest against the curtailment of his visit was broken up by the police, and the angry organizers decided, with the cooperation of a middle-class barrister, Edmund Beales, to form a political association to secure working-class rights. It was inaugurated as the Reform League in February 1865, with Beales as president and Howell as secretary. Applegarth became a foundation member; he had already written an address for an earlier reform organization founded in Manchester in 1862, and he warmly welcomed the new league, which, under the direction of its barrister-president and bricklayer-secretary, harnessed London labour to the cause of political reform. A new period of movement was beginning in English politics. The league issued its first address in May; Palmerston died in October, and before the next year was out the league had raised the London crowds and the trades to a greater pitch of enthusiasm for reform than there had been since the 1840s.

In the political agitation which was stirring again, Applegarth realized the importance of close cooperation with the middle classes. His own purpose was to build up the influence of the skilled artisans in 'the interests of the toiling masses of our fellow countrymen', but he saw that this purpose could become effective only if the support of middle-class reformers like Bright was secured. There were difficulties in creating a working alliance, for the middle classes of the North and Midlands had their own organization, the Reform Union, set up in Manchester in the same year. It inherited the methods and some of the personnel of the Anti-Corn Law League and could mobilize large funds in the cause of reform. But there was some difference of outlook as well as of membership in the two organizations. The Reform Union began by recommending household suffrage; the league pressed for manhood suffrage, although one trade unionist told a packed meeting that 'if they went to the House of Commons and asked for manhood suffrage they might as well stay at home and whistle jigs'. Even Bright, who was the most militant middle-class reformer, did not go far enough for some of the working-class radicals.

Three factors brought the two organizations close together: the defeat of the relatively moderate Reform Bill introduced by Russell and Gladstone in 1866; the split in the Liberal ranks between reformers and defenders of the old order; and the advent of a Conservative government in June 1866. Beales, faced with a parliamentary crisis, declared the willingness of the league to accept household suffrage as the basis of continued agitation, on the grounds that it would unite reformers and serve as 'a link between Manchester, Birmingham, and London'.

It was between the autumn of 1866 and the spring of 1867 that the Reform League reached the zenith of its power. Circumstances rather than leadership gave the reformers their opportunity. The winter was a hard one, and the harvest had been ruined by heavy rains. Bread prices rose in consequence, as did the price of milk and meat, which had been affected by a serious cattle plague in the home counties. Business conditions too were depressed. The failure of Overend and Gurney's Bank in the City and a rise in bank rate curbed credit expansion and ushered in a series of industrial and commercial bankruptcies. Finally, to add to the distress, cholera, the regular harbinger of political excitement, made another of its dramatic appearances. The political equilibrium of mid-Victorian England was being shattered in a moment of maximum social tension.

Unemployment, hunger, and disease were concentrated in London, where the Reform League was already most popular. In the East End of London, in particular, the distress was so acute that, as one writer put it, 'no one can sound the depths of its absolute, deplorable misery'.

What gave the league its greatest opportunity in such a situation was neither the misery nor the panic but the resentment caused by some of the speeches in Parliament during the debates on Gladstone and Russell's Reform Bill. The brilliant but acrid speeches of Robert Lowe, which battered the working classes with abuse, captivated the House but enraged the London population. The gap between Parliament and people grew wider than it had been since 1832. The Reform League began to play a similar role to that of the National Political Union thirty-five years before on the eve of the first Reform Bill, and Applegarth, as the man in touch with innumerable labour organizations, became a second Francis Place. This time, however, there were many Francis Places, for the labour movement was far stronger than it had been in the England of William IV, and the active and well-informed labour leader was ceasing to be an exception in politics.

In July 1866, before the economic and social situation suggested real danger, the league decided to hold a mass evening demonstration in Hyde Park, after the workers had left their places of employment. It had already held rallies in Trafalgar Square, but Walpole, the new Conservative Home Secretary, and Sir Richard Mayne, the commissioner of police, were afraid of rioting in the park and banned the meeting. On the night of 23 July the reform leaders were denied entry to the park, which they claimed as a legal right. The crowd of between one hundred and two hundred thousand people clearly sympathized with the reformers, and under their pressure the park railings began to give way. Applegarth, who had ridden in the same carriage as Beales and Howell, was the first man to be forced against the railings as the crowd pushed through. In the meantime, Beales had lost his gold watch and chain, which were stolen during the skirmishing.

The Hyde Park incident was hardly a riot, and the league could not be blamed for failing to control such a large number of people, but there was considerable fear among leaders of the government and the ruling classes of an outbreak of working-class violence. The trade-union leaders were attaching themselves more firmly each day to the crusade for reform; and the small group of revolutionaries associated with Marx were working behind the scenes, persuading themselves that they were playing a strategic part in a movement which had now reached 'immense and irresistible dimensions'. Marx was writing hopefully to Engels that 'the Englishman first needs a revolutionary education, and two weeks would be enough for this if Sir Richard Mayne had absolute control'. Even Goldwin Smith, the liberal professor, was expressing alarm lest 'the struggle may in the end cease to be one between parties in Parliament and become one between classes, the class represented by the House of Commons on the one side, and the class represented by the trade unions on the other.'

There were three important reasons why, despite the tension, the political struggle did not turn into an open class struggle – three reasons which are fundamental to an understanding of mid-Victorian England. The first was the leadership of Bright, who, though a middle-class manufacturer himself, believed that it was essential to secure the wholehearted support of the trade unions both in London and in the provinces. He saw that only a conjunction of the Chartist and Anti-Corn Law League traditions could overturn the half-reformed constitution. He had laboured for middle-class–working-class cooperation ever since the repeal of the Corn Laws in 1846 in the belief that only such cooperation could liberalize the organization and policy of government. The ghost of the Anti-Corn Law League lingered in the offices of the Reform Union in Manchester; while in London, to many of the workers, 'the blood of the Chartists of '48' was the seed of 1866. For a few months two traditions converged. Bright, as an outstanding orator and the undisputed radical leader in Parliament, had many working-class enemies, particularly in the North, but men like Applegarth were willing to serve him.

The second reason was the political strategy of the Tory, Disraeli, who was watching and waiting, not only in 1866, but throughout the whole of the previous twenty years. In his estimate of the situation in 1861 Goldwin Smith had written that 'the true statesman would rather drag the working men within the pale of the constitution by force than suffer them to organize themselves into a separate community outside it'. Disraeli was ready to drag, or rather to cajole, to tease, and to manoeuvre his party into accepting a complete change in the structure and balance of the constitution.

The third reason is the most important of the three. The English working class was not revolutionary, although for a moment it seemed as though it might become so; the trade unions were not the cells of socialist conspirators either in the provinces or in London. Nor were they shock troops. 'If the railings – and it was touch and go – had been used offensively and defensively against the police and about twenty of the latter had been knocked dead,' wrote Marx in a description of the Hyde Park riots, 'the military would have had to "intervene" instead of only parading. And then there would have been some fun.' That 'touch and go' echoes across English history. It was the hinge on which Marx's wishful thinking always turned. In England the wish was never capable of becoming a fact. The workers did not pick up the railings and use them offensively, or even defensively, against the police; they demanded their rights and secured them, but even when they were provoked they never flirted with the thought of 'a really bloody encounter with the ruling powers'.

To understand the English working classes in the middle years of the century, there is little need to go beyond Applegarth. He believed in the class from which he sprang and considered it as a class and not as a conglomeration of individuals; but he held that it could advance only by education and superior organization, not by picking up railings in Hyde Park or by accepting a 'scientific' theory of tactics and objectives. He would collaborate with Marx, or with the positivist intellectual, Professor Beesly, as he collaborated with Mundella, but he looked beyond them, prompted by both his experiences and his sympathy. The trade union which he helped to create was to be a stable organization, justified by its practical results, as much a creature of law as 'all corporations and every club among the upper classes in Pall Mall and St James's'. When he looked to the future, Applegarth did not see a utopia but a land of more equal opportunity, where unionists were full, responsible citizens, exercising an active influence in national affairs and building with care and vision a cooperative commonwealth.

CHAPTER EIGHT

John Bright and the Creed of Reform

There are in an old poem that I read with great pleasure many years ago – the *Faerie Queene* – two lines which I think may teach us something in our present position –

> 'No fort so fencible, no wall so strong
> But that continual battery may rive.'

I feel certain that the fort of selfishness and monopoly cannot be held for ever, and that the walls of privilege cannot through all time resist the multitude that are gathering to the assault. In all the nations of the world of this day, I believe the powers of good are gaining steadily on the powers of evil. I think it is eminently so in this country.

JOHN BRIGHT (1865)

I

John Bright was the most important figure in the history of mid-Victorian radicalism. His career spans the period from the free-trade agitation of the 1840s to the home-rule dispute of the 1880s. His life is in itself a chapter of English history. 'The history of the last forty years of this country,' he told his Birmingham constituents long before his political battles were over, 'is mainly a history of the conquests of freedom. It will be a grand volume that tells the story, and your name, and mine, if I mistake not, will be found on some of its pages.'

Yet Bright was never an important or effective cabinet minister. He prided himself that he was a plain citizen, 'dwelling among his own people'. All titles he disliked, even necessary ones. Happier in the public meeting than in the 'warm precincts of the Treasury', he preferred manipulating opinion to mastering administration. His justification was a simple one:

'Parliament had no more power than the smallest vestry until public opinion had become convinced.' Even in private conversation he was always conscious of his audience and the need to convince it. An American journalist, George W. Smalley, who first met him in 1866, has left an unforgettable account of the occasion:

It was a low room, rather crowded, with two jets of gas flickering in the face of the orator. His hair even then was grey, though abundant, the complexion florid, and the rather irregular but powerful features gave you at first sight an impression of singular force and firmness of character. So did the whole man. The broad shoulders, the bulk of the figure, the solid massiveness of his masterful individuality, the immovable grasp of his feet upon the firm earth, his uprightness of bearing, the body knit to the head as closely as capital to column – all together made the least careful observer feel that here was one in whose armour the flaws were few.

This was an American picture of Bright in the middle sixties, when he was clearly the man of the hour; in the fifties and early sixties he was by no means so congenial a figure to many English writers and politicians. There seemed to be too much firmness and bulk, too thick an armour; his radicalism seemed to admit of no doubts. His politics were concerned not with expediency but with moral principles, and, though the principles were always stated in majestic language, the language bore little relation to the detailed logic of particular situations. In a shrewd but hostile picture of Bright, which sharply contrasts with that painted by Smalley, Trollope wrote:

I think that when once he had learnt the art of arranging his words as he stood on his legs, and had so mastered his voice as to have obtained the ear of the House, the work of his life was not difficult. Having nothing to construct, he could always deal with generalities. Being free from responsibility, he was not called upon either to study details or to master even great facts. It was his business to inveigh against evils, and perhaps there is no easier business. ... It was his work to cut down forest trees, and he had nothing to do with the subsequent cultivation of the land.

Mid-Victorian intellectuals could forgive anything except unbounded self-confidence; they liked doubt, for doubt was the evidence of subtlety. They profoundly mistrusted Bright, who appeared never to have had a doubt in his life. At the same time mid-Victorian politicians liked elasticity, even if elasticity led to inconsistency. Palmerston was admired for his tricks, and Russell was forgiven for his scrapes; Bright did not worry whether he was admired or not, and he never needed to be forgiven for either inconsistency or mischief. He did not fit easily into the England of Bagehot and Trollope; it was only before their time and when their world was breaking up that he came into his own.

There was a further reason for mistrusting him. In his appeal to the electorate, and more dangerously to the non-electors, he seemed to play deliberately on class antagonisms. The reason Palmerston gave for not including Bright in his cabinet of 1859 was that he was a danger to social peace. 'It is not personalities that are complained of,' Palmerston said. 'A public man is right in attacking persons. But it is his attacks on *classes* that have given offence to powerful bodies, who can make their resentment felt.' Bright was never able to live down his bitter oratory of the 1840s, when he built up the political consciousness of the middle classes by attacking the aristocracy as a moribund social caste. In the 1850s and 1860s it seemed as though he were intent on building up the political consciousness of the working classes as well, on welding an alliance between manufacturers and artisans against landlords and statesmen. With no respect for the traditional deference structure of English society, he appeared to be anxious to substitute in its place a society not unlike that of America. Democratizing English parliamentary institutions was merely one aspect of a bigger assault on English society.

Most of the mid-Victorian attacks upon Bright were understandable but unfair. In the first place his self-confidence had its limits. As a sincere Quaker he never lost a genuine spiritual humility. When late in life he was offered a position of responsibility in his local meeting house, he replied that the labours of his career had taken him 'out of the way of service for our little Church and have to a large extent unfitted me for it. I feel that there is nothing but the humblest office – shall I say that of doorkeeper? – which I could properly undertake.' Even during the Crimean War, when he was absolutely certain of the righteousness of his cause and expressed himself with un- qualified self-assurance, he was afraid of the temptation to which his successes as an orator were exposing him. Unpopular in the country, he feared the implications of the respect people felt for his speeches in the House of Commons. Compliments offered him by senior politicians of different parties provided too much 'food for vanity and self love' and created and fostered 'a foolish pride'. Bright's inner uncertainties were concealed from his supporters as well as from his enemies, but, as occasional remarks in his *Diary* reveal, they were never completely absent when he worked out his own calcula- tions.

The second charge – that he fomented class antagonism – is easier to deal with. Far from accentuating class conflicts on the eve of the second Reform Bill, Bright did much to soften them. He set out to influence workingmen and, not without diffi- culty, won their confidence. In consequence, Marx referred to him scathingly as 'Father Bright' and held him largely res- ponsible for 'the period of corruption' in the middle years of the century during which the workingmen became 'hench- men of the capitalists'. If middle-class politicians like Bright had refused to interest themselves in the agitation by artisans for an extension of the suffrage, the year 1867, despite the working classes' lack of revolutionary fervour, might have been one of bloodshed rather than reform.

It is true that throughout the whole of his life Bright was a bitter critic of the existing establishment, both ecclesiastical and civil, and that he thundered against the privileges of par- sons and squires; but he never wished to see a complete trans- formation of English institutions, even a complete middle-class transformation. Bagehot was right when he detected in Bright an essential conservatism, and so was the *Spectator* when it talked about 'a sort of moderation in him', provided only that people were willing to meet him half-way. Bright himself went so far on one occasion as to claim that he was 'the perfect Con- servative. I should like to know what there would have been left of Conservatism for Conservatives to conserve at this hour but for me,' he declared. As early as 1859 he told Conservative members of Parliament that he professed 'to be in intention as Conservative as you. I believe infinitely more so, if you look twenty or thirty years into the future.' It was the Tory party and not the Radical party which was the 'turbulent party of this nation'. In later life he went further still. 'I am in favour,' he exclaimed, 'of the constitution, which has come down to us from our forefathers, with such amendments as circumstances and our own experiences seem to warrant.' The English constitution, which he did not hesitate to call 'ancient and noble', had not been based, nor should it be based in the future, on universal suffrage; it depended upon a balance of classes, not on the dominance of one over the rest. 'I do not pretend myself to be a democrat. I never accepted that title, and I believe those who knew me and spoke honestly of me never applied it to me. What I am in favour of is such freedom as will give security to people, but I am not in favour of that freedom that will destroy it.'

Such inherent conservatism was concealed from the eyes of most spectators between 1846 and 1867. During those years Bright seemed anxious to keep domestic politics in movement, while other men wished to keep them in repose. He refused to welcome any diversion of public interest to questions of national prestige or colonial expansion. The only good thing about the Crimean War, he believed, was that it had produced a demand for administrative reform – and Florence Nightingale. Although he interested himself in one great foreign cause, the American Civil War, he did so not because it was a foreign cause but because it was for him a battle in which all men were implicated. There was no political constitution in existence, he believed, 'in the preservation of which the human race is so deeply interested' as the American constitution. When news arrived of the surrender of General Lee and his army to General Grant, Bright saw the issue of the struggle in universal terms. 'Slavery has measured itself with Freedom, and Slavery has perished in the struggle. . . . This great triumph of the Republic is the event of our age, and future ages will confess it, for they will be better able than this to estimate the gain to freedom and humanity which will spring from it.'

Bright lacks the attractive simplicity of Lincoln chiefly because he was too enmeshed in the economic philosophy of the English manufacturing interest, but he shared the same belief in human rights and liberal government. Though he and Lincoln never met, they were friends, exchanging across the Atlantic the 'good wishes of all men who love Liberty'.

In English politics the importance of Bright was that he turned liberalism into a creed, that he made men seek reform because reform was 'right', and that he refused to separate the spheres of morality and politics. Moreover, he did all this at a time when the mood of the informed men of the age disposed them to prefer subtle calculations of political expediency to adherence to general principles of conduct. He was freely accused of making discontent, but he created no discontent which was not already there beneath the surface. It was his mission to guide the discontented towards a definite goal and to force the contented to realize that they also could not afford to ignore the creed of reform.

2

Bright accepted the articles of the creed in his youth. His family was a Quaker family which had moved from Wiltshire to Rochdale, a small Lancashire town on the edge of the Pennines, a few years before he was born. He always bore the double imprint of his religion and his birthplace. 'I could not be otherwise than Liberal,' he once said. 'I was then, as I am now, a member of the Society of Friends. ... Belief in the equality of all men in the sight of heaven, and in equal rights of all men before earthly governments, naturally leads to a strong sympathy with the great body of the people.' Bright sprang from Puritan and martyrs' stock; 'the persecutions they had endured and their principles of equality and justice' drove him to liberalism by necessity as well as by inclination. Unlike Gladstone, he had nothing to unlearn before he became a Liberal; he had merely to remember.

Yet traditionalist Quakers had chosen to be select rather than popular and were anxious to remain 'quiet in the land' rather than discontented. Bright, even in his youth, tried to teach them a civic gospel. He castigated those Quakers of whom he disapproved with as much vigour as he castigated the bishops, and he spoke of some Quaker institutions with little more respect than he spoke of the House of Lords; but he remained a Quaker until his death and was buried in 1889 in the graveyard of the Rochdale Meeting House, which he had attended as a child. In fifty years of endeavour he built a new political tabernacle, but he never felt any temptation to seek a new spiritual home.

The Quaker origins of his liberalism and his lifelong sympathy with nonconformity explain the religious core of his conception of government – liberal government grounded in responsibility, self-respect, and justice. He had only one criterion of statesmanship which he applied at all times: 'In working out our political problem, we should take for our foundation that which recommends itself to our conscience as just and moral.'

Particular problems all demanded a common approach. Of the repeal of the Corn Laws, he said in later life: 'You find it in Holy Writ that the Earth is the Lord's, and the fulness thereof. We have put Holy Writ into an Act of Parliament.' During the Crimean War he pleaded with hostile audiences: 'You profess to be a Christian nation. ... Within the limits of this island alone, on every Sabbath, twenty thousand – yes, far more than twenty thousand – temples are thrown open, in which devout men and women assemble that they may worship Him, who is the Prince of Peace. Is this a reality or is your Christianity a romance?' Dr Robert W. Dale, the great Congregationalist minister in Birmingham, tells a story of 'the extraordinary effect' of Bright's first speech in Birmingham after he became a member of Parliament for the city. The audience had come expecting some fierce onslaught on the privileged classes; they found themselves surprised and awed by Bright's tone of moral earnestness. 'We rebuked ourselves,' Dale declared 'with the words of the Prophet, "Surely the Lord is in this place and I knew it not".'

It was this moral fire which impressed Gladstone and drew

him close to a man whose religious views were quite different from his own. 'The supreme eulogy which is Bright's due,' he said, 'is that he elevated political life to a higher elevation, and to a loftier standard, and that he has thereby bequeathed to his country the character of a statesman, which can be made the subject not only of admiration and of gratitude, but of reverential contemplation.' The Queen admired Bright for the same reasons, but Palmerston was never impressed; when he sarcastically called Bright 'the Honourable and Reverend gentleman', he was deliberately attacking those qualities which Gladstone and the Queen came most to appreciate. To Palmerston, Bright was a humbug, and a dangerous humbug to have in the House of Commons.

If the pull of 'an omnipotent and eternal moral law', as he saw it, was the first great influence on Bright, the second was the tug of locality. In his youth he looked at the world from Rochdale, a textile town on the edge of the moors, representative, in his own words, of 'the millions of Lancashire, whose industry had not only created, but sustained the fabric of national power'. Until he was thirty, Bright took no part in political activities outside Rochdale, Burnley, Bury, and the neighbouring Lancashire towns, the cotton towns of a new age. Although one of the first effects of his association with the Anti-Corn Law League was increased travel, and election in 1842 for the city of Durham, he returned to Lancashire and became member for its great cotton capital, Manchester, in 1847. 'I am induced to consent to become a candidate for the suffrages of Manchester,' he told the electors, 'in the belief that to a large extent my sympathies accord with theirs, and because my sympathies are bound up in an especial manner with the advancement of that great and industrial population of which Manchester may be deemed the centre.' It was from Manchester that the gospel of free trade was proclaimed and 'the deliverance of the country' effected in 1846. With the election of Bright, wrote the *Manchester Times*, 'the city now stands forth to the world', crowning 'the new alliance of industrial independence with political power'.

With Rochdale and Manchester behind him, Bright

approached politics in a very different way from Trollope and Bagehot. There was less deference in Lancashire than in most parts of the country. Indeed, Bagehot, who married the daughter of a prominent member of the league, asserted that Lancashire was more egalitarian than any other part of England. 'Lancashire is sometimes called "America-and-water",' he wrote; 'we suspect it is America and very little water'. Bright did not worry about the ingredients; he was only anxious that Lancashire should become a larger ingredient in the English democratic mixture.

The harmony between Bright and his background was more than a harmony of thinking. During the days of his Rochdale apprenticeship he was shaping his character as well as his attitudes in the rugged mould of the industrial North. His education, begun in Quaker schools at Ackworth and York, was continued in the Rochdale Literary and Philosophic Society, the Rochdale Temperance Society, the Order of Rechabites, the Bible Society, and even the local cricket club. Agencies of this kind moulded many other political figures of the period; for Bright they took the place of a university. The industrial North in the bleak age of the nineteenth century was not merely a land of slag heaps and dark satanic mills; it was a land of chapels and clubs, of co-operative and friendly societies (the Co-operative Movement began in Rochdale with the pioneers of 1844), of small but energetic social and religious groups, of intense and variegated loyalties. Bright grew up in such a world. It was in odd breaks at his father's mill that he first studied statistics, political economy, and social theory; in the evenings he put his teaching into practice and learned how to address an audience without being tempted to run away.

Religion and locality together inspired Bright to take part in his first two exercises in political agitation: the battle against church rates in Rochdale and the national battle against the Corn Laws. The first venture, limited though it was in scope, tested all Bright's powers; it turned into a fierce struggle in which the contestants rose far above the normal stature of local leaders. When Bright became a leading propagandist for the league, he had already received a sound basic training.

The origins of the quarrel were not unusual in industrial communities. All parishioners were traditionally expected to pay church rates in order to maintain the fabric of their parish church, the local centre of the established Church of England, and to provide what was necessary for the decent celebration of its services. From the 1830s onward dissenters were increasingly loath to fulfil this obligation. They were building large numbers of new chapels of their own and were full of a natural zeal for their own mission. Why should they be compelled to pay twice, they asked, once as nonconformists for their own chapels and a second time as citizens, for churches of which they did not approve? The question became particularly bitter in Rochdale in 1834, when the vicar, who had been the chairman of the Lancashire County Magistrates at the time of the massacre of Peterloo, attempted to increase the rate. Bright described the subsequent squabble about 'this miserable question' as 'a stand-up fight'.

By 1840 Bright had become a leading participant in the debate, a redoubtable opponent for Dr John Molesworth, a new vicar who had come straight from the serene cloisters of Canterbury to the noisy alleys of a very raw Rochdale. Molesworth was shocked by what he saw: 'Plainly as Dissent has lately shown the cloven foot,' he wrote in his parish broadsheet *Common Sense*, 'yet its rampant malice and would-be tyranny as here exhibited would scarcely be credited in districts where its mob rule is more circumscribed.' Bright retaliated, when words of this kind were uttered, by drawing upon the services of Ebenezer Elliott, the Corn Law rhymer:

> When palaced paupers, sneering, beard the town,
> They preach the church tax in a text like this –
> No text more plain – 'To Caesar give his own!'
> Ah, serviles, knavishly the mark they miss.
> And give to Caesar *ours* – not *theirs*, nor *his*!

In 1840 and 1841, after he had stirred up local opinion to fever pitch, Bright won the battle of the Rochdale church rates. Although a bill abolishing church rates in all parts of the country was not passed until 1868, the most dramatic of all church-rate controversies had ended in a victory for nonconformity. Bright looked forward to a greater victory. 'The time is coming,' he told the men of Rochdale, 'when a State Church will be unknown in England, and it rests with you to accelerate or retard that happy consummation.'

From church rates Bright turned not to disestablishment as an immediate objective, but to free trade as the condition of all national progress. The Anti-Corn Law League mobilized the same two forces of dissent and local feeling in Lancashire as the opponents of church rates had done. It was founded in Manchester in 1839, after industrial England had been plunged into deep depression. Two years later Richard Cobden and Bright made a solemn vow never to rest until the Corn Laws were repealed. For five years they battered against 'monopoly', claiming that only total repeal would relieve the burdens of businessmen and the distress of the working classes. They gained their chief support in the North of England, where new industrial wealth was freely contributed to sustain the agitation. Economic arguments were given the necessary religious colouring to appeal to as wide a northern audience as possible. 'Blessed is he that giveth the corn and cursed is he that withholdeth it.' 'When Jacob saw that there was corn in Egypt he said unto his sons: Why do you look one upon the other? Behold, I have heard that there is corn in Egypt; get you down thither, and buy for us there, that we may live and not die.' There was only one proper conclusion to devise from such texts: 'As a nation of Bible Christians, we ought to realize that trade should be as free as the winds of heaven.'

The amalgam of biblical rhetoric and economic theory turned explosive when it was fused by social jealousy. The manufacturers of Lancashire were anxious to vindicate in face of the landlords – 'titled felons' or even 'landed vampires', they called them – their rightful claims to political and economic power. The year 1832 had given the middle classes the vote; only the repeal of the Corn Laws could confirm the reality of middle-class power. Protection seemed to the manufacturers merely a 'protection of native idleness at the expense of the impoverishment of native industry'. A landlord Parliament should be made to yield, but it would only do so if the demand for free trade was wielded as a bludgeon.

Bright was more eloquent than any other spokesman of the league in clarifying these political and social implications of the repealers' case. As he told a Manchester audience in 1849:

The Anti-Corn Law League will henceforth stand before the world as a sign of a new order of things. Until now, this country has been ruled by the class of great proprietors of the soil. Every one must have foreseen that, as trade and manufactures extended, the balance of power would, at some time or other, be thrown into another scale. Well, that time has come, and the rising of the League . . . was sufficient to have pointed out to any statesman that the power of the landed aristocracy had reached its height and that henceforth it would find a rival to which eventually it must become subjected. We have been living through a revolution without knowing it.

The revolution of the 1840s was the prelude to all Bright's work in the 1850s and 1860s. His share in the success of the league was smaller than that of Cobden; his share in following up the work of the league, after 1846, was far greater. Until the Corn Laws were repealed, it was Bright's task to excite the emotions after Cobden had convinced the understanding. 'The Corn Law has scourged you with thongs,' he shouted; 'it has lashed you with scorpions. It has made your trade fluctuating and hazardous. It has deprived you of political independence. It has surrounded you with discontented and impoverished labourers.' After the Corn Laws were repealed, it was his task to continue the battle against the landlord and the parson on a new front. 'The League is the foe of aristocratic injustice, and the State Church is the creature and tool of the aristocracy.' No single measure taken by Parliament could settle the whole social question. When respectable men in Rochdale and Manchester refused to pay a penny in church rates and contributed sometimes several thousand pounds to the Anti-Corn Law League, something, in Bright's opinion, was wrong with England. It was his mission, he believed, to put it right.

3

He had no doubts about the necessary items in a further political programme – an extension of free trade, a reduction of taxation, changes in the laws relating to the holding of land ('free trade in land', he called it), a cheaper foreign policy, and an extension of the suffrage to increase the power of the large populous districts at the expense of the countryside. There is an air of crude self-interest about these proposals, but Bright saw them all as moral issues and stated the case for them in terms of justice and freedom.

The programme soon began to be called the programme of the Manchester School. It had been a familiar maxim twenty years before that 'the school master now walks abroad in English politics'; by 1848 it was clear that the men of Manchester were dictating the main outlines of the syllabus. 'We are called the Manchester party,' said Bright, speaking at the Free Trade Hall in Manchester in 1851, 'and our policy is the Manchester policy, and this building, I suppose, is the school room of the Manchester School.'

The influence of the Manchester School depended upon the power of the cotton manufacturers. In the 1850s raw cotton was England's greatest import and manufactured cotton goods were England's greatest export. The trade was still expanding. There seemed to be an analogy between the character of the cotton products and the men who made them: 'They are not luxuries, such as can be laid aside without privation, but articles of prime necessity to men of all ranks.' The businessmen of Manchester were proud of their contribution to social and economic progress.

Our treasures of iron and coal, our crystal mountain streams, and convenient outlets to the ocean, could hardly have failed to render us distinguished in the annals of commerce, but if Providence had never planted the cotton shrub we should in all probability never have known that prodigious expansion of trade which has distinguished the last hundred years.

Cotton provided 'the magic impulse which has been felt

during that period in every department of national energy, which has affected more or less our literature, our laws, our social condition, our political institutions, making almost a new people.'

Bright began all his thinking with such a picture of the relation of cotton to progress in his mind. His father was a cotton-spinner, and his brothers remained active in the family business at the time when Bright was becoming a politician. Bright kept in close touch with them. The noise of a cotton-mill could always be heard in the classrooms of the Manchester School, and the smoke of mill chimneys was behind every agitation. The direct influence of the business background on the syllabus of the school can best be seen in the attitude the teachers adopted to factory legislation. Freedom of trade, they thought, was an essential element in the freedom of the individual, and the state had no more right to limit hours of work in the factories than it had to interfere by protective measures in the network of buying and selling. Bright consistently opposed factory legislation, first, on the grounds that a reduction of hours would mean a reduction of wages and, later, after the repeal of the Corn Laws, on the grounds that 'all legislative interference with the labour market, all attempts of Government to fix the wages of industry, all interference of a third party between employers and employed, are unjustifiable in principle and mischievous in their results'. He was a benevolent employer, but he believed that no employer should be compelled by the state to become benevolent. Quite frankly, he stated that he had never professed

to keep on my manufactory for the benefit of my workpeople, or for the sake of clothing my customers. My object is, by the expenditure of capital, and by giving labour to a business, to procure for myself and family a comfortable income, with a hope of realizing something like a competency at a late period of my life.

The state had no right to interfere with such private striving. When representatives of the landed interest, like Ashley, took up the cause of the factory operatives and demanded state interference to protect them, Bright accused them of bias and deliberate ignorance.

When they view from their distant eminence the state of the manufacturing districts [they] look through the right end of the telescope; what they see is thus brought near to them and is greatly magnified. But when they are asked to look at the rural districts, they reverse the telescope, and then everything is thrown to the greatest possible distance, and is diminished as much as possible.

Did not the manufacturers know best?

The operatives did not always think so, and they persisted in demanding factory legislation. They eventually secured it in 1847 and 1850, with the help of a group of sympathizers in Parliament, some of them manufacturers themselves. Yet even in the 1850s and 1860s, when men like Sir James Graham, who had opposed the ten-hours bills in the 1840s, were converted, Bright continued to oppose factory legislation. Nor did he ever admit the right of the state to interfere with the smoke of the large towns or even the public health conditions of local communities. 'Hands off!' remained his slogan. He made many enemies as a result of his obstinacy; although his own employees in Rochdale on more than one occasion expressed complete approval of his conduct as an employer, working-class opposition to his attitude on factory questions persisted. In 1911 the Rochdale Trades Council, for instance, refused to send representatives to the centenary celebrations of Bright's birth on the ground that 'John Bright was a capitalist, and an employer of labour, who opposed industrial legislation and was against shortening the hours of labour for children'.

But Bright's attitude to state interference was consistent even when his own personal interests were not directly involved and when his opinions might have been expected to predispose him to support economic legislation. He believed in temperance, for example, but he could never be induced to support a permissive drink bill allowing local authorities to stop the liquor trade. 'The trade of the licensed victualler is a trade that has been permitted and is now permitted,' he said, 'and I think Parliament and the Law are not justified in inflicting upon it unnecessary difficulties and unnecessary irritation.' Restrictions on drinking should not be introduced in an attempt to make men sober. '*Law* must be founded on broad and general principles, such as are consistent with political economy, but individuals may use their own discretion as to what they abstain from, and men may persuade each other to do many things which it would not be proper for the law to compel them to do.'

The opposition of Bright and most of the other leaders of the Manchester School to state interference drove a wedge between the manufacturing middle classes and the working classes. The wedge was always an obstacle to Bright in his efforts to secure political cooperation. Economic interests and political principles cut across each other and made it impossible for the Manchester School ever to attract broad ranks of operative opinion.

A more serious obstacle to the success of the school was a division within the middle classes themselves. Not all Manchester men, and certainly not all middle-class manufacturers in other parts of the country, were prepared to support the full programme Bright wished to realize after 1846. Cobden himself was suspicious of Bright's belief in the working classes as a political force; many other manufacturers were uninterested in 'Free Trade in land'; and, above all, large numbers of manufacturers supported instead of opposing Palmerston's foreign policy. They were not mere 'economic men' seeking a cheap foreign policy which would keep taxes low; they were Englishmen whose loyalty to their country and belief in its destiny made them sensitive to any challenge to its honour and prestige. They were not all like the famous Manchester man whose only remark on being shown the uniform worn by Nelson at Trafalgar was: 'Was the uniform manufactured in the West Riding of Yorkshire or in the West of England?'

There was another division in the middle classes, which Matthew Arnold stressed. One half was 'serious' and the other half was 'gay' and even 'rowdy'. The real strength of the English middle classes lay in the serious portion, but in times of stress the 'gay' half might well take the initiative. Bright came to realize this himself when the Crimean War broke out, and Palmerston was able to exploit middle-class support in the country against the motley band of his parliamentary enemies. The 'comic premier ... a gay old Tory of the older school, disguising himself as a Liberal and hoaxing the Reform Club', was not incapable of hoaxing the men of Manchester.

4

The campaign of the Anti-Corn Law League had concluded with a triumph. Cobden and Bright were heroes, at least for the middle classes of the North. The Crimean War, by contrast, turned them both into national outcasts. Exultation gave way to humiliation, leadership of opinion to dogged resistance to the voices of the crowds. It was a sign of Bright's greatness that he did not hesitate to express his unpopular opinions as vigorously as he had canvassed his popular programme in the previous decade. 'Even if I were alone,' he exclaimed in one of his famous war speeches, 'if mine were a solitary voice, raised amid the din of arms and the clamours of a venal press, I should have ... the priceless consolation that no word of mine has tended to promote the squandering of my country's treasure or the spilling of one single drop of my country's blood'.

In his short speech in the House of Commons after Bright's death, Gladstone dwelt for some time on Bright and Cobden's renunciation of popularity during the Crimean War. 'I felt proudly,' he said, 'and have never ceased to feel, what must be the moral elevation of men who, having been nurtured through their lives in an atmosphere of popular approval and enthusiasm, could at a moment's notice consent to part with the whole of that favour which they had heretofore enjoyed, and which their opponents might have dreamed was to them as the very breath of their nostrils.'

Bright's opposition to the Crimean War was not based upon complete pacifism. He did not accept the doctrine of non-resistance in all circumstances. 'I have not opposed any war on the ground that all war is unlawful and immoral,' he once wrote to a friend. He rather examined the specific situation in 1854 and reached the conclusion that this particular war was both un-necessary and criminal.

The background of his opposition to the Crimean War is complicated, not simple. As a Quaker, he had a natural dislike of bloodshed and violence, and many of his Quaker friends were prepared to oppose the war merely because it would involve the loss of life. The Quaker 'Meeting for Sufferings' decided, for instance, in January 1854, on the very eve of the war, to send Joseph Sturge, Robert Charleton, and Henry Pease, three of their most notable members, to Moscow to discuss with the tsar the possibility of maintaining peace. Bright approved of the mission, which, as the members themselves predicted, could do nothing to stop the drift to war. After war had broken out, the small group of Quakers continued to act as 'the soul of the peace movement', and Bright found consolation, when he was pilloried by the public, in the knowledge that he could retreat from the turmoil into the spiritual peace of a small community which shared his deepest convictions.

If Bright was not a complete pacifist, his approach to the Turkish question was very strongly influenced by moral considerations. In the summer of 1836 he had visited Constantinople, Jerusalem, and the Holy Places, and many other parts of the Turkish Empire. The remarks which he made in his *Diary* show that before the Anti-Corn Law League was set up, and before he had met Cobden, he had convinced himself that Turkey was a barrier to social progress in the Middle East. Cobden reached the same conclusions analytically at about the same time. In his pamphlets *England, Ireland and Russia* (1835) and *Russia* (1836) he derided balance-of-power arguments in foreign policy and strongly attacked attempts to bolster Turkey against the expansion of Russian commerce and possibly Russian troops. There would be little harm, he said, if the Russians occupied Constantinople. 'Religion, language, national character, and the plague, all oppose the claim of the Turk to preference over the Christian rival.' Commercial interests were also involved, for the Russians would be more likely than the Turks to turn Constantinople into a great trading city. Britain would then take its share in the newly provided opportunities. 'Cheapness, and not the cannon and the sword, is the weapon through which alone we possess and can hope to defend our commerce.'

The Anti-Corn Law League systematized this philosophy of

foreign relations. Peace and free trade were held to be inextricably interrelated. The greatest result of free trade, indeed, would be 'to draw men together, to thrust aside the antagonism of race, and creed, and language, and unite us in the bonds of eternal peace'. 'I believe,' said Cobden at Manchester in 1846, 'that the desire and the motive for large and mighty empires, for gigantic armies and great navies, for those materials that are used for the destruction of life, and the destruction of the rewards of labour, will die away.'

Between 1846 and 1851 Cobden and Bright were able to rally a considerable body of opinion to press for 'a peace policy'. International peace conferences were held in 1843, 1848, 1849, 1850, and 1851. A Peace Society organized propaganda, and in 1849 and 1850 Cobden brought forward resolutions in Parliament itself in favour of arbitration as a method of settling international disputes. At the 1849 Paris Conference Victor Hugo told the delegates in his opening address to look forward to the day when cannons would be relegated to their proper places in museums. A year later a more important figure than Victor Hugo spoke in much the same vein: Prince Albert talked of 'that great end to which all history points – the realization of the unity of mankind'. Not far from the Great Exhibition, which was dedicated to the gospel of peace, Joseph Sturge leased a house in which he gave a series of receptions to canvass peace, temperance, and antislavery. These high hopes of 1851 wilted in 1852 and 1853. Radicals were plainly dividing into two hostile camps, not the camps of the serious and the gay, but of the 'pacifists' and the crusaders. It is significant that, when Kossuth visited England, the Peace Society tried to warn people against treating him like a romantic hero: Palmerston knew better. He was more interested in the Radicals who supported Kossuth than in Kossuth himself.

Kossuth's visit aroused popular hostility towards the Russians and enthusiasm for the Turks. The Turks had sheltered Kossuth in 1849, when Austria and Russia were hunting him down; the moral was not left unexplained by his supporters. Turkey was a haven of refuge; Russia was a citadel of tyranny and its tsar a despot and a bully. The stereotypes were completely different from those of Bright, who believed with increasing conviction that 'the Turkish Empire is evidently approaching decay. Within itself it contains the seeds of decay, as all despotisms do.' Bright and Cobden both tried to present this point of view to the public in 1854 and 1855, but they met with little success. When war broke out, their arguments appeared almost treasonable to full-blooded supporters of the struggle. It was not only the enthusiastic followers of Urquhart who writhed when they heard the Turkish Empire described by Bright as 'one of the most immoral and filthy despotisms over one of the fairest portions of the earth', or the contest dismissed by Cobden, in one of his less pro-Russian moods, as 'a war in which we have a despot for an enemy, a despot for an ally, and a despot for a client'.

Even Manchester, which had supported Cobden and Bright so enthusiastically a few years before, and had returned Bright unopposed at the general election of 1847, swung round between 1852 and 1855 to wholehearted support of war against Russia. The swing was first discernible as early as 1850; when Bright was expressing scepticism about Palmerston's policy of 'meddling everywhere', his scepticism was 'much condemned in Manchester by men who ought to know better'. 'They seemed to wear their principles but loosely,' Bright complained, 'and expect me to do the same.' By 1853 there was as enthusiastic a war party in Manchester as in any other English city, although the resistances to it were greater than in Birmingham or Sheffield. After war had started, Bright's effigy was burned in Manchester, while the crowd chanted:

> To Brighten up the Quaker's fame,
> We'll put his body to the flame,
> And shout in mighty England's name,
> 'Send him to old Nicholas.'

Scurrilous pamphleteers joined in sneering at the 'buttonless, broad-brimmed, unbaptized, and heartless humbug'.

Although public opinion was strongly opposed to Bright and Cobden during the war, Bright actually increased his reputation in the House of Commons. 'My position in the House,' wrote Bright in his *Diary* in August 1854, 'not worse but better, notwithstanding my opposition to policy of Govt and House. ... Have met with many marks of respect and good feeling from men of all parties.' Bright's enhanced stature was the result partly of his oratory, partly of the general political situation. His oratory was universally admired even when his arguments were deemed unpalatable. During the league agitation he had not reached the heights of his eloquence; the war gave him his opportunity. The strength of the opposition which confronted him brought out his full powers. Nothing short of greatness could have saved him from ridicule or humiliation in 1854; but, when the waging of war proved more difficult than had been anticipated and involved a far greater loss of life than had ever been thought likely, members were ready to listen to him. They were emotionally prepared for speeches heavy with emotion and would rush into the House when it was announced that Bright was about to take part in a debate. There were tears in some members' eyes when he reached the great sentences of his most impressive peroration: 'The angel of death has been abroad throughout the land; you may almost hear the beating of his wings.'

Members of Parliament felt a sense of deep responsibility in 1855, almost a sense of guilt, and Bright was able to exploit this sense to the full. Even Lord Stratford de Redcliffe, the British ambassador in Constantinople, who has often been considered to be the villain who caused the Crimean War, declared on visiting Sebastopol soon after its fall that 'John Bright is fully borne out by all this. If this is a sample of the effects of war, who would not be willing to join his peace party? It is more like the crater of a volcano than a ruined city'.

The sense of guilt was accompanied by a general political confusion, which afforded a second opportunity for Bright. When Palmerston replaced Aberdeen in 1855, he did so not because he was a hero but because there was no alternative. Bright detested Palmerston and consequently found it possible during the war to reach temporary agreement with other members whose objections to Palmerston were the product of political calculation rather than sincere conviction. With

Disraeli, Bright was always on good terms throughout the war. They shared confidences and even talked, as they had once talked perhaps rather whimsically in 1852, about 'a reconstruction of parties' and a coalition of former protectionists and Manchester men. Disraeli appreciated Bright almost as much as he appreciated himself: 'I have always thought Gladstone, Bright, and myself the three most energetic men in the House,' he told the Saxon minister in July 1855. 'Bright is sometimes blunt, but his eloquence is most powerful. He has not the subtleness of Cobden, but he has far more energy, and his talents are more practically applied.' After Bright had made his 'Angel of Death' speech, Disraeli told him that he would have given all that he had to have made a speech of the same eloquent simplicity. But Bright was prepared to talk with many other disgruntled members as well as with Disraeli; more than once he had long discussions with Layard, the chief supporter of a more vigorous war than Palmerston was prepared to wage, and with Roebuck, who had views on the war quite different from those of the Manchester School. In a fluid parliamentary situation, when Palmerston's government was by no means secure, Bright figured in most political calculations. His abilities were generally advertised, and even Delane murmured that 'Cobden and Bright would be our ministers now but for their principle of "Peace at all price".'

Public opinion was less easy to convince than 'the men who knew' in Parliament. In the country it seemed that Bright was merely 'playing the game of the despot kings':

> This broad-brim'd hawker of holy things,
> Whose ear is stuft with cotton, and rings
> Even in dreams to the chink of pence. . . .

The Peace of Paris, which Cobden and Bright welcomed, was unpopular; and, after Palmerston had shown between 1856 and 1857 that he did not intend to become a pacifist himself now that hostilities were over, Bright and Cobden were once again ready scapegoats. Bright, physically exhausted by the political struggle, was taken ill and had to travel abroad; while Palmerston, profiting from increased popularity, was able to gain new supporters even in Manchester, where he received an enthusiastic welcome in 1857. In the elections of that year Bright was bottom of the poll, nearly three thousand votes below his leading antagonist. In 1852 he had secured a majority in every ward except one; in 1857 he was in a minority in every ward. The defeat was not made more palatable by the knowledge that one of the victors was 'a vain man who ate and dined his way to a knighthood through the Mayoralty of Manchester'. The Manchester School had been renounced by Manchester: 'We have brought what is true into our School,' Bright wrote, 'but the discipline was a little too much for the scholars.' The same moral was drawn by spectators: 'The town which has won with such effect so great a fame in the electoral field,' exclaimed the *Daily News*, 'now sinks back into insignificance, preferring local thrift to the world-wide honour of being represented by the most distinguished man in Parliament.'

Bright was not alone in eclipse; in other cities of the North of England, Manchester men were defeated also. The results were depressing to contemplate. Cobden, beaten at Huddersfield, complained that 'the most warlike returns' had come from the most popular constituencies, 'the least warlike from the most aristocratic counties'. The Crimean War seemed to have reversed the direction of English politics. 'Was there ever anything,' asked Macaulay, 'since the fall of the rebel angels, like the smash of the Anti-Corn Law League? How art thou fallen from Heaven, O Lucifer!'

Macaulay, despite his dislike of the league, wished that Bright and Cobden had been returned; so did most politicians in Parliament. Even *The Times* and the Conservative newspapers regretted the defeat. 'Rarely have politicians retired from the parliamentary stage,' commented the *Saturday Review*, 'attended by so general an expression of respect and esteem as that which Mr Cobden and Mr Bright have received from those who were most opposed to the ideas and principles by which their careers were guided.'

In the moment of despair Cobden lost heart and suggested that, while people were growing conservative and aristocratic with prosperity, honest men were not in demand in govern-

ment. 'Foolish notions' were abroad, which it would be difficult to check. Bright, recovering from his illness, was more
optimistic. 'Ten years hence,' he wrote to Cobden, 'those
who live so long may see a complete change in the public mind
on the questions on which the public mind has recently been so
active and so much mistaken.' He was determined to take an
active part in changing the public mind and to start a new
crusade for parliamentary reform, the biggest casualty of the
war. The battle for reform was not terminated; it was beginning. Manchester might be 'passionate and ungenerous', but
England could still be stirred.

5

It was in such a mood that Bright accepted the invitation of
Birmingham Radicals to become a candidate for the great
metropolis of the Midlands, 'the home of the most convinced,
intelligent, and rational Radicalism in all England'. In August
1857 he was returned unopposed for Birmingham, which he
continued to represent without interruption until his death
thirty-three years later. The switch was of national significance.
Manchester had dominated English reform politics in the 1840s;
Birmingham took its place in the later nineteenth century. Early
Victorian England was symbolized by the one; late Victorian
England, by the other. But Bright was never at home in Birmingham in the same sense that he had been at home in Manchester in 1847. He continued to represent Manchester ideas in
a Birmingham setting; it is significant that in his Birmingham
speeches he always referred to 'your city' and not to 'our
city'. But he found it – and left it – unlimited in its approval of
his influence and example.

In one respect his move to Birmingham assisted his efforts to
extend the suffrage. The social structure of mid-nineteenth-
century Birmingham was more congenial to a middle-class–
working-class Radical alliance than the social structure of
Manchester. Both cities were industrial as well as commercial
centres, but in Birmingham there was 'less aristocratic snobbery' and more class cooperation. While, in Cobden's phrase,

'the great capitalists of Manchester form an aristocracy, individual members of which wield an influence over sometimes two thousand persons', in Birmingham businessmen and workingmen were not separated by high walls of social privilege. Workshops were small, and manufacturers were often skilled artisans who had risen by their own efforts. The middle classes were ready to work heartily with the working classes and from 1830 onward had put their trust in 'a thorough union'. It was this thorough union which Bright himself was most anxious to build up not only in Birmingham but throughout the whole country. It was, in his view, a precondition of any further extension of the franchise.

The reform issue he had clearly stated in 1849, when, along with Cobden, he set up the Parliamentary and Financial Reform Association to advocate a double programme of tax reduction and franchise extension. At that time he worked with Hume and Roebuck in supporting the Little Charter – household suffrage, the ballot, triennial Parliaments, and a more equal distribution of seats. The association lost its grip on opinion – even Manchester opinion – during the Crimean War, and it was officially dissolved in 1855. Bright's election for Birmingham revived the agitation, and in October 1858, at the first meeting at which he addressed his Birmingham constituents, he pressed for a new movement to secure reform. 'If your great town,' he told his audience, 'with its great constituency, is only to send two men to Parliament, whilst an equal population and property in some other part of the kingdom is to send twenty men to Parliament, then I say that the franchise is of little avail.' Between the sessions of 1858 and 1859 Bright addressed great popular meetings on the same subject in Manchester, Edinburgh, Bradford, and other towns, as well as Birmingham, and claimed that they had 'exceeded in numbers and in influence almost every meeting that was held by the Anti-Corn Law League'.

Many Radicals, like Roebuck, who had opposed him during the Crimean War, took part in this campaign. It seemed as though the Radical splits were being patched up and the conflicts of 1854 and 1855 were being forgotten. But the campaign had a very limited success outside the large cities: 'The middle classes are against Brightism – witness their able organ, the *Economist*,' wrote Disraeli, 'and the educated classes are against it, as is proved by the articles in the *Saturday Review*. That the opinion of the country is the same is sufficiently proved by the tone of *The Times*.' *The Times* was very sure of the mood. 'The more Mr Bright talked of reform,' it commented, 'the less the country seemed to desire it. He frightened and disgusted the upper classes without conciliating the lower.' He might try to convince himself that there was a 'steady, ever-growing, irresistible tide of public opinion', but outside the large cities there was little to justify such a claim.

The reformers, unable to stir opinion, were having to employ the unconvincing arguments that the best time to carry through Radical changes in the suffrage was not when there was enthusiasm but when there was no public excitement at all. 'It appears that there are two periods,' wrote one shrewd Tory, 'two states of the public mind, equally propitious to changes in the representative system – one when people are quiet, the other when people are agitated.' It was like the old drinking song:

> Friends and neighbours, I've been thinking
> What's the fittest day for drinking;
>> Sunday, Monday,
>> Tuesday, Wednesday,
>> Thursday, Friday,
>> Saturday, Sunday,
> I find, after all my thinking,
> These are the fittest days for drinking.

The tranquillity of the public did not prevent statesmen of all parties from proposing reform bills as part of the game of parliamentary manoeuvring. Russell had already brought forward one abortive bill in 1852 and had withdrawn a second bill, with tears in his eyes, because of the outbreak of the Crimean War in 1854. In 1859 Derby and Disraeli produced a Tory reform bill which Bright described as 'a Spanish feast – a very little meat and a great deal of table cloth'; a year later Russell produced yet another bill which was withdrawn after the House had shown no particular interest in it. In 1861 both

Parliament and the public were so quiet that Russell, the chief Whig enthusiast for reform, announced that the ministry did not intend to waste time by introducing another reform bill. He was quickly dismissed by Bright as 'a bankrupt tradesman, who, having carried on his business for many years by fictitious credit, at length called his creditors together, glad of an opportunity of getting rid of his obligations.'

In an effort to interest the public in the creed of reform, Bright laid great emphasis during these years on the association of franchise reform with fiscal improvement. Only a popular House of Commons, he maintained, would check the extravagant expenditure of the governing classes and reduce indirect taxation. Such arguments were emotionally unexciting; they did not stir working-class opinion at all, any more than criticism of the Crimean War, on the grounds that it doubled the national debt and greatly increased the burden of taxation, had stirred the middle classes in the 1850s. The creed of reform possessed a singular unattractiveness when it was expressed in terms of pounds, shillings, and pence. If it were to capture opinion, it would have to become an issue of right and wrong rather than of hard cash. It would have to reach men's hearts as well as their pockets. A similar raising of the tone of argument had been necessary before the demand for the repeal of the Corn Laws could change from the cry of a pressure group into a wholehearted crusade.

When Bright took up the issue of reform again on a large scale in 1865, he was in a better position to enlist enthusiasm. Three important developments between 1861 and 1865 changed the whole picture – the American Civil War, the conversion of Gladstone to belief in parliamentary reform, and the death of Lord Palmerston.

The American Civil War was a war which Bright strongly supported; while it lasted, he was able to rally large numbers of working-class people instead of antagonizing and dividing them as he had done during the Crimean War. He depicted the issues of the war in the same simple terms as Palmerston had employed during the Crimean War, but this time the colours were those of class rather than nation. The war was a battle between aristocracy and democracy; the cause of the North was the cause of the worker and the manufacturer. As John Morley once said, partisanship on the American issue veiled a hidden English civil war, and the triumph of the North was 'the force that made English Liberalism powerful enough to enfranchise the workmen, depose official Christianity in Ireland, and deal a first blow at the landlords'.

From the start Bright realized the moral issues of the struggle. Cobden at first was more doubtful. He was disposed to sympathize with the seceders in the South on the grounds that they were free-traders throwing off the yoke of a protectionist government. Bright converted him, and, though he was not able to convert Gladstone, he counteracted the effects of Gladstone's declaration of faith in the emergence of a southern nation with his impressive alternative picture of

one vast confederation, stretching from the frozen north to the glowing south, and from the wild billows of the Atlantic westward to the calmer waters of the Pacific main ... one people, and one language, and one law, and one faith, and over all that wide continent the home of freedom and a refuge for the oppressed of every race and of every clime.

He persuaded workingmen of the glory of this vision and enlisted their energies to help make it a reality. He found some of his most lively supporters in his native Lancashire, even though the cotton areas were badly hit by the cutting-off of raw-material supplies from the South. A larger cause triumphed over the immediate claims of self-interest.

During the Crimean War, Bright had refused to mobilize the enthusiasm of the nation because he thought the cause was unjust, and less generously because he held that it was not his duty 'to make this country the knight-errant of the human race, and to take upon herself the protection of the thousand million human beings who have been permitted by the Creator of all things to people this planet'. On that occasion it was left to men like Roebuck to appeal to the sentiments of sympathy and chivalry. But by a quixotic twist of attitudes Roebuck was the great supporter of the South during the American Civil War, even going so far as to demand the recognition of the

South by the British government and to indulge in private diplomacy with Napoleon III in an effort to bring about an armistice on the other side of the Atlantic. Roebuck found so little support in the House of Commons in June 1863 in the course of the debate on his motion to secure recognition of the South that he did not press it, but, before he had time to withdraw, Bright had completely pulled his arguments to pieces. 'He shook Roebuck as a terrier shakes a rat,' said one who heard the debate. In fact, he finally shook him out of that reputation for radicalism which had hitherto always clung to him even in moments of temporary aberration.

When the Civil War ended, Bright had established his position as the leading popular politician in the country, and he had drawn the working classes and the trade unions into politics. The way was prepared for an agitation to extend English democratic rights – rights which Lincoln had himself propounded in a famous letter to the workingmen of Manchester.

The American Civil War persuaded Bright to change his arguments in demanding an extension of the suffrage. Hitherto he had complained of 'the secret and irresponsible doings of the Foreign Office' and the consequent burdens of taxation; now he spoke of moral challenge.

The class which has hitherto ruled in this country has failed miserably. It revels in power and wealth, whilst at its feet, a terrible peril for the future, lies the multitude that it has neglected. If a class has failed, let us try the nation! That is our faith, that is our purpose, that is our cry: Let us try the nation!

There was one further difference between his speeches on reform before and after 1865. In his early speeches he had emphasized the need for a redistribution of seats in favour of large towns and had attacked the 'dead body' of the county representation; in his speeches after 1865 he laid greatest stress on the extension of the suffrage to the working classes as the first and indispensable element of reform. More anxious to win the support of the working classes in the acquisition of additional power in the large cities, he was shifting the foundations of his agitation from interest to justice.

The change in approach was partly the result of changes in

the parliamentary situation, particularly the increasing interest of Gladstone in questions of franchise reform. Bright had learned to appreciate Gladstone during the Crimean War. At that time Gladstone was a Peelite, not a popular Liberal politician. As late as the spring of 1860 he was still a member of the Carlton Club. He was drawn more closely into popular politics by his sympathy not with the Americans but with the Italians, a people for whom Bright cared very little, and by the series of free-trade budgets which he introduced as Chancellor of the Exchequer between 1860 and 1865.

Gladstone was never a 'mystery man', like Disraeli, but in the early sixties his actions were often unfathomable to his fellow-parliamentarians. He was, in fact, reaching the years of decision which were to determine his place in history. 'I feel within me the rebellious unspoken word,' he wrote in his *Diary* at the end of 1860. 'I will not be old. The horizon enlarges, the sky shifts around me. It is an age of shocks; a discipline so strong, so manifold, so rapid, and so whirling that only when it is at an end, if then, can I comprehend it.'

The shocks began to echo outside the pages of his *Diary* in 1864. It was then that he made his famous remark in the Commons that 'every man who is not presumably incapacitated by some consideration of personal unfitness or political danger, is morally entitled to come within the pale of the constitution.' This was far from a revolutionary speech, and it simply expressed Gladstone's view that the question of reform could not be postponed any longer; but it had far-reaching results. Palmerston complained that it was 'more like the sort of speech with which Bright would have introduced the Reform Bill which he would like to propose, than the sort of speech which might have been expected from the treasury bench in the present state of things'. The complaint was misplaced, but Bright himself commented that it marked the beginning of a new era in the reform question.

A year after this famous speech Gladstone moved one step further along the road to reform; defeated by the Oxford University electors at the general election of 1865, he turned to the industrial North and became a member for South

Lancashire. For the first time in his life he was now the representative of a great popular constituency, and he felt free to act without restraint. 'Keep him in Oxford and he is partially muzzled,' Palmerston had said to Lord Shaftesbury, a few days before the election, 'but send him elsewhere and he will run wild.' If he did not run wild, he certainly began to express opinions which would have seemed shocking to himself a few years before. Although he was still only very indirectly associated with Bright, he was now subject to the same influences which had turned Bright into a reformer.

Gladstone's father had been a Liverpool merchant, and his own sense of a Lancashire background – 'Oxford on the surface, Liverpool below' – inspired him to a new feeling of identity with his county. The conduct of the general body of the operatives of Lancashire during the cotton famine forced him to feel that 'it was a shame and a scandal that bodies of men like these should be excluded from the parliamentary suffrage'. He looked to the working class with increasing confidence, 'strong conviction, and an overpowering sense of the public interest'.

But he could become an active reformer only when Palmerston had disappeared from the political scene. 'The life of Lord Palmerston,' it was generally admitted, 'was a security against the introduction of a measure of reform.' For twenty years he had kept the waters of politics still. 'When the old pilot dropped off,' wrote one nineteenth-century writer, 'the ship of State, though steered with energy and skill, left the protection of the harbour and encountered rough weather in the open sea.' 'The truce of parties is over,' wrote Disraeli on Palmerston's death in 1865. 'I foresee tempestuous times, and great vicissitudes in public life.'

The immediate effect of Palmerston's death was to disorganize and demoralize the House of Commons. The Parliament of 1865 had 'no faith in any principle, no enthusiasm for any cause, and no fidelity to any leader'. Both Lord John Russell, the new Prime Minister, and Gladstone, the leader of the government in the House of Commons, were anxious to dispel the confusion by introducing a new reform bill. Naturally their attention turned to Bright, the one unquestioned reformer of the previous twenty years. For the first time the possibility of including him in the cabinet was seriously considered. 'If we can get him to renounce his allegiance to President Johnson,' wrote Russell to Gladstone, 'and to be a loyal subject to Queen Victoria, there are few better speakers in the House of Commons, or anywhere else – but he must grow tamer than he is before he ceases to be the wolf of politicians.' They did not include him, but they knew that they could rely upon him to support them in any far-reaching reform bill they might propose. And, even though they might fail in their own attempts, they knew that Bright would persist in his determination to alter the whole balance of English politics. He had no fears, as many of the Whigs had, of making a leap in the dark. To him a comprehensive reform bill was a leap into the light: 'The case for a parliamentary reform is more glaring and undeniable if possible than our free trade cause was.'

6

In the crucial battles for franchise reform in 1866 and 1867 Bright could rely upon the cluster of new urban Radical organizations which had grown up in the 1860s. There was always an alternative England to Trollope's 'Barsetshire'. The 'populous districts', as the large cities were called, were never completely quiet in the mid-Victorian period even when they appeared to be quiescent. When in 1864 Palmerston visited Bradford, for example, he was given a very different reception from that which he received in his own small Devonshire constituency of Tiverton. Working-class people greeted him in silence, and the middle-class leaders told him bluntly that 'the people of Bradford have extreme opinions'. 'We hope that when you return to London,' one of them went on, 'you will go to your right hon. colleague, Mr Gladstone, and tell him that he did not make so great a mistake as you thought when he made his Reform speech.'

After Palmerston's death, urban radicalism became noisier in places more inhibited than Bradford. Some members of Parliament stood as 'non-electors' candidates,' and at many of the city meetings the majority of those present were non-electors. Manhood suffrage societies and political unions sprang up in towns as far apart as Norwich, Leeds, and Bristol. Large bodies like the Reform Union and the Reform League drew on the support of such local organizations.

After Gladstone's speech introducing his reform bill in March 1866, *The Times* wrote, in the same strain as it had written in 1860: 'There is no applause, not even an echo. We have listened in vain for the faintest note of approval, or the contrary, or bare recognition from the provinces.' This time the comment was wrong. Within a fortnight resolutions of support for Gladstone had been carried at mass demonstrations in Manchester, Birmingham, Edinburgh, Leeds, Liverpool, and Rochdale. At the very moment when Conservatives were claiming that 'England is now satisfied with her institutions', the supporters of change were preparing for a final struggle.

It soon began to be clear that the opponents of reform in the House of Commons included not only members of the Conservative party but also a sizeable group of Liberals whom Bright christened the 'Adullamites'. At first he claimed they merely consisted of a party of two – Horsman and Lowe. 'This party of two reminds me of a Scotch terrier, which was so covered with hair that you could not tell which was the head and which was the tail of it.' But eventually he had to concede that it consisted of at least 'forty thieves'. Ironically the existence of the Adullamites assisted rather than handicapped the reformers; Lowe's rhetoric stirred the working classes not to defend but to attack: 'It is Mr Lowe's speeches,' said Forster, 'that have aroused the working classes from their apathy, and enlisted them one and all in the cause of reform.' After Lowe had talked of the 'venality and corruption' of the lower orders, Bright made the most of the vituperation. 'I would recommend,' he said, 'that these passages from that celebrated and unhappy speech should be printed on cards, and should be hung up in every room in every factory, workshop, and clubhouse, and in every place where working men are accustomed to assemble.' Bright had little difficulty in turning Lowe into the most unpopular man in the country. Victory, he argued, was just round the corner. 'The men who, in every speech they utter, insult the working men, describing them as a multitude given up to ignorance and vice, will be the first to yield when the popular will is loudly and resolutely expressed.'

The more powerful were the arguments advanced by the opponents of reform in the House of Commons, the stronger were the speeches Bright made to attack the unreformed House of Commons at mass meetings in the country.

Parliament is never hearty for reform, or for any good measures. It hated the Reform Bill of 1831 and 1832. It does not like the Franchise Bill now upon its table. It is to a large extent the off-spring of landed power in the counties, and of tumult and corruption in the boroughs; and it would be strange if such a Parliament were in favour of freedom and of an honest representation of the people. But notwithstanding such a Parliament, this bill will pass if Birmingham and the other towns do their duty.

The bill did not pass, though Birmingham and the towns did their duty. Because it did not pass, popular interest in reform grew. When Gladstone's government was defeated in June 1866, and Derby and Disraeli returned to power, Bright addressed meetings of almost every section of the reform movement. The Conservatives and Adullamites were branded as enemies of the people. 'The accession to office of Lord Derby,' he said, 'is a declaration of war against the working classes. The object of the reformers was not to overturn the British constitution but to 'restore it in all its fullness, with all its freedom, to the British people'.

The object of the reformers was in effect secured in the summer of 1866. After the Hyde Park 'riots', the *English Leader* remarked that the reform question had been reduced 'to one simply of date and extent'. After Bright had addressed a crowd of over two hundred thousand people in Birmingham in August, *The Economist* commented that the Conservatives could not shelve reform now, even for one session.

The burst of popular agitation was the prelude to the debate on reform in the House of Commons. But, noisy though opinion was, it could not hinder the debate from continuing or silence the critics of the measure. The Reform Bill of 1867, as it finally emerged, was as much a product of Tory flexibility as of Radical principles. And Robert Lowe, afraid of Tory democracy as much as of militant radicalism, opposed it to the last.

Bright claimed much of the credit, particularly in the eyes of the crowds. The *Manchester Examiner* was expressing a commonly held view when it stated that the bill had passed because the people had been called in to redress the balance in the Commons. 'The nation decreed its own political organization. Mr Gladstone and Mr Bright were organs of its will.'

That Gladstone profited in public esteem, and not Disraeli, was unfair to Disraeli – but no one could deny the influence of Bright. With pardonable exultation Bright himself took credit for the final result. 'It is discovered in the year 1867,' he said, 'that my principles all along have been entirely constitutional and my course perfectly patriotic. The invective and vituperation that have been poured upon me have now been proved to be entirely a mistake.'

CHAPTER NINE

Robert Lowe and the Fear
of Democracy

Sir, it appears to me we have more and more reason every day we live to regret the loss of Lord Palmerston. The remaining members of his government would seem, by way of a mortuary contribution, to have buried in his grave all their prudence, statesmanship, and moderation.

ROBERT LOWE (1866)

I

John Bright guided the forces of change in English politics, and the Reform Bill of 1867 was his greatest triumph. Robert Lowe gave strength to the forces of resistance, and to him the Reform Bill was a national disaster.

Lowe's resistance did not spring from naked self-interest or blind prejudice. Although he was member of Parliament for a pocket borough, Calne, not even his worst enemies claimed that his opposition to reform was based merely on a desire to protect that which was his own or that which was his patron's. There was less self-interest in Lowe's approach to politics than there was in that of Bright. He attacked reform not as a Whig apologist defending an order, but as an intellectual pleading for government by the educated against government by the masses. The only aristocracy he recognized was the aristocracy of intellect; mere lineage was unimportant. 'All knowledge,' he once said, 'except heraldry, has some use.' In 1866 and 1867 it was reason, not passion or personal property, which persuaded him that 'the greatest happiness of the greatest number' could not be secured by an extension of the suffrage to the working classes.

Lowe established an ascendancy in the House of Commons during the debates of those years because he asked one bold question which was in the back of many of the members' minds: 'Is England to continue a monarchy in which the aristocratic and democratic elements of the nation have ever harmoniously blended? Or is it, in spite of all experience, to adopt a lower form of civilization?' Interest in this question was so great that Lowe, by intellectual brilliance alone, was able to secure command of the House. His chief opponent, Gladstone, stated many years later that in the whole of his experience no one had ever surpassed Lowe's achievement, and, in recommending him for a viscountcy in 1880, he pressed his claims 'as a tribute to his former elevation, which, though short-lived, was due to genuine power of mind. ... It seemed to me that a man who had once soared to those heights trodden by so few, ought not to be lost in the common ruck of official barons.'

Ironically, as Bright realized, the very lucidity of Lowe's arguments and the brilliance of his exposition assisted rather than hindered the cause of reform. The more he chilled the imagination of his hearers in Parliament and frightened them into deep gloom, the more he fired the working classes to a feverish enthusiasm for reform. Had he not made his powerful speeches in the Commons attacking the working classes, the Reform League would have lacked a convenient scapegoat. The demand for reform grew stronger the more keenly Lowe prosecuted the attack.

Lowe's personality was as important as his speeches in provoking the anger of his opponents. He was, on the surface at any rate, a hard man who did not appear to consider the feelings of others. He liked to be rude, and he enjoyed an argument for its own sake. There were scores of anecdotes about him circulating not only in the clubs but in the streets. Once, when travelling with the Lord Chancellor, he arrived by cab at the railway station some time before the train was due to start. To pass the time, he said, 'Let us have a row with the carman about the fare.' To the Lord Chancellor's consternation he had a very effective row. Years before, when he had been an examiner at Oxford, he was once asked, while an oral examination was in progress, how he was getting on. 'Excellently,' he replied; 'five men plucked [failed] already, and the sixth very shaky.' He felt a terrible temptation to fail people for the rest of his life, and any shakiness on the part of his enemies – or even his friends – brought out the devil rather than the angel in him.

His choice of arguments was clever but often offensive, and he made no concessions to the mood of his audience. 'He cannot help being brilliant,' wrote Bagehot. 'The quality of his mind is to put everything in the most lively, most exciting, and most startling form. . . . He startled those who do not like to be startled, and does not compose those who wish to be composed.' He disliked the slow, the dull, and the unenlightened, even when they were members of Parliament. 'Brute votes' did not interest him. 'Look at that fool throwing away his natural advantages!' he exclaimed when a deaf member of the House of Commons put up his ear trumpet. In 1866 and 1867 he managed to win over many members of Parliament and to impress the rest, but he did not make many permanent friends. He moved more easily in intellectual than in political circles, and, after several years of high office between 1868 and 1874, the last years of his life were years of total political eclipse. His light had always come from the moon rather than the sun, but now the moon was completely blotted out; he was generally regarded as a Cassandra seeking confirmation of his early prophecies of doom in all the political changes of the day.

Many of his political weaknesses were the result of physical infirmity. He was an albino, so shortsighted that it was a wonder he was ever able to read a book at all. His brilliant achievements at Winchester and Oxford were a triumph of mind over physique: It was said that he would have taken even higher honours than he did at Oxford if he had not rubbed out with his nose what he had written with his pen. With such a combination of an acute mind and exceptional shortsightedness, it is not surprising that Lowe cared little for the values of the playing field, which in his view merely 'opened to dullness its road to fame'. He preferred the caustic wit of the First Class men to the team spirit of the First Football Fifteen. He always liked to walk, or to run, alone. 'Outstripping others in the race,' Gladstone wrote to him in a very frank, fault-finding letter in August 1873, 'you reach the goal or conclusion before them; and, being there, you assume that they are there also. This is unpopular.'

Lowe blamed his political unpopularity on his physical constitution. 'With a quiet temper and a real wish to please,' he remarked in his short typewritten fragment of an autobiography, 'I have been obliged all my life to submit to an amount of unpopularity that I really did not deserve, and to feel myself condemned for what were really physical rather than moral deficiencies.' This self-judgement was naïve. Lowe suffered from mental shortsightedness; he could never see his own faults, nor could he understand why his brilliant and carefully contrived schemes often went astray. 'His self-delusions about his own faults and merits are extraordinary,' wrote his friend Lord Granville, 'praising and condemning himself in wrong directions.' It was not only that 'the clearness, power, and promptitude' of his intellect was a handicap to him in dealing with lesser men; what was a far bigger hindrance to smooth relationships was a sharpness of tongue and an irresistible flash of contempt. He seemed to prefer conflict and animosity to unity and understanding. As early as 1856, for example, when as vice-president of the Board of Trade he introduced a bill to abolish local dues on shipping in Liverpool, he was so tart in his speeches and so provocative in his criticism of parties interested in the question that the bill was thrown out. His chief opponent, Sir Frederick Thesiger, was able to say, 'Lowe and I have thrown it out'. A few years later, between 1861 and 1864, he managed to provoke the unanimous opposition of all parties interested in the question of education, from the High Anglicans to the militant dissenters, and, for good measure, the inspectors of schools as well.

Lowe loved to test the superior qualities of his mind in sharp encounters with vested interests, for which he had a Benthamite sense of repugnance, and with parliamentary opponents, whom he regarded as ill-informed laymen. No one doubted his brilliance, but Lowe was never happy himself unless he was displaying it. His 'quiet temper' and 'real wish to please' were very rarely displayed outside the pages of his own unpublished autobiography.

In 1866 and 1867 he enjoyed the fight against reform even when he felt most gloomy about the consequences of a reform bill. In contrast to many Whigs, who were afraid of the political turmoil which they knew would follow Palmerston's death, Lowe confessed that he was glad that stormy times lay ahead. 'Poor Macleay used to say I was always fond of hot water, and lately it has not only been cold, but stagnant.' The hotter the water became, the cooler were Lowe's arguments and the more icy was his oratory.

2

Taken together, Lowe's speeches on reform set out the most comprehensive case against democracy expressed in the House of Commons in the nineteenth century. The first occasion on which he publicly stated his views was in 1865, when a private member, Edward Baines, brought forward a borough franchise extension bill. Although many 'Liberals' opposed Baines, Lowe feared that, once Palmerston was dead, a government reform bill would be introduced; and he ventured to predict

that if they (the great Liberal party) unite their fortunes with the fortunes of Democracy, as it is proposed they should do in the case of this measure, they will not miss one of two things – if they fail in carrying this measure they will ruin their party, and if they succeed in carrying this measure they will ruin their country.

It was after Gladstone and Russell had introduced their bill as soon as they could in March 1866 that Lowe, who had not been given office in the new government, first dazzled the members of Pariament with his rhetoric and challenged Gladstone's leadership. The bill was moderate, its central feature being a seven-pound property franchise in the towns in place of the existing ten-pound franchise, but Lowe wanted no reform bill at all, not even a moderate one. In discussions with the Conservative Adderley before the details were announced, he promised the support of a sufficiently large group of Liberals to overturn the government if it brought forward a bill. 'What bill do you mean?' Adderley asked. 'Any bill that lowers the borough franchise by one sixpence,' replied Lowe. In such an intransigent mood he revelled in the beginnings of the great debate. 'Mr Lowe is the great reputation of the Session in the House of Commons,' the *Spectator* noted. 'No stranger goes there without looking for the white gleam, or rather flash, of his striking head, or listening anxiously for the cold, sardonic ring of his lucid voice, penetrating it with a shiver of half-mocking intelligence.'

Lowe soon gathered around him a small group of members of the Liberal party who were opposed, like himself, to any lowering of the franchise. They included Lord Elcho, Lord Grosvenor, and Mr Horsman; 'unattached' men or unrepentant Palmerstonians who felt no special loyalty to Russell or Gladstone; and some of the members for small boroughs who feared changes in the distribution of seats. In all, they numbered more than forty, and they were not without influential supporters outside, like Delane, who believed that they were capable of becoming 'a third party'. These were the men Bright had christened the 'Adullamites', dismissing them as a cabal, collecting in their cave 'every one that was in distress and every one that was discontented'. But they were more influential than that. Lord Elcho's home was a very comfortable cave and appealed to some Liberals outside it whose loyalty to the government kept them from organized opposition. When Gladstone's bill was put to the vote in April, it was carried only by 5 votes (318 to 313), with 32 Liberals voting against it. Lowe, 'the prince of the revolt', was 'flushed, triumphant, and avenged. His hair, brighter than silver, shone and glistened in the brilliant light. His complexion had deepened into something like a bishop's purple.' Members asked each other, 'Who would have thought there was so much in Bob Lowe?'

The government's majority was so small that it seemed unlikely that the franchise bill would survive the committee stage. In an attempt to meet the arguments of men like Lord Grosvenor, who had refused to consider changes in the franchise without also considering changes in the distribution of seats, Gladstone and Russell introduced a redistribution bill in May 1866. It did not abolish small boroughs, but 'grouped' them together; the transfer of power to large urban electorates was severely restrained. At the end of May the two modest reform bills were incorporated in one single bill, which the government prepared to pass on to a committee.

At this point Conservatives and Adullamites united again to defeat the government on an unimportant Conservative amendment by 248 votes to 238. Unimportant though the issue was, the moral strength and authority of the government were further reduced. A more damaging amendment to abolish 'grouping' was proposed by Hayter, a disgruntled representative of a small borough. Lowe backed him, but Hayter withdrew his amendment for fear of further splitting his party. It was no surprise when the government was finally defeated on an important amendment moved by an Adullamite in June. When the figures – 315 to 304 – were announced, Lowe and the denizens of the cave stood up and waved their hats in triumph over the heads of their own party.

The Queen, who as usual was more preoccupied with questions of foreign policy than reform, was anxious that Russell should remain Prime Minister; but after a short exchange of courtesies Russell told her bluntly that 'there are things which can and cannot be done. To acquiesce in a further limitation of the enfranchisement... would cover us with shame and WOULD NOT SETTLE THE QUESTION.' He refused to recommend a dissolution – on the interesting grounds that the southern counties were apathetic in the cause of reform – and in consequence Derby and Disraeli accepted the task of forming a new Conservative government.

Lowe and his Adullamite colleagues had shown little enthusiasm for Disraeli in the complicated Conservative–Adullamite negotiations in the spring of 1866. They refused in June to join the new Conservative cabinet, although a few of them thought that, unless they associated with Derby, 'next year we may see a worse measure of reform carried than would have been borne now.' Lowe himself was willing to give 'unofficial support' to Derby, but within a few weeks he began to realize that the new government was unlikely to prove a bulwark of the constitution. 'I hold Bright and his mob in such sovereign contempt,' he wrote to his Conservative brother in October, 'that I require no external support to fortify me against their abuse. What I am afraid of is your friends the Tories, and, above all, Dizzy, who, I verily believe, is concocting a very sweeping Bill.'

By February 1867 his suspicions were confirmed. It was clear that Derby and Disraeli were anxious to settle the question of reform themselves and, if necessary, to outbid the Liberals. 'The reign of reason seems over,' wrote Lowe. 'Everybody is determined to settle the question of reform, and they hardly seem to care how.'

In attacking Disraeli, Lowe was angrier than he had been in attacking Gladstone. He claimed that the Conservatives were knaves and traitors as well as fools. 'We have inaugurated a new era in English politics this session,' he told the members of Parliament in 1867, 'and depend upon it, the new fashion will henceforth be the rule and not the exception. This session we have had not what we before possessed – a party of attack, and a party of resistance. We have, instead, two parties of competition, who, like Cleon and the sausage-seller in Aristophanes, are both bidding for the support of Demos.' Lowe not only refused to appeal to Demos; he tried to prevent other statesmen from making the appeal as well. He was as proud of his lone superiority – *Athanasius contra Mundum* he saw himself rather than Adullam in the cave – as Bright had been of his loneliness in the Crimean War.

He maintained his opposition to reform to the very end. When the Tory Disraeli gloried in his triumph in carrying a Radical reform bill, Lowe commented bitterly that 'England had gained a shameful victory over herself' and referred to 'the shame, the rage, the scorn, the indignation, and the despair with which the measure was viewed by every Englishman who is not a slave to the trammels of party or dazzled by the glare of a temporary and ignoble success'. He realized by then that he had made a serious miscalculation in 1866. Frightened as he was, even then, of Disraeli's unscrupulousness, he had never thought it possible that, if Russell and Gladstone were defeated, Disraeli would be prepared to go even further than Bright. He never forgave Disraeli during the rest of his life. Nor did Disraeli ever forgive him for his relentless criticism. The mutual dislike went deeper than a mere difference of opinions. Disraeli dismissed Lowe's speeches in 1867 as those of an inspired schoolboy, while Lowe, going one stage further back, called Disraeli's arguments in 1875 'lispings of the nursery'. When Disraeli was made an earl in 1876, Lowe wrote to his brother, 'I am glad Dizzy is out of the House. It may stave off a little longer electoral districts and universal suffrage.' Dislike turned into hatred. Two or three years before Disraeli died, a friend asked him whether there was anyone in London with whom he would not shake hands. Reflecting for a moment, he answered, 'Only one,' and named Robert Lowe.

3

Lowe's political calculations were faulty in 1866 and 1867, but his analysis was, within its limits, convincing. He began by challenging the reformers to state why they wished to tamper with the constitution. 'The burden of proof of existing institutions is in their favour'; it was for the reformers to say why the institutions should be modified. They were reluctant to do this, however keen they were to stir the crowds at public meetings. 'I find nothing so difficult as to get a Reformer to assign his reasons. The plan is to assume that there are reasons. Bring in the Bill, *solvitur ambulando*, by walking into the subject.'

When they tried to give reasons for reform, they could not agree among themselves. Radicals, like Bright, talked of the necessity of reform: the unenfranchised were thundering at the gates, and it was a matter of prudence as well as of justice to let them in. More moderate Liberals, like Gladstone, talked of the inevitability of reform: 'Time is on our side. The great social forces which move onwards in their might and majesty, and which the tumult of these debates does not for a moment impede or disturb – those great social forces are against you; they work with us; they are marshalled in our support.' Intellectuals, like Mill, were 'sentimental advocates of democracy'; they had forgotten their Benthamite political calculus and were relying upon intuition. 'Our business,' they said, 'is to elevate the working classes.' Lowe criticized all types of reformers. The question of reform was not one of sentiment, of rewarding, punishing, or elevating, but a practical matter of business and statecraft. 'What we have to do is to find out any practical evil in the working of our institutions, and then to suggest a remedy for it.' The test of reform should be its effect on Parliament, the governing body of the nation, not on the class which received the franchise. 'The end being good government, in which of course I include stable government, before I give my assent to the admission of fresh classes, I must be satisfied (not on *a priori* but on experimental grounds) that their admission will make the government better or more stable.'

Lowe did not admit that there was a case for reform comparable with the case in 1832. The grievances which were complained of in 1832, he said, were practical grievances, while those of 1866–7 were theoretical. The political system as it was actually operating in 1866 was reasonably satisfactory, as satisfactory as any political system could be. 'This House holds – not only in England, but throughout the whole world – a position far above that ever held by any other deliberative Assembly that ever existed.' The ten-pound householder suffrage had served 'as one of the most respectable institutions that any country ever possessed. The seven Houses of Commons that have sat since the Reform Bill have performed exploits unrivalled, not merely in the six centuries during which Parliament has existed, but in the whole history of representative assemblies.' Useful reforms, such as the introduction of free trade and limited liability, had been carried; new classes had been hitched to the constitution; and a proper balance of interests among different groups in the community had been maintained.

The alternative to the existing House of Commons was not a House of Commons elected on a slightly more open franchise, but a democratic House of Commons elected by the masses of the people. It would be impossible to determine the franchise for long by drawing a new property line at the seven-pound voter or the six-pound voter. The tendency of all reform was towards democracy. 'It is trifling with the House,' said Lowe in 1866, 'to suggest that when you have passed this Bill you will have settled anything; all that you do is to unsettle everything, perhaps to lay the foundation of a real agitation, because people, when they find that so much will be gained with such little trouble, will be encouraged to ask for a great deal more.' The result would be not only political but social democracy, for it was only too easy to destroy the work of centuries within a few months. 'Democracy you may have at any time. Night and day the gate is open that leads to that bare and level plain, where every ant's nest is a mountain and every thistle is a forest tree.'

Democracy would have three disastrous consequences. First, it would transfer political power to the ignorant. Intelligent government would then be impossible. 'If this House means to maintain the great power and influence which it exercises over the executive government it must beware of putting itself on too democratic a foundation.' Second, it would destroy real leadership. 'If you form your House solely with a view to numbers, whatever other good you obtain, you will destroy the element out of which your statesmen must be made. You will lower the position of the executive government, and render it difficult, if not impossible, to carry on that happy union between the two powers which now exists.' Third, it would lead to the canvassing and carrying of policies which would undermine national unity and prosperity. The working classes would use the franchise as a means to an end. The machinery of the state would be employed to assist strikes, to abolish free trade, even to lead the country to war. 'Once give working men the votes, and the machinery is ready to launch those votes in one compact mass upon the institutions and property of this country.'

Lowe went on to point out that democracy would not be in the best interests of the provident section of the working classes themselves. The merit of a limited franchise was that the suffrage had to be earned. Thrifty and industrious workers had already won the vote or were winning it each day under the half-reformed constitution. The way to elevate the working classes was not to bring down the franchise 'to the level of those persons who have no sense of decency or morality' but to keep it as a privilege of citizenship. Universal suffrage could only create 'that sort of elevation which has resulted in Australia in the franchise being so despised that people hardly care to pick it out of the gutter'. When, in Australia, one statesman had 'hit upon the happy device' of requiring a shilling fee for registration of voters, 'the effect was magical. I am informed that it diminished the personal voters by one half. A franchise which in the estimation of those who have it is literally not worth a shilling, cannot be an elevation of the working classes.'

4

Lowe's opposition to reform was founded on experience as well as logic. There were three features of his own history which made him suspicious of democratic government.

The first was his memory of Australia. It was in New South Wales that he served his political apprenticeship from 1842 to 1850. For eight years he wrestled with the problems of a colonial community, originally serving as a Crown nominee on the Legislative Council and finally emerging as the 'popular favourite' of the Sydney electorate.

All Lowe's abilities and weaknesses were apparent in his Australian record, a complete career within a career. His speeches and journalistic articles anticipated his performances in England. Brilliant and incisive, they spared no one, not even the governor, his old friend and patron. The first Anglican bishop of Sydney was described as 'arrogant', and his clergy were dismissed as 'trembling, crouching, sneaking bigots'. Sydney Corporation was castigated as 'an engine of corruption', and paid commissioners recommended as efficient replacements of idle mayors, aldermen, and councillors. There was merciless radicalism in many of his remarks and policies, and he soon acquired the title of 'the Cromwell of the

Antipodes'. His enemies, unable to hold their own with him, called him 'the most quarrelsome man in the new world'.

For a brief spell he was a popular hero, almost a demagogue. At the election of 1848 he staged his own private revolution. Breaking with officialdom and with the rural squatter groups, he stood as the people's candidate in the large urban constituency of Sydney. His allies were the skilled artisans, his enemies 'the petty aristocracy', and his election was a victory for 'democracy'. A year later he reached the pinnacle of popular success. On one glorious day in June 1849, 'one of the few heroic moments in Australian history', he harangued at Sydney Circular Quay an excited crowd which had gathered to protest against the unloading of a ship bringing transported convicts from England. Speaking from the top of an omnibus, Lowe attacked not only the governor and 'the parasites and sycophants' who surrounded him but also Earl Grey, the Colonial Secretary in London. The transportation system and the colonial system were equally worthy of condemnation. 'England herself is but part of the Empire,' he maintained, 'and when she treats us as if she were the whole she is actuated by a narrow and provincial spirit.'

One old woman in the crowd was so stirred by Lowe's rhetoric that she shouted, 'Ah! bless his dear old white head' – an unusual benediction for him. The enthusiastic gathering was roused to the point where it dragged Lowe's carriage through the streets of Sydney. The convict ship did not land its human cargo at the harbour, nor was it ever possible again for the Colonial Office in London to extend its transportation system. Lowe had earned his place in Australian history as a pioneer of representative government in New South Wales.

Basically, however, his philosophy was not unlike that which he later expressed in 1866. 'I care not for mere names,' he told the Australians; 'I look to the substance, and the constitution of England was framed not for the assertion of mere abstract principles, but to guard and maintain the substantial benefits of free government. Let pot-house politicians indulge in rhetorical flourishes concerning venerable institutions and consecrated principles – principles violated before the ink was dry in which they were acknowledged – but give me the application of the general principles of the British Constitution to the useful and the new.' The difference between England and Australia was that the 'useful and the new' seemed less synonymous in an old country like England, where the 'pot-house politicians' talked not of 'venerable institutions' and 'consecrated principles' but of Radical reform.

Even before he left Australia, Lowe had begun to change. His local popularity did not last, and when he left for England in January 1850 there were no mass demonstrations. Although his first public speech in England on his return was at a meeting of the Society for the Reform of Colonial Government, he soon passed from colonial questions to English domestic issues. As the blue skies of Australia faded from his mind, his memories became increasingly selective. He recalled the crowds as crowds of ignorant enemies, the Australian constitution as a dangerous experiment in democracy, and the squatters as 'an important and useful element in colonial society' and 'a necessary prop of colonial institutions'.

When he thought of Australia in 1866 and 1867, it was not in terms of an omnibus at the quayside but of a distant country managed by the mob. 'In the colonies they had democratic Assemblies. And what is the result? Why they become a curse instead of a blessing.' The only way to save them from anarchy was to relieve them from universal suffrage.

Victoria and New South Wales are both governed by universal suffrage and it is as much as we can do to prevent them from going to war with each other. . . . If you want to see the results of democratic constituencies you will find them in all the assemblies of Australia and in all the assemblies of North America.

America was a more familiar example to English audiences in 1866 and 1867 than Australia, although both were frequently discussed. The cry of 'Americanizing the constitution' was freely used against Bright, and Lowe was one of the makers of it. In 1856 he had visited America and added personal knowledge of another 'new country' to bolster his case against democracy. On the voyage out he studied De Tocqueville; once in the United States, he was shocked by much that he saw. There seemed an utter absence of distinction, a complete lack of a leisured class, a wide range of corrupt institutions, and an anxiety to kowtow to the multitudes. Everyday life was full of lessons. He was alarmed, for example, to observe a passenger on a railway train asking his fellow-passengers in turn which man they thought should be President. This was not the right way to secure effective political leadership or to develop 'pure' government. And there was a terrible nemesis in store. 'It is impossible for universal suffrage to continue where there are so many poor who will want to divide or destroy property.'

As a result of his career in Australia and his visit to America, Lowe became 'a mine of useful information on *colonial* and *new country* subjects'. Much as he disliked and feared democracy in 'new territories', he hated it much more in crowded England, where there was a shortage of land, a pressure of population, and an inherited social structure. The most serious danger came from the English poor. In an unreformed Parliament the worst abuses of the political system were concentrated in those parts of the country where the working classes were strongest. 'If you want venality, if you want ignorance, if you want drunkenness, and facility for being intimidated; or if on the other hand, you want impulsive, unreflecting, and violent people, where do you look for them in the constituencies? Do you go to the top or to the bottom?' In a reformed Parliament such classes would hold power.

Lowe's personal experiences in England provided the third element in his personal case against democracy. In Australia he had been 'a stranger, a cork floating on the ocean; one who might be here today and gone tomorrow'; in America he had been a temporary visitor; in England he was at home. And his first memories of home disposed him to think ill of crowds. As a young man he had watched Reform Bill mobs sack Colwick Hall in Nottinghamshire; as an undergraduate at Oxford he had been taught, like Gladstone, that democracy meant the government of the rich, who were few, by and for the poor, who were many. When a member of Parliament for Kidderminster, he had been struck on the head by a stone thrown in an election riot. 'The bribe and the beer-barrel' were effective political weapons in Kidderminster, as they were in Trollope's Beverley. English experience convinced Lowe that democracy could never mean government of the *best*.

Many members of Parliament who were unable to argue the case against democracy in such intellectual terms were able to share some of Lowe's fears for the future. Even Radicals like John Stuart Mill and John Bright had spoken about the dangers of extending the suffrage. Mill had written both in *Political Economy* and in *Representative Government* of 'the extreme unfitness [of] the labouring classes . . . for any order of things which would make any considerable demand on either their intellect or their virtue'; while Bright had conceded the existence among the working classes of what he called a 'residuum', a group 'which it would be much better for themselves if they were not enfranchised, because they have no independence whatever, and . . . much better for the constituency also that they should be excluded'. In the House of Commons a persuasive Lowe was able to turn on Bright and warn him that free trade, too, was in peril if the working classes secured the vote, adding, 'If we have a precious jewel in the world, it is our free trade policy.' Turning towards Gladstone, he was able to remind him that as late as 1865, just before he began to concoct his reform bill, he (Gladstone) had said:

It has been our privilege to see a process going forward in which the throne has acquired broader and deeper foundations in the affections of the country; in which the law has commended itself to the respect and attachment of the people; in which the various classes of the community have come into close communion, the one with the other; in which the great masses of our labouring fellow-countrymen have come to be better supplied than they were in the time of their immediate forefathers, and in which, upon the whole, a man desirous of the welfare of this kind, looking out on the broad surface of society, may thank his God, and say, 'Behold, how good and pleasant a thing it is for brethren to dwell together in unity!'

Why should the surface of English society be disturbed? Why should the underlying unity be destroyed?

5

Behind Lowe's political arguments was a profound suspicion of the working classes as a whole. He admired those provident individuals among the workers who had acquired middle-class respectability, but he considered that specifically working-class organizations, like the trade unions, were anxious 'to make war against all superiority; to keep down skill, industry, and capacity; and to make their members the slaves of clumsiness, idleness, and ignorance'. The routine of the trade unions implied restriction and protection; rules relating to piecework, for instance, could not be justified by any economic arguments. But behind the routine there was 'a system of terrorism'. Granting the franchise to the working classes would mean arming the terrorists with the vote. Political power would automatically be used in the interests of crude class domination. Not only would the constitution be swamped by numbers; society would be torn apart.

To those thinkers like Mill who denied that, if the working classes were given the vote, they would act together, Lowe pointed to existing working-class cohesion in the field of labour relations. He recognized, as did the middle-class supporters of the trade unions, that 'nothing is so remarkable among the working classes of England as their intense tendency to associate and organize themselves'. He differed from Hughes and Harrison, however, in fearing rather than admiring such mutual cooperation. 'It is impossible to believe that the same machinery which is at present brought into play in connexion with strikes would not be applied by the working classes to political purposes.' It was idle to assume that artisans and unskilled labourers would continue to defer to their betters.'You know very well that they will soon possess the secret of their own power, and then what is to prevent them using it?' Once the suffrage had been extended, nothing could prevent the rise of a separate Labour party. Neither Liberals nor Conservatives would satisfy trade unionists for long. 'They will say, "We can do better for ourselves. Don't let us any longer be cajoled at elections. Let us set up shop for ourselves."'

Lowe pressed these views on Parliament with great determination, but he was anxious that they should reach a wider audience. In 1867, after the passing of the Reform Bill, he wrote an interesting article for the *Quarterly Review* which related questions of labour very directly to questions of reform. He foresaw the rise of unskilled labour and refused to believe that 'the aristocracy of labour' would long remain in control of the trade-union movement. Trade unions, he said,

are rapidly taking possession of the mind of the unskilled assistants of the higher class of operatives. ... A Trades' Union is in this respect similar to a great military power. It not only possesses great offensive force itself, but is the cause of the creation of great offensive force by others. Every trade can collaterally exercise so much influence on other kindred trades, and directly so much influence on the employers of labour, that it drives all those with whom it comes in contact to imitation. The more the Union spirit spreads, the more is it likely to spread. It is a machine excellently qualified for political action, and we cannot doubt that the new Reform Bill will give an additional impulse to this species of association.

In addition to looking far ahead into the future, Lowe reviewed in detail the events and attitudes of 1866 and 1867. He discussed the Sheffield and Manchester outrages, and he examined Applegarth's evidence before the royal commission. His approach was analytical, but he could not keep out of the picture the lurid details of cloak-and-dagger unionism in Manchester and Sheffield.

Needles are put by the thousand into the clay to lame the hands of those who load it. ... Watchmen are wounded in the head with slugs – a policeman is murdered outright. ... We read of stabs with knives, of pistols discharged, of persons who cannot swim thrown into deep water, of waylaying and beating; and one person nearly killed because he was taken for another.

Admitting that 'a vast interval separates such an association as the Amalgamated Carpenters and Joiners from the Bricklayers of Lancashire or the Saw Grinders of Sheffield', Lowe added that 'they all contain within them the germs and elements of crime, they are all founded on the right of the majority to coerce the minority, on the absolute subjugation of the one to the many, and the employment of such means as may be necessary in order to give effect to these false and dangerous principles'.

The Amalgamated Society of Carpenters and Joiners spent one third of its income in supporting strikes; it rejected piecework; it enforced its rules, no matter how strong the minority opinion. Lowe conceded it to be 'one of the most moderate, best regulated, and best conducted of existing Trades' Unions'; if it could not stand the application of ordinary economic principles, no other union could. Yet, when Lowe examined the approach of the A.S.C.J. to questions of wages and competition, he came to the conclusion that it was 'utterly reckless' of the degree to which it increased the expenses of production and 'deliberately blind' to the problems of foreign competition. The subscriptions of the union were wasted in

pretending to do that which the laws of demand and supply are already doing, or in ruining that very fund out of which the support of the contributors must come. ... We do not denounce these Unions as wrong or selfish, but as an enormous blunder, a gigantic miscalculation, based on fallacies the most obvious and mistakes the most easily detected.

With great difficulty England had accepted the principles of free trade. 'Now there is growing up in the midst of us a monopoly of labour far more oppressive and indefensible than the monopoly of trade we have abolished.' Lowe condemned the well-regulated unions in the name of political economy, just as he condemned the terrorist unions in the name of law and order. The fact that Applegarth's union was founded in direct defiance of economic principles weighed gravely against it on the grounds of justice, fairness, and expediency. 'Political economy is not exactly the law of the land, but it is the ground of that law. It is assumed as its basis and foundation.' If the skilled unionists had their way, the good effects of free trade would be undone and economic progress would be jeopardized; if unskilled unionists began to increase in numbers, the ruin of England as a commercial and industrial power was certain.

Lowe's conclusion was a simple one: all societies formed in restraint of trade should be declared illegal, and magistrates should be given powers of summary jurisdiction over their members.

The law will then be adequate to the mischief. If it can be enforced, society will have freed itself from a great peril; dangers to our manufactures and commerce, the amount of which no man can measure, will have been arrested, and a demoralization which threatens to lower the character of the English operative to the level of the Thug of India will have been stayed; if not, we must be prepared to see our prosperity wither and perish under the ruinous influence of persons as ignorant of their own true interests as they are careless of the feelings and reckless of the interests of others.

It was natural that such views, so clearly and forcibly expressed, should win Lowe the support of many manufacturers and provoke the sharpest possible opposition from labour leaders and sympathizers of every kind. A Leeds manufacturer wrote to him, saying that the unions were doing incalculable injury to trade and that there was hardly a man among them who ever received as much during a strike as he had paid in. 'The poor fellows are the willing dupes of a few idle demagogues.' Since the demagogues had taken over, the word 'master' might as well be expunged from the social vocabulary. A Yorkshire surgeon went further and attacked not only the unionists but the workers as a whole. 'I know more than one butcher,' he wrote, 'who last year sold weekly from three to seven legs of first-rate mutton to the ironworkers to feed prize dogs, and during the last strike in the same town, one personally known to me was getting two, or sometimes three, legs weekly for the same purpose. . . . Surely I may express surprise that such men are to be put in possession of a responsible privilege affecting the whole community.'

Working-class opposition to Lowe was converted into hatred in 1866 and 1867. The Reform League directed much of its propaganda against him as it strove, in his phrase, 'to make me an object of the hatred, perhaps a mark for the vengeance, of my fellow-countrymen'. Lowe was indifferent to threats of violence. 'I am like Caesar in one respect,' he wrote in April 1866; 'at least I receive warnings to take care of my life and always to go to the House in a cab.' There was no violence. The only injury which Lowe suffered in 1866 was a bad fall from a railway platform when, because of his shortsightedness, he stumbled over a bag of books and had to have his hand tightly bandaged. Like Marx, Lowe was perhaps disappointed that there was not a little more evidence of a revolutionary spirit among the working classes.

One member of the Reform League tried to make him think again about his social presuppositions. Joseph Guedalla, a member of the executive of the Reform League, wrote a very modest and quiet letter to him in January 1867, asking him whether he would not consider modifying his views of working-class organization. 'Surely you will be ready to confess that the recent gatherings have been characterized by uniform decorum and good conduct, by an entire absence of drunkenness, violence, turbulence, and the other vices enumerated by you.' Self-control and intelligence had been demonstrated even by the crowds. 'The moment has arrived,' Guedalla concluded, 'when you may well undo what threatens to be a fatal work, and gracefully retract accusations which only enemies of English freedom, English character, and English institutions could hail with pleasure or satisfaction.' Lowe flatly refused to argue with Guedalla or with the league. 'With such a body and its leaders, of whom you appear to be one, I have no courtesies to interchange. When I think proper to give an opinion on the recent popular demonstrations, it is not to the Reform League that I shall offer it.' The crispness of Lowe's reply concealed profound emotion. Lowe chose to argue that the league had been misrepresenting him on the basis of one of his speeches in Parliament, the speech relating to corruption and venality among the poorer voters in the constituencies; in fact, the league was judging him by his speeches as a whole, and he was doing little to contradict their main charge that he was an enemy of the working classes.

Lowe's picture of the working classes was very sharply criticized by writers far less interested in popular agitation than Guedalla. Richard Monckton Milnes, who had been created Baron Houghton in 1863, and R. H. Hutton, later the editor of the *Spectator*, were two of a distinguished group of contributors to *Essays on Reform*, an influential collection of studies published in 1866. Hutton admitted that the artisans were less thrifty, less disposed to be guided by those who were their superiors in culture, less cautious in their political in- stincts, and less attached to the political institutions under which they lived than the middle classes, but he went on to praise the solidarity and vigour of workingmen. Their organizations proved their class patriotism; this class patriotism could be turned to national account.

> Only the working class have got a clear conception how much individuals owe, by way of self sacrifice, to the larger social organization to which they belong. . . . What I think may fairly be hoped for, is the diversion of some of this high *esprit de corps* from the narrow organization of the Trade Society to the wider organi- zation of the nation.

It was certain that the working classes would demand stronger government. They would not feel that 'wholesome dread of a strong central power' which the middle classes had felt. But this, to him, was a ground for optimism rather than fear. A stronger state was necessary to carry further reforms without which England would be torn by social jealousy and economic conflict.

Houghton made the point even more strongly:

> The real danger to England now is not from the working class, for no working class in any country was ever more peaceably dis- posed than ours is, but from the isolation of classes, caused by the extinction of the yeomanry and the growth of a manufacturing population, and from the alarming increase in the political, and still more in the social, power of wealth.

This danger was not to be met by treating classes as hostile bodies and playing one off against another. Nor could it be removed if the narrow franchise were maintained. It would only disappear if the working classes were admitted to a share in political power in the same way that the middle classes had been admitted in 1832.

Neither Houghton nor Hutton feared the swamping of the constitution. For them, social safeguards still seemed strong enough to guarantee peaceful progress. They refused to prophesy about the distant future, 'for in politics nothing is more certain than that it is impossible to predict how political and social forces will adjust themselves under a new Constitution'. It seemed likely that, for a time at any rate, there would be no drastic changes. As another of the essayists, Leslie Stephen, put it:

England is still an aristocratic country ... because the whole upper and middle, and a great part of the lower, classes have still an instinctive liking for the established order of things; because innumerable social ties bind us together spontaneously, so as to give to the aristocracy a position tolerably corresponding to their political privileges. If this instinct ever dies out, so that the political ceases to be the expression of the social organization, it will be utterly vain to boost it up by legislation; any such expedients will be temporary and cause sufficient irritation to ensure their downfall; it is because the correspondence has become palpably imperfect that some Reform is now imperatively demanded.

Such a conclusion shocked Lowe. He was pessimistic about the future of English society and the possibility of retaining safeguards once the door to democracy had been opened. Only one new safeguard seemed to him worthy of serious attention – the extension of popular education. Although he never used the phrase which is usually put into his mouth. 'We must educate our masters', he did declare, as soon as the Reform Bill was passed, that it was now essential 'to compel our future masters to learn their letters'. Like a good Benthamite, he turned to education as a condition of all improvement, although as an experienced politician he was not very sanguine about the outcome.

6

Lowe had interested himself in educational questions long before 1867. In Australia he had tried to introduce a comprehensive system, and on his return, between 1859 and 1864, he was vice-president of the Council and in charge of education. His ideas on education were as clearly defined as his ideas on the suffrage, and he was unwilling ever to change them.

He drew a sharp distinction between education for the rich and education for the poor; but he was unhappy about the existing provision of services for both sections of society. Although he was a brilliant product of Winchester, he felt no enthusiasm for the public schools or for the classical form of education which they provided. Education at Winchester was 'coarse and brutal', even though Winchester was considered one of the best of the schools. Tradition should have little importance in education.

Political economy made him as suspicious of the public schools as he was of the trade unions; they were endowed bodies, and all endowments were dangerous. 'Endowed schools are the eldest sons of education'; they became comfortable homes for men of inferior ability. There was no reason why education for the rich should not become more competitive. Formal rules and statutes should give way to the natural interplay of supply and demand. 'No one believes that if an endowment were given for supplying the City of London with meat or bread, its effect would be to make the meat or bread of London better.' Education was like bread; if there was free trade in corn, there should be free trade in schools.

The first effect of a more competitive educational system would be a change in the curriculum of the schools. Although an outstanding classical scholar himself, and a one-time coach of Latin and Greek at Oxford, Lowe came to detest classical studies in the schools. Dead languages, he believed, were less important than living modern languages, and living modern languages were less important than science. 'To acquire the scientific habit of mind,' he said, 'is the one invaluable thing in life.'

After the passing of the Reform Bill the need for more scientific knowledge, he believed, had become urgent. With the advent of the democratic franchise, it was suicidal for the young men of the upper classes to spend the best years of their lives studying Latin and Greek. Unless the landed gentry wished to abrogate its position as a ruling class, it was necessary that its members should be taught something about the lords of the Treasury in London as well as about the archons of Athens, something about physics and chemistry as well as Tacitus and Cicero. Lowe was a powerful and consistent advocate of educational reform. In the middle of the debates on the Reform Bill, he found time to address the banquet of the civil engineers, where he described classical studies as 'a minute analysis of the forms of expression and the modes of thought which were used by people many thousand years ago, and concerning which there was much controversy and no certainty would be arrived at'. It is not surprising that Lowe became as unpopular with fellows of Oxford colleges and masters at public schools as he was with trade-union leaders in London.

Education for the poor also needed reform. For Lowe, it was to be simple basic education, primarily in the three R's – reading, writing, and arithmetic. His career as vice-president of the Council reveals clearly his attitude towards state-provided instruction, which was carried out before the Education Act of 1870 by government subsidies to voluntary bodies. Necessary though it was in England as well as Australia, its purposes should be clearly defined and its costs assessed scientifically. Lowe cooperated with Gladstone in cutting down the cost to the government of education and introduced the system of payment by results. Grants to elementary schools with more than a hundred pupils were to be made only if the children passed an examination in reading, writing, and arithmetic.

Three factors influenced his decision to introduce a 'revised code' along these lines. The first was 'the battle for thrifty husbandry'. In 1860 the education grant was reduced for the first time since 1834. The second was efficiency; examination was deemed a more efficient test of good school management than inspection. The school inspectors dealt in abstract phrases like 'general efficiency', 'moral atmosphere', 'tone', and 'mental condition'; examiners dealt in marks. If education costs were to be cut down, then it was necessary to find a simple test – a good Benthamite test – which would enable government grants to be distributed fairly. 'If education is not cheap it should be efficient: if it is not efficient it should be cheap.' The third was distaste for subsidized 'luxury'; all educational frills were thought unnecessary. Lowe sympathized with the view of his Conservative predecessor, Adderley, that 'any attempt to keep children of the labouring classes under intellectual culture after the very earliest age at which they could earn their living, would be as arbitrary and improper as it would be to keep the boys at Eton and Harrow at spade labour'.

Lowe was a tidy administrator but, even in 1861, a bad politician. His educational proposals were sharply criticized on all sides, and in 1864 he was forced out of office by a coalition of enemies. Charges made against him of mutilating and falsifying the reports of the school inspectors were unfounded, but he resigned after the House of Commons had passed a vote of censure. His revised code stayed, and even after the passing of Forster's Education Act of 1870, the first comprehensive national education act, it was still considered the task of the elementary-school teacher 'to bring up the children in habits of punctuality; of good manners and language; of cleanliness and neatness; and also to impress upon them the importance of cheerful obedience to duty, of consideration and respect for others, of honour and truthfulness in word and act'. The purpose of elementary education, in a phrase of H. G. Wells, 'was to educate the lower classes for employment on lower-class lines, with specially trained, inferior teachers'.

There was one final consideration which influenced Lowe in his approach to elementary education: he was not anxious, either before or after 1870, to see 'a completely bureaucratic system of national education' in England. In his approach to the problems of the best way of distributing the educational grant of 1861, he showed fears of educational centralization. A single system of schools unified under rigid public control meant dangerously strong government. Lowe's Benthamism did not lead him, like Edwin Chadwick, towards an efficient autocratic state; rather it made him afraid of too great a concentration of power at the centre. Despite his utilitarian approach to religion, he praised 'the invaluable superintendence of the gentry and the clergy, the zeal of religious conviction, the harmony with the present state of society, and the standard already reached' in the existing educational system; and he feared that these qualities would all be sacrificed if the instruction of the poor were placed 'in the hands of indifferent and incompetent local bodies, or of a central department which shall henceforth take charge of what used to be the work of free and spontaneous growth, the formation of English character and habits of thought'.

There was a danger that a democratic electorate might tamper not only with the property system but also with the educational system in such a way that the unity of society would be further undermined. Although Lowe believed that it was necessary 'to compel our future masters to learn their letters', he felt that it might be dangerous if they attempted to learn much more. He was too honest a believer in the merits of educational progress to press this argument to its conclusion. Adderley did not scruple to do so. 'The educating, by the artificial stimulus of large public expenditure, a particular class out of, instead of in, the condition of life in which they naturally fill an important part of the community, must upset the social equilibrium,' Adderley maintained. 'It is clearly wrong to attempt to keep ordinary children of the working class at school after the age at which their proper work begins, and there are some kinds of work which must begin very early.' Education, like society, was to remain stratified; the elementary school should not be organized in order to change the world but to keep it exactly as it was.

7

Lowe's belief in sound administration and cheap government might have made him the favourite of the middle classes. He never found it easy to understand why many of them seemed to prefer Bright. 'I was one of those', he said at Liverpool in 1867, '– and they were very few indeed – who lifted their voices in favour of the middle class not so much for their sake as for the sake of the country. . . . I never met with the slightest encouragement or support from those whose cause I was pleading.'

This lack of sympathy increased his sense of isolation. He always defended the claims of the ten-pound householders, a group of people who had 'discharged their duty in a manner which almost defies criticism'; and he frequently quoted Aristotle's remark, 'Happy and well-governed are those States where the middle part is strong and the extremes weak.' While a don at Oxford, ten years before the repeal of the Corn Laws, he was attacked by many respectable parents for teaching their sons 'the heresy of Free Trade'. In Australia, his criticisms of the Colonial Office were not unlike those of Bright, and in similar language he thundered against 'horse-racing dukes, fox-hunting squires, and blackleg baronets'. In England he was always active in supporting those parliamentary measures which assisted middle-class interests. During the Crimean War, for example, he stressed the need for reform both in the civil service and in the army. After the war ended, he introduced in the Commons the Limited Liability Bill of 1856. His sympathy for middle-class ambitions is reflected in all his speeches of this period. 'Until merit is the only avenue to public office,' he exclaimed, 'we are fighting with a leaden sword against a man who uses a steel one.'

His approval of middle-class aspirations was even more clearly demonstrated after 1868, when he became Chancellor of the Exchequer in Gladstone's great Liberal government. While he was at the Treasury between 1868 and 1872, he attempted to implement a policy which would satisfy the most ardent supporters of orthodox political economy. He took a penny off the income tax in 1869 and abolished the shilling duty on corn, the residual element of the old protectionist system. The duty on fire insurance he also abandoned on the grounds that it was 'a tax upon prudence'. In 1870 another penny off the income tax seemed to forecast the total abolition of the tax within a few years. In 1871, however, he suffered a serious setback when he had to increase the income tax and introduce a new tax on matches which created surprising popular opposition; and in 1873 he was moved from the Treasury to the Home Office. As usual, he had impressed himself with his achievements far more than he had impressed the public. According to the touching words of his own epitaph:

> Twelve millions of Taxes I struck off,
> Left behind me six millions of gains;
> Of Debt forty millions I shook off,
> And got well abused for my pains.

During his years in office after 1868, he drew close to Bright's foreign policy as well as to Bright's economics. In 1870, for example, he very strongly opposed the British purchase of the Suez Canal shares on the grounds that he did not believe that the returns 'would pay the interest of the money considering all that remains to be done' and that 'we should be involved yet more deeply than at present in the politics of Egypt and might very probably find ourselves driven to an occupation'. 'I hold to the policy of avoiding entangling occupations of territory,' he told Granville, 'which can only result in scattering our forces and leaving us weak at home without making us strong abroad.' When Disraeli actually bought the shares in 1876, Lowe strongly objected and contrived to annoy not only the public but also his old friend Lord Rothschild, from whom Disraeli had raised the money, and who did not like Lowe's reference to the £100,000 commission on the deal. By attacking Disraeli's bill to confer on the Queen the title 'Empress of India', he succeeded in alienating the Queen as well. His views on India were as firm as his views on the absurdity of the royal title. ' I do not think India worth the sacrifice implied in a permanent occupation,' he had written categorically in 1870.

His detailed knowledge of 'new countries' and his opposition to spending large sums of taxpayers' money made him an even more vigorous critic of 'imperialism' than Bright. He was one of the first Englishmen to give prominence to the word 'imperialism', treating it as savagely as a twentieth-century Marxist. In the 1870s he looked forward to a time when the British dominions overseas would be completely free to manage their own affairs, although he was not optimistic about the results. 'I am averse to setting up a consular jurisdiction in Fiji,' he wrote in 1871, 'which I believe would be both costly and unsatisfactory. . . . I think it would be far better to annex Fiji to New South Wales or Victoria. They are quite silly enough to take it and would govern it much better than we should. I am much against forming new Colonies, but see no objection to adding troublesome places like this to old ones.'

The stout advocacy of such views won Lowe the good will of nobody. Although he often expressed opinions in keeping with those of the old-fashioned Radicals, he never made any attempt to flatter middle-class audiences. He was contemptuous of *nouveaux riches* who were Tories 'because they think it genteel'; but he did not care overmuch to win the support of the Liberal middle classes either. He always preferred to move in small circles than to mix with people whom he considered his intellectual inferiors.

Perhaps the turning-point of Lowe's later career was his refusal in 1859 to stand as an opponent of John Bright at a Birmingham election. He rejected an offer made to him by a group of local Liberals, even though his sponsors offered to pay all his election expenses. He had no desire to repeat his experiences in Sydney. Instead he chose to stand for the pocket borough of Calne, which was in the safe keeping of the Marquis of Lansdowne. It is unlikely that Lowe would have won an election in Birmingham against John Bright, but, by failing to do more than curtly acknowledge the offer, he made it possible for Bright to lampoon him in the House of Commons in

1866. 'The constituency which the right hon. gentleman represents,' Bright remarked, 'consists of a hundred and seventy four men, seven of whom are working men; but the real constituency of the right hon. gentleman is a member of the other House of Parliament, and he could send in his butler or his groom, instead of the right hon. gentleman, to represent the borough.' There was no effective reply to this charge in 1866.

Lowe's refusal to take his chances with a large electorate may have been determined by his sense of physical deficiency; but, whatever its cause, it became a serious handicap to him as a politician. When, after the second Reform Bill, he was returned as member for the newly created University of London seat, it was possible for Disraeli to taunt him too, for Disraeli was able to say that, if he had not created a new constituency for the University of London electors, Lowe would have been left without a place in the Commons. 'The right hon. Robert Lowe by kind permission not of the Marquis of Lansdowne but of Mr Benjamin Disraeli'; there was no taunt more crushing.

Lowe turned eagerly from the shifting world of politics to the world of the civil service, to the permanent element in each department of state. He was always on terms of the closest friendship with civil servants, and they were unhesitating in their admiration not only of his tidy mind, but also of his 'kindness of heart and freedom from spleen and malice'. Surrounded by papers in his office and with good officials at his shoulder, Lowe was always at his ease; the trouble came from vested interests, ruthless politicians, and dull members of Parliament. In twentieth-century circumstances he might have been a distinguished civil servant himself, preparing memorandums which inferior men could later sift and publicize. As it was, even in the mid nineteenth century, he moved easily in the ill-defined territory between the realm of the civil servant and the realm of the politician. By advocating the extension of the system of competitive examination to all departments of the civil service, he was pointing the way forward to the permanent and independent civil service of the twentieth century. He was, indeed, one of the first persons to apply the phrase 'head of the whole Civil Service' to the Permanent Secretary to the Treasury, and his contribution as a minister to effective civil service reform was substantial.

But there was a fatal flaw even in his approach to the civil service. He advocated an improvement in the machinery of government without wishing to give the machinery more tasks to perform: 'Our business is to diminish, not to increase, the duties and responsibilities of government,' he wrote in 1873. He trusted the civil service at the same time that he feared democracy. Administration reform was to be a substitute for, not a complement of, political reform. His civil service was to have little, not much, to do. The logic was defective. It was only after he had passed from the political stage and his great enemy Disraeli had launched the first programme of social legislation between 1874 and 1880 that the civil service could begin its period of spectacular expansion. The pressure of interests and the clamour of voters were to be as important as logical analysis in the making of the design of the new civil service, what Graham Wallas boldly described as 'the one great political invention in nineteenth-century England'. Lowe's great bogy, the growth of 'state socialism', was the greatest effective challenge to old administrative methods; and the Fabians, not the Benthamites, were to lead the way into the twentieth century. Neither Lowe's intellect nor his imagination was powerful enough to discern such a sequel to the Reform Bill of 1867. It was Disraeli's vision, conditioned by tradition as well as by calculation, which was to prove more sensitive to the claims of the future.

CHAPTER TEN

Benjamin Disraeli and the Leap in the Dark

What an unknown world we are to enter. .... If the gentry will take their part they will be adopted as leaders. If we are left to demagogues, God help us!

GATHORNE HARDY

I

When Benjamin Disraeli, Earl of Beaconsfield, died in 1881, the French newspaper *Débats* remarked that both in office and in opposition he had stood out as 'the most trusted representative, the staunchest champion of that non-exclusive Toryism which has known how to modify and transform itself daily, and which has enabled the aristocracy of England to remain Liberal without ceasing to be Conservative.'

Disraeli would have welcomed such a Continental verdict, for he always liked to consider his career as an English statesman against a European background. Unembarrassed by English prejudices, he understood them sufficiently well to know how to exploit them in others; cool and detached in his own calculations, he discovered the secret of inspiring enthusiasm in his followers. His aim was to educate 'his party', and the first lesson he taught was that the party could not hold together on the principle of stubborn resistance against the spirit of the age. Change was the order of the day. Conservatives had to accept the necessity for change and to adapt their tactics accordingly – attacking, defending, snatching advantages, and chasing opportunities as occasion demanded. Conservatism could survive only if it considered something more than conservation. The historic past was alive, but it was also dead. After the second Reform Bill of 1867 had been attacked by both the Whig *Edinburgh Review* and the Tory *Quarterly Review*, the two great organs of traditional English politics, Disraeli compared them to two old-fashioned rival posting-houses. They had each described his policy as dangerous, revolutionary, and precipitate. So, said he, 'you may behold the ostler at the Blue Lion and the chambermaid at the King's Arms, though bitter rivals in the bygone epoch of coaches and post-horses, making up their quarrels and condoling together in the street over their common enemy the railroad.'

Intelligence and dexterity allied with creative imagination formed an unusual blend of qualities in an English party leader. Disraeli was as much of a 'mystery man' to many of his own supporters as he was to Gladstone and Bright. He had made his debut in English politics in 1832 at the age of twenty-eight as a romantic dandy flirting with radicalism; after more than thirty years of striving, he still remained a 'stranger' to many of his mid-Victorian contemporaries. The radicalism had blossomed out into Toryism, but it was a Toryism of imaginative opportunism rather than principle, an opportunism which mystified and shocked. Yet his strength in 1867 lay in his force of character as much as in his intellectual brilliance, for he had risen to be leader of his party in the House of Commons in the teeth of prejudice and without the support of the crowds. Only supreme confidence in himself could have overcome the obstacles which confronted him.

His achievement was the reward of genius and pertinacity, although it did not conform to the texts and homilies either of *Self-Help* or of the Victorian public school. He had been educated first at a small private school at Walthamstow, managed by a Unitarian, and then at home in a rich Jewish household. Neither setting had much in common with Arnold's Rugby. Two of the heroes of his novels, Contarini Fleming and Vivian Grey, fight and thrash the biggest boy in their schools, but they hardly do it in the spirit of *Tom Brown's School Days*. Disraeli believed not in thrift but in destiny, 'in that destiny before which the ancients bowed'. The stars, he knew, were with him in his adventures; by 1867 he had lived long enough to see his impossible wishes come true.

It was Disraeli's individual contribution to the history of

mid-Victorian England to carry the Reform Bill, which, after years of detached debate, finally gave the vote to the working classes of the towns. He carried the bill not as a Radical but as a Conservative, showing a willingness in the process to go further even than John Bright in his acceptance of the need for remodelling the constitution. One of the brilliant satirical magazines of the period, the *Tomahawk*, coupled the names of Bright and Disraeli in an imaginary letter from Bright to Disraeli written after the bill had passed the Commons: 'We have had a very hard struggle to carry our Bill,' Bright is made to say, 'and as it left the Commons, spite of one or two blemishes, it promised to effect our object by transferring power from the hands of those who may be clever enough to see through us, to the hands of those who are sure to take us at our own valuation.' Other writers saw Disraeli merely as the putative father of the bill, Bright as the real one. 'This offspring is a stolen child,' exclaimed Bernal Osborne, one of the political wits of 1867. 'The right hon. gentleman has stolen it, and then, as the *School for Scandal* has it, he has treated it as the gipsies do stolen children – he has disfigured it to make it pass for his own. But the real author of this Bill is ... the Member for Birmingham.'

For those who view English history through Radical eyes the granting of the suffrage to urban artisans in 1867 was the great landmark in the making of modern democracy. But for Disraeli, too, the Reform Bill was a dazzling personal triumph. He had carried Conservative supporters with him in passing a reform bill which changed the whole political atmosphere in England. After twenty years of struggle as one of the leaders of a minority party after the repeal of the Corn Laws, he felt the full excitement of riding on the crest of the parliamentary wave. 'For him,' as Herbert Paul aptly said, 'the supreme test of human affairs was success.' The material results of victories were less satisfying than the simple pleasure of having succeeded. 'It was not his Bill (as it finally passed), but it had passed, and he, not his adversaries, sat upon the Treasury Bench. "Sing, riding's a joy! For me, I ride."'

Disraeli's victory was all the more exciting because it was gained against heavy odds. The Conservatives were in a minority in the House of Commons. If all the opposition groups had voted against them, they would have been defeated by about seventy votes. Clever tactics were necessary to keep the Liberal party divided and the Conservative party united. In a Parliament which cared little for party discipline the situation was always strategically open, and, if Disraeli had not been a master-strategist, no Conservative Reform Bill could have been passed.

The secret of his success lay in his intimate knowledge of the House of Commons and the procedures it followed. He was, as Froude has said, 'a child of Parliament'. It was Parliament and the confidence of Parliament which gave him his place in the state. He handled Parliament far more effectively in 1867 than Sir Robert Peel had handled it in 1846. Although dissident Tories complained that he was re-enacting the great betrayal of 1846, they were unable to exploit the situation as he himself had exploited circumstances twenty-one years before. He was always in control, even when he seemed to be most dependent upon the Radicals.

The Reform Bill which was eventually carried was the half-accidental result of the balance of forces in the House. It could not have been passed in a House dominated by the 'monolithic' party blocs of the twentieth-century English system of government. No single member of Parliament in February 1867, including the party leaders themselves, could have prophesied the final collective result. Disraeli, however, insured his own control of events by approaching the question of reform in an ingenious way. He wanted at all costs to maintain political power for the Conservative government. He did not want to try to dictate a settlement; rather he was prepared to allow the House of Commons considerable freedom to do what it wished. There was only one proviso: initiative should not pass from him to the Liberal party.

Maintaining control was made far easier by the way in which he framed his own bill. In its origins it was not a democratic measure. Two criteria of reform were laid down – household suffrage, based on personal payment of rates to the local authority, and, to prevent it from being too revolutionary, necessary constitutional guarantees on which the extension of the suffrage was dependent, such as special franchises for privileged groups and dual voting. The Liberal party was confronted with serious tactical dilemmas when it considered the Conservative proposals. The Radicals wanted to scrap the guaranties; the Adullamites wanted to scrap both guaranties and household suffrage. The moderates did not want the guaranties, but they did not want complete household suffrage either – that is, what would be left if the guaranties were withdrawn. With such divided aims, the Liberals were in no mood to accept leadership from Gladstone or from anyone else. Tactics became more difficult to evolve than principles were to defend, particularly when choices were offered not between the simple alternatives of good or bad but among complicated preferences for various goods and evils. Disraeli split his opponents from the moment he introduced his bill, and he had the Machiavellian advantage over them that he never needed to concern himself unduly about the relationship between tactics and principles. By introducing distinctions which few of his opponents accepted, like that between personal rating and rate-compounding (the former, paying rates direct to the local authority, and the latter, paying them as a weekly supplement to the landlord's rent), he confused his enemies in their purposes and made them fight not against him but among one another. The one clear line which they might have taken – to unite in throwing out his bill and substituting a measure of their own – was barred by the knowledge of the failure of Russell and Gladstone's bill in 1866.

2

When Russell and Gladstone were defeated in 1866 and the opposition leaders, Derby and Disraeli, took their places, it was agreed that the reform issue could not be shelved for long. At first Derby, the Prime Minister, refused to commit himself and said that he would only proceed if he could find a course of action which would command general support; but it was not long before several Conservatives expressed their interest in a settlement of the question. The Queen, too, was clear that a new reform bill was necessary. 'If the question of Reform be not taken up in earnest by her Ministers with a view to its settlement,' she wrote to Derby in October 1866, 'very serious consequences might ensue.'

In the autumn of 1866 Disraeli was far less convinced of the urgent need for reform than some of his colleagues. When Derby wrote in December that he was reluctantly coming to believe that 'we shall have to deal with the question of Reform', Disraeli replied that 'observation and reflection have not yet brought me to your conclusion as to the necessity of bringing in a Bill for Parliamentary Reform, but I hope I say this with becoming diffidence'. Derby continued to press – 'we must deal with it, and that immediately' – but down to the end of 1866 Disraeli was anxious to postpone rather than force the issue.

His change of mind came when he appreciated the extent of parliamentary and extra-parliamentary support for a new reform bill. The apathy of the previous year had been blown away both in the Commons and in the country, and Disraeli formed a revised estimate of the state of opinion. 'He would not admit in the autumn,' wrote Buckle, 'that the success of the agitation which Bright was conducting showed that the country had determined to obtain Reform; but by January he found the evidence conclusive.' By January 1867 he had become convinced that the right procedure for his party to adopt was not to set up a royal commission on the subject, which would have delayed the passing of legislation, but to introduce general resolutions on reform and eventually a comprehensive reform bill. In making his new assessment, he was as strongly influenced by reports from the provinces as by first-hand evidence from the campaign of the Reform League in the capital. The economic situation favoured a sharp spasm of political radicalism, and 'the people' were showing 'in an unmistakable manner that the Reform issue be trifled with no longer'. The more active public opinion became, the more tempted was Disraeli to resort to a policy of parliamentary opportunism.

The Queen's speech, drafted for her by the government, at the opening of the February session of Parliament forecast measures which, 'without unduly disturbing the balance of political power, shall freely extend the elective franchise'; it was followed up six days later by the government's introduction of general resolutions on the need for reform. The resolutions were extremely general. They included, for instance, as the first clause, 'The number of electors for counties and boroughs in England and Wales ought to be increased,' and, as the ninth clause, the delightfully vague suggestion that 'it is expedient that provision be made for the better prevention of bribery and corruption at elections'. The resolutions were deliberately general; they were designed not to illuminate but to conceal. Pious platitudes were all that a divided cabinet could agree upon. 'I think resolutions are only safe as long as they are general,' wrote Cranborne, one of the opponents of reform within the Conservative government. Behind the scenes there was a widening difference of opinion between those Conservatives who wanted at most a 'small' reform bill and those who wanted a comprehensive 'great plan', as Disraeli was already beginning to conceive it. Only the resolutions could reconcile irreconcilable opinions.

The House of Commons as a whole wanted something more substantial than vapid generalizations. Gladstone, Bright, and Lowe agreed that it was essential for the Conservatives to declare their real intentions. Lowe hoped that he would then be able to trounce them; Bright, that he could advocate in their place 'a substantial and satisfactory Bill'; and Gladstone, that he could hold the Liberals together as a party whatever was proposed. 'The crisis is serious,' wrote Lord John Russell. 'We must allow no peace to the dishonest, fraudulent attempt to shut England out of good Government.' Already, however, some Liberal tacticians were beginning to realize that the real danger of the future lay not in milk-and-water Conservative proposals but in an all-out attempt to carry a comprehensive bill which would go much further than the Liberal bill of 1866 itself. The only bill that the Conservatives would be capable of carrying would, as Gladstone put it, 'be larger and not smaller, than would have been, or even would be, accepted from us.'

Lowe and Bright, for opposite reasons, wished to vote against the Conservative resolutions. Lowe was irritated that Derby, who had defeated the moderate Liberal measure of reform in 1866 with the support of the Adullamites, was now preparing to introduce a reform bill of his own; Bright was suspicious of Conservative intentions, believing that the administration was 'bitterly hostile to Reform' and anxious 'to murder the cause and the question by a course contrary to Parliamentary usage and odious in the sight of all honest men'. The moderate Liberals, who did not share the extreme feelings of either Bright or Lowe, were not anxious to launch a frontal attack on the resolutions; they preferred to bide their time until the government announced details of their proposed bill.

If the tactics of the moderates had been defeated within the divided Liberal party in February 1867, and a conjunction of Adullamites and Radicals had joined the moderates in attacking the government from the start, Disraeli would have had no chance of introducing a comprehensive bill. Tory democracy would have been stifled at its birth. But, of course, his strength, as he himself well knew, lay in the weakness of the Liberal party.

Before he could introduce a comprehensive reform bill, he had to compose the differences within his own party. Some Conservatives, particularly General Peel, the brother of Sir Robert Peel, refused to accept any increase in the number of artisan voters, even the granting of the franchise to selected working-class groups with educational or property qualifications. Others, while prepared to accept 'fancy franchises', were not prepared to consider any changes which would produce democratic domination in a large number of constituencies. Working agreement was reached within the government however, on 23 February, on the basis of carefully prepared electoral statistics, and the cabinet decided that Disraeli should introduce a 'large' reform bill two days later.

During the week-end of the twenty-third to the twenty-fifth more than one member of the cabinet spent a miserable arithmetical Sunday making precise calculations of what the government's proposals implied. Three influential ministers were not satisfied with the answers to their sums. On the morning of the twenty-fifth Disraeli received a note from Derby, written at 8.45 A.M., telling him that Cranborne, Carnavon, and Peel were strongly opposed to the bill and were threatening to resign. 'Utter ruin,' added Derby. 'What on earth are we to do?'

'Stabbing in the back,' commented Disraeli. But he was not too wounded to act. A hastily summoned cabinet, which could not be collected until the early afternoon, decided in ten minutes to maintain unity by reverting to a small bill instead of the large one. Disraeli went down quickly to the House of Commons and introduced a measure completely different from that which he had planned to introduce less than twelve hours previously. He had found it necessary to be an opportunist in relation to his party as well as to the opposition.

The measure which he introduced provided for a six-pound rating franchise in the boroughs, designed to add 130,000 voters to the list; four new fancy franchises, based on education, savings-bank deposits, investment in the public funds, and amount paid in taxation; and a twenty-pound rating franchise in the counties. In all, 400,000 new voters would be added to the electorate.

Bright, Lowe, and Gladstone all poured scorn on these proposals, and those Liberals who were neither Adullamites nor Radicals agreed that they would now oppose the reform resolutions when they were to be discussed the following week.

Disraeli realized that there was little point either in attempting to press the resolutions or in pushing the small bill. Backed by many members within his own party, he decided instead to reintroduce the large measure. 'All I hear and observe,' he wrote to Derby on 28 February, 'more and more convinces me that the bold line is the safer one, and, moreover, that it will be successful.' Derby agreed, although it was known that, if the large bill were reintroduced, Cranborne, Carnavon, and

Peel would resign from the government. On 2 March they did resign. Reform now seemed to be more important than party, though Derby, like Disraeli, was aware that few members of the Conservative party were likely to follow an anti-reform line. Most of them shared the opinion of Gathorne Hardy, 'Lord Derby is to be pitied, but feels it a profound duty to the Queen to go on, and I for one will go with him.' The vacancies in the cabinet were filled by the promotion of three ministers to higher posts and by the introduction of three new men to cabinet rank.

The way was now prepared for Derby's and Disraeli's ideas and tactics to go forward without fear of cabinet division. A few days after Cranborne's resignation, his wife met Derby at a party. 'Is Robert still doing his sums?' asked the Prime Minister.

'Yes,' replied Lady Cranborne, 'and he has reached rather a curious result – take three from fifteen, and nothing remains.' Her repartee was more effective than her judgement. In the exercise in power politics which was about to begin, the government was strengthened rather than weakened by the loss of three men of rigid principle. Take three from fifteen, and anything was possible, even the spectacle of a Conservative administration carrying a Radical measure. It was not long before Cranborne was commenting rather wearily that he wished Gladstone's safe and conservative Reform Bill of 1866 had been carried. 'I sometimes hear the Bill of last year mentioned with a feeling of regret and perhaps something like penitence,' he wrote, 'for I feel that if we had accepted that offer, though perhaps I might not have been standing on this side of the House . . . the prospects of the British constitution would have been a good deal brighter than they are now.'

A Radical reform bill, however, was the end and not the beginning of the story. The second bill which was introduced by Disraeli on 18 March, while comprehensive in character and designed to establish the House 'on a broad, popular basis', was still not an experiment in democracy. Like the small bill of February, it included checks and counterpoises and suggested no extensive redistribution of seats. The franchise in the boroughs was to be based on personal rating. All householders paying their own rates and possessing a residential qualification of two years were to be given votes. Lodgers and those ratepayers who compounded their rates along with their weekly rents were not to be given votes. The county franchise was to be lowered from a rental qualification of fifty pounds to a rating qualification of fifteen pounds. Special franchises were to be introduced for particular groups. Graduation from a university; fifty pounds in the funds, the Bank of England, or a savings bank; and membership of a learned profession were also to confer the right of voting. Two hundred thousand additional people were to be enfranchised who paid twenty shillings a year or more in direct taxes. Dual votes were to be conferred on those individuals who possessed special as well as property qualifications.

Disraeli claimed that 237,000 urban ratepayers would get the vote for the first time, 100,000 belonging to the specially privileged groups, and another 171,000 in the counties. In addition, the twenty-shilling direct taxation franchise would give about 200,000 members of the middle classes a second vote. The final result of the passing of the bill would be a new social balance within the electorate, which would insure a fair and stable settlement. No class would be preponderant; representation would rest with the nation. One quarter of the voting power would belong to the aristocracy, one quarter to the working classes, and the remaining half to the middle classes. Parliament would not become a mere representative assembly based on the brute force of number; it would mirror social interests and at the same time ensure the continuation of good government.

3

From this bare outline of events and proposals, some of the reasons why Derby and Disraeli produced a reform bill can be deduced. One reason was pressure from outside, a subsidiary factor but an important one in determining the timing of events Disraeli's conversion to the belief that a reform bill was urgently necessary was influenced by statements made to him by his friends concerning 'the unanimity with which all classes ... desire a Reform Bill – from Lord Shaftesbury to the Shropshire rustic'. The Reform League too was sufficiently influential for some writers to claim that the Hyde Park rioters really carried the Reform Bill of 1867 just as the Birmingham Political Union carried the Reform Bill of 1832.

More important than external pressure was the desire of the Conservative leaders to secure a comprehensive settlement. Reform had been toyed with for many years; it now seemed possible at last to get the issue out of the way. Conservatives like Lord Malmesbury believed that the boldest course was the safest and that it was preferable to follow a line of action which would be simple and direct, not 'complicated, invidious, and incomplete'. Settlement of the question appealed, indeed, as Lady Gwendolen Cecil has written, to all types of politician – 'to the easy-going man who wanted quiet times and a safe seat, to the indifferent man who was bored to exasperation by the prolonged controversy, to the earnest-minded man who saw in its continuance a bar to all useful legislation'. Party leaders, 'accustomed to measure the forces at their command', were beginning to recognize that, if they did not carry reform, their successors certainly would. They were anxious to secure credit while credit was good, and to prevent their rivals from capitalizing on what was now beginning to be recognized by ambitious politicians on all sides as an inevitable development.

But there was more to the motives of Derby and Disraeli than the attempt 'to dish the Whigs', or, as Disraeli put it, 'to terminate the monopoly of Liberalism'. They were fascinated by the thought of comprehensive reform for its own sake. In this there was more consistency in their position than has sometimes been conceded. Derby, as Lord Stanley, had helped to draft the Reform Bill of 1832; he had stood out in Parliament at that time as the 'Prince Rupert of debate'; he had displayed great sympathy for the poor of the London slums; during the cotton famine he had shown great solicitude for the Lancashire artisans; and in 1864 he had rubbed elbows with Garibaldi. Finally, as George Saintsbury put it, 'in addition to a genuine wish to get the question done with and out of the way, a little of the *après moi le déluge* feeling entered into his motives. There was to the last a great deal of boyishness in Lord Derby; and this boyishness took, among other forms, the form of being ready to act in a sort of "here goes" and "in for a penny in for a pound" spirit.' It was he who wrote, when he had made up his mind to introduce a new bill, 'of all possible hares to start, I do not know a better than the extension to household suffrage'. As for Disraeli himself, in addition to delight in mischief ('*Schadenfreude*', Carlyle called it), there was a remarkable continuity in his ideas on reform – a continuity which was only broken sharply on one occasion, during the debates on Gladstone's Reform Bill of 1866.

The nature of his continuity can best be discerned in a volume of his speeches which he published in January 1867, under the title *Speeches on Parliamentary Reform*. The volume was designed as propaganda to demonstrate the facts of Disraeli's career as a reformer. It was 'a complete and consistent record' the editor wrote; it would enable the country to see 'with what justness it has been asserted that the Tory party are disqualified from dealing with the most difficult of modern political questions', that of reform.

When the propaganda element is discounted, the speeches speak for themselves. As early as April 1851 Disraeli protested against 'what is popularly understood as the principle of finality', the unwillingness to tamper with the act of 1832. In 1852 he stated that he had always been in favour of extending the suffrage to include more sections of the working classes. In the same year, while attacking universal suffrage and constant tampering with the constitution, he was prepared to consider sympathetically the claims of non-electors. In 1854 he opposed Russell's Reform Bill on the grounds that, since the country was faced with war, it should not make war on itself, but he added that 'you can never obtain such a change as you desire until the great preponderance of public opinion demands it'. Three years later at Aylesbury, he condemned 'bit-by-bit reform' and indicated his preference for 'a complete measure'. 'A bold and decided course' would put the Conservative party on its legs and 'greatly help the country, and secure the State'.

In 1858, summing up the various attempts at reform down to that date, he claimed that, from the moment that Lord John Russell and many of the Whigs abandoned finality, he too, and the Conservative party with him, 'held ourselves free to consider the question of Parliamentary Reform upon its merits'. If any future plan were brought forward to change the parliamentary constitution of this country, 'we were open to offer those suggestions which, to our minds, might appear to lead to a settlement most conducive to the public weal'.

The Conservative minority government of 1858–9 introduced a reform bill after considerable discussion as to whether it should be large or moderate. 'Our fear,' wrote the Whig *Edinburgh Review*, 'is that, like new converts, they may propose wild and fantastic measures intended to captivate the tastes of the uneducated classes, and though Conservative in name, they become destructive in reality.' In bringing his bill before the Commons, Disraeli vindicated the right of the Conservative party to deal with a subject 'which touches the interests of all classes and all individuals, and in the wise and proper settlement of which the very destiny of this country is concerned.' Although the bill proposed 'fancy franchises', it equalized voting conditions in town and country (a reform not achieved until 1884) and set out to be 'a conclusive settlement', not a mere parcel of palliatives. Disraeli even talked, in language later picked up by Gladstone, of opening avenues to the mechanic 'whose virtue, prudence, intelligence, and frugality entitle him to enter into the privileged pale of the constituent body of the country'. He insisted, however, that mechanics should enter the pale as individuals and not as a multitude, otherwise they would become the predominant class, swamping the rest. When Bright protested against 'fancy franchises', Disraeli retaliated that alliteration was not an argument in legislation but 'a very popular form of language among savages'. He underlined the right of the Conservatives to change the constitution just as much as the Whigs or the Radicals. All parties had their share in 'the pedigree of progress'. The same arguments he reiterated in 1865 in the debates on Baines's bill: 'It has always been clear,' Disraeli said, 'that if you deal with the subject popularly called Parliamentary Reform, you must deal with it comprehensively.'

These speeches taken as a whole suggest, first, a refusal to leave reform to the Whigs or to the Radicals; second, a willingness to accept a substantial measure of reform; and, third, a hankering after a comprehensive settlement. The comprehensive settlement, Disraeli believed, would not be incompatible with Toryism. Indeed, reform would produce its best results if it were fitted into a Tory context. Disraeli's speeches reflect his political calculations and are best considered as forensic orations of a leading counsel, but his imagination was engaged as well as his reasoning when he talked of an extension of the suffrage. He had begun life as a Radical, and in the famous *Runnymede Letters* of 1835 and the *Spirit of Whiggism* of 1836 he maintained with great force that Toryism was the really democratic political philosophy of the English people; the word 'democratic' was not considered in these studies, as it was in 1867, as a bogy word but as the opposite of his own bogy word 'oligarchic'. Liberties and rights, he claimed, were preserved not by revolutionary parties and radical republicans but by historic institutions and traditions. The monarchy of the Tories was more democratic than the republic of the Whigs; it recognized the nexus of rights and duties. An extension of the suffrage could not by itself sever the ties of a highly integrated society. Even if constitutional arrangements were changed, the social system was a guaranty of national stability. 'I do not believe,' he argued, 'that any scheme of the suffrage, or any method of election, could divert [the power of England's natural aristocracy] into other quarters. It is the necessary consequence of our present social state. I believe the wider the popular suffrage, the more powerful would be the natural aristocracy. This seems to me an inevitable consequence, but I admit this proposition on the clear understanding that such an extension be established on a fair, and not a factious basis.'

This line of argument, totally opposed to that of Lowe, Disraeli abandoned only once, in 1866, when he made his most conventional Conservative speeches against reform, probably for strictly party reasons, to help defeat Gladstone. By 1867 he had returned to his instinctive position, and seven years later he reflected that his zeal for Tory democracy had served as the consistent element in all his work: 'I have for forty years been labouring to replace the Tory Party in their natural and historic position in the country.'

Instinct and imagination were as strong with Disraeli as was calculation, though it is difficult to disentangle the operations of the three different forces. It may have been either instinct or calculation which accounted for Disraeli's curious friendship with John Bright in the 1850s and 1860s. Although their political positions were far apart, their personal relations were good. The dandified Tory in a bright waistcoat and the quiet Quaker in a broad-brimmed hat often shared confidences with each other. During the Crimean War they were on very friendly terms; even in 1867, when Bright believed that Disraeli was merely using the reform question to cling to power, he did not turn against him. In a conversation in the spring of 1867 Disraeli recalled to Bright that earlier talk they had had in 1852 when they had both objected to 'Whig deception' in government. He went on to describe his approach to reform. 'He said he did not care much for the counties: the Working-Class Question was the real question, and that was the thing that demanded to be settled.' Bright promised Disraeli that he would not indulge in factious opposition. 'I told him,' he recorded in his *Diary*, 'that people said that he and I always fought with gloves on, but sometimes I had been tempted to take them off.' He replied that there had 'always been something of sympathy between us,' which, added Bright, 'I suppose is true – tho' our course and aims have seemed so different. . . . As we were talking Mr Brand, the Opposition Whip, went by, and Disraeli said, "He will think it is a Coalition" – that he and I should be seen in conversation in such a crisis as this. At parting, he pressed my hand with an apparent earnestness of feeling, saying, "Well, whatever happens, you and I will always be friends."'

Bright was always a friendly foe; Lowe was unpalatable even as a friend. Disraeli's estimate of the two personalities and the causes they represented influenced his attitudes in 1866 and 1867; it made him averse to any combination with the Whigs or the Adullamites and tempted him, even before he saw the full possibilities, to go all out for a major resettlement.

4

The nature of the ultimate re-settlement was very different from that envisaged by the Conservative party in March 1867. In the course of the debates on reform between March and July, the Conservative Reform Bill was totally transformed. A series of amendments was carried which not only swept away the original safeguards but deliberately shifted the whole balance of political power in Britain.

The reason for the transformation was the parliamentary confusion in the House of Commons. The Liberals became so divided on tactics that it was possible for Disraeli to win votes, as Bernal Osborne pointed out, by the unsportsman-like practice of cross-fishing, by which both sides of the stream were swept, and fish attracted from every direction by a display of different coloured baits.

Tactical dilemmas made it necessary for the parties to hold frequent meetings either inside the House of Commons or in the houses of their leaders. So frequent did these meetings become that one Whig critic, Homersham Cox, the first historian of the reform bills of 1866 and 1867, believed that the dignity and independence of the House as a whole was being undermined.

Disraeli was willing to take the risk of dislocating his own party if he could further disorganize his antagonists in the process. The task of disorganizing them was not difficult. Lowe and Bright both wished to oppose the second reading: Lowe, because the leaders of the government were 'by the contagion of their own immorality, breaking up and democratizing everything around them'; Bright, because they were not democratizing enough. Gladstone, as parliamentary leader of the opposition, attempted to lay down a party line which would satisfy both sides. He wanted to restrict the franchise to exclude those ratepayers who were paying less than five pounds a year in rates but at the same time to enfranchise every householder above this line, whether he paid personal rates or compounded his rates through his landlord. In suggesting this 'compromise', he succeeded in satisfying neither Radicals nor Adullamites, although Bright, who shared his distrust of the 'dregs of the working classes', the residuum, came to his support. Opposition to Gladstone ranged from murmuring and scuffling of feet at party meetings to voting with Conservatives in the lobbies. 'I can hardly speak a word in the Commons,' Gladstone wrote in March, 'especially if it in any manner oppose or reflect on Disraeli with any confidence that some man will not rise on the Liberal side to protest against it. It is an almost unexampled position – a party of vast strength is completely paralysed by internal dissension. But for myself I think the best course is to avoid all acts of leadership which can be dispensed with.'

Ten days later he forgot the 'best course' and made an attempt to lead the party by suggesting that an amendment should be introduced embodying his own notions concerning both suffrage restriction and compounding. Forty or fifty Liberal members of Parliament, meeting in the tearoom of the House of Commons, decided to oppose him. They included a sprinkling of Adullamites, led by Lord Elcho; a Radical group, led by Henry Fawcett, the blind member for Brighton and professor of political economy at Cambridge; and several Russell Whigs who 'cannot bear Gladstone as their Leader'. The motives of the tearoom group were very mixed. Lord Elcho claimed in a letter to Cranborne that 'it is composed of men acting with the fear of a coming democracy and Trades Union tyranny before their eyes'; Fawcett had only one aim, 'to get the largest measure of reform, whether it should come from the hands of the Government or from the Opposition'. Disunited though they were in principles, the tearoom group were united in dislike of Gladstone's tactics, and they forced him to withdraw his proposal to introduce a party amendment to Disraeli's bill. This was the first real breach in the defences of the opposition.

Having failed to carry the party with him, Gladstone proceeded to act on his own. He proposed an amendment in committee to admit the compound householder as well as the personal ratepayer to the franchise. It was generally known that he wished to change the franchise along these lines only if it were also restricted along other lines; and, consequently, he was able to secure the support of some dissident Conservatives who did not like reform at all. Private preferences were very difficult to sort out at this stage, and the lines of party division were very confused. Disraeli was in a position to exploit the divisions to the utmost. In a speech which he himself described as 'marvellous and memorable' he broke through the ranks of his enemies. Although 7 Conservatives voted with Gladstone, his amendment was defeated by 310 votes to 289; 45 Liberals voted against their party leaders – 25 Adullamites, 12 Radicals, and 8 members of the tearoom party – and nearly 20 others abstained. The result of the division was 'a smash perhaps without example', and the House immediately adjourned for the Easter recess with Disraeli the master of the situation. It was being freely said in the lobbies that he 'would hold Gladstone down for twenty years'.

It now seemed certain, as Disraeli put it, that reform could be carried 'in a canter'. 'There are no doubt breakers ahead,' he wrote, 'but I feel great hope of our overcoming them, and of realizing the dream of my life, and re-establishing Toryism on a national foundation.' After the Easter recess, however, it was the Radicals who took control of the situation. They succeeded with little difficulty in carrying amendment after amendment against the government. During the process of revision the Reform Bill took on an entirely new shape.

Their first amendment, proposed by the Radical member for Tower Hamlets, the great London constituency, reduced the period of residential qualification for voters from two years to one. Disraeli opposed the amendment, but was beaten by 81 votes. The following night he announced that the government had decided to accept the change.

A second amendment, proposed by the Radical member for a second London seat, Finsbury, extended the borough franchise to lodgers who had occupied rooms for the whole of the preceding twelve months. The amendment was not put to the vote, for Disraeli at once accepted it. At this stage he did not very much care what particular Radical clauses were passed; what was important was that a bill of some kind should go through while a Conservative government was in power. At the very moment when Conservative speakers in the Commons were attacking the principle of offering the franchise to every 'migratory sojourner in a borough', Disraeli was writing flippantly to Stanley: 'I wish, in the intervals of settling the affairs of Europe, you would get up an anti-lodger speech or a speech on the subject either way; as I think our debates want a little variety.'

The third Radical amendment was far more important than the other two. A Newark solicitor, Hodgkinson, proposed an amendment which abolished the distinction between compound householders and personal ratepayers altogether within the boundaries of parliamentary boroughs. The technical question of compound rating had been discussed in the House of Commons for many weeks, and on more than one occasion the House had refused to give the vote to compound ratepayers. The question was of great practical importance, since there were nearly a half-million compounders in England and Wales, comprising thirty-five per cent of the total number of householders. The frequency of compounding (i.e., paying rates to the local authority not directly but through the landlord) varied very much from place to place. In Brighton, for instance, where there was a great deal of compounding, only fourteen new electors would have been added to the electorate on the basis of Disraeli's personal rating proposal, whereas in Sheffield, where almost all tenants paid their own rates, the whole body of householders would have been granted the vote. Disraeli tried to justify this variety of franchises, but Liberals as a whole disliked patent inequalities founded on accident rather than principle. It was, however, difficult for them to know what to do. They did not accept the distinction between personal ratepaying and compound ratepaying as a proper test of fitness for political power; many of them would have preferred, as did Gladstone and Bright, a division between ratepayers of all types based on the amount of rates paid, to a division between different categories of ratepayers. But to admit this would have meant challenging Disraeli's slogan of 'household suffrage'. The government was, as Gladstone admitted, 'bowling us over by the force of the phrase'.

Hodgkinson's amendment provided a way out for the Liberals. The mover himself thought that it would be defeated by about a hundred votes. Instead, to the astonishment of a small House, Disraeli accepted it; three hundred thousand new voters were added to the franchise as a result of its passing. The worst fears of Lowe were realized. The Conservatives were making a desperate attempt to win the support of Demos. Power was being transferred, as Cranborne pointed out, to 'those who have no other property than the labour of their hands. The omnipotence of Parliament is theirs.'

Hodgkinson became 'immortal', as Argyll put it, as a result of his success. His amendment virtually established complete and unlimited household suffrage as the foundation of the borough franchise in England and Wales. The concession of the lodger franchise, the abolition of compounding restrictions, and the cutting-down of the period of residential qualification opened the borough franchise so wide that the fancy franchises lost all their point. Practically everyone who might have qualified in terms of a fancy franchise now qualified in any case. Unostentatiously, therefore, Disraeli eliminated all the fancy franchise clauses which provided a link with his earlier efforts at reform. The bill in its new form went further than any bill which Bright had ever sought to introduce.

But there was more to come. The conditions of the franchise had been radically altered; so too were the clauses relating to distribution of seats. In the past the Conservatives had always held firm on this question and had refused to increase the representation of the cities and large populous districts in the House of Commons. But notions of balance were cast on one side in May and June 1867. Samuel Laing, an independent Liberal who had supported the Adullamites, proposed a more drastic scheme of redistribution than any the government had brought forward. He moved to increase the number of boroughs to be redistributed to thirty-eight by taking away one member from boroughs with an electorate of less than 10,000, instead of 7,000 as the government suggested. The extra seats gained were to be handed over in the form of second members for towns of over 50,000. Despite the opposition of Disraeli, Laing's amendment was carried by the large majority of 127 votes, 72 Conservatives voting with Laing against the government. The process of educating the Conservative party in the political facts of life had clearly gone a very long way. Although Radical amendments to disfranchise all boroughs with a population of less than 5,000 were defeated – with Liberal help – and a new clause providing a third member for large cities was lost by 8 votes, Disraeli made a backstairs compromise by offering third members to Liverpool, Manchester, Birmingham, and Leeds. It was this unsavoury 'surrender' which bestirred General Peel to comment that the proceedings on the bill had taught him three things – that nothing had so little vitality as 'a vital point'; that nothing was so insecure as 'a security'; and that nothing was so elastic as the conscience of a cabinet minister.

The bill, as it finally emerged from the Commons in July, was thus different at almost every point from the bill as it was first introduced. It was far more democratic than Disraeli, or, indeed, most of his opponents, had ever intended. Yet for Disraeli himself its passing was a parliamentary triumph of the highest order. A minority government had smashed the opposition and had carried its reform bill against all the expectations of its enemies; the greatest joy of the victory was the consciousness of an opponent outwitted and outmanoeuvred. It was not surprising that Bernal Osborne declared that Disraeli was the greatest Radical in the House. It was not surprising either that orthodox Conservatives like Lord Cranborne claimed that the monarchical principle was dead, the aristocratic principle doomed, and the democratic principle triumphant, all because of a 'political betrayal, which had no parallel in our annals, and which had struck at the roots of that Parliamentary confidence upon which alone the strength of our representative system was maintained'.

5

Why were the Conservative backbenchers prepared to accept changes suggested by the Radicals with little opposition and at times with wholehearted concurrence? Three obvious answers stem from the preceding analysis. They shared Disraeli's and Derby's desire to settle the reform question; they felt the exhilaration of the battle and revelled in the buoyant high spirits of the debates; and they were anxious to 'dish the Whigs'. After all, they had been members of a minority party since 1846, and their short-lived share in government had depended upon parliamentary sufferance, not upon public support. In 1867, at the end of the struggle, Derby stated quite frankly, some said cynically, that the intention that had been uppermost in his mind when he took office the previous year had been to avoid at all costs being ousted by the reunited Liberals; his purpose was 'to take such a course as would convert the existing majority [the Liberals] into a practical minority'. He was determined not to be a stopgap, as he had been before in 1852 and 1858, acting as Prime Minister until it suited the Liberal party to forget their dissensions and bring forward a reform bill which would oust him from office and place them in power.

Derby's strong feelings on this subject provided a guaranty that, once reform had been introduced, it would not be abandoned. Many of the rank-and-file members of his party felt the same way, and in their case feelings were intensified by fear of a dissolution of Parliament. When Derby first told his supporters of the nature of the reform bill he proposed to introduce, he added that if its central provisions were rejected, the government would dissolve. Such a penal dissolution would mean that every member who voted against the government would, if his cause succeeded, subject himself to a fine of several hundred pounds. It is not surprising that representative rural Tories, including some who, like Henley, had refused to support the bill of 1859, rallied to the government.

Fear of a dissolution was real, but the positive drive for

reform came from the enthusiasm generated by Disraeli's handling of the question, particularly in the vital stage before 'the Conservative surrender' after the Easter recess. It was then that Disraeli played upon dislike of Gladstone with such consummate skill that he made most of his backbenchers share his delight in dividing the Liberal party. His outstanding speech just before the Easter recess, which was largely responsible for the bill continuing to go through, was described by Stanley as 'one of the best you have ever made. . . . It has pleased all our friends. . . . After our troubles it has come like the warm weather after frost and snow.' Although frequent capitulation to the Radicals after the Easter recess made some of his followers restive, they were by that time in the mood for political education. The mind of Parliament had been prepared; now it was time for action, not purposeful action, but a series of mental jerks, depending upon almost limitless resilience. The better the training, the more convincing was the exercise.

The Conservatives did not make up one single team. There were many different groups in 1867, although most of them used the Carlton Club as a common social and political centre. Most of the ultra-Tories had died or disappeared in the previous ten years, but the biggest group still consisted of those whom Bernal Osborne described as 'the stupid, heavy country gentlemen'. Some of the members of this group were by no means completely well disposed to Disraeli. He was disliked by the ordinary member of Parliament for his reserve and mistrusted by many of them as a Jew and a 'mystery man'. 'They did his bidding' – one of them said in retrospect – 'for the party has always followed its leader, but they hated it; and very many, including myself, felt that there was something like a repetition of Sir R. Peel's betrayal.' That there was no large-scale rebellion was important. Horsman, Lowe's friend, had estimated that forty to fifty Tories would follow Lord Cranborne, but they never did so. There was no 'Cranborne Cave' comparable to the cave of the Adullamites; nor was Cranborne temperamentally suited or of sufficient political experience to play the same part in 1867 which Disraeli had played in 1846.

Bagehot suggested that it was the stupidity of most of the

Tories which insured the success of Disraeli's tactics in 1867. They did not know what was happening. Chancing to visit a purely agricultural and Conservative county, he asked the local Tories, 'Do you understand this Reform Bill? Do you know that your Conservative Government has brought in a Bill far more Radical than any former Bill, and that it is very likely to be passed?'

The answer I got was, 'What stuff you talk! How can it be a Radical Reform Bill? Why, *Bright* opposed it!' There was no answering that in a way in which a 'common jury' could understand. The Bill was supported by *The Times* and opposed by Mr Bright; and therefore the mass of the Conservatives and of common moderate people without distinction of party, had no conception of the effect. They said it was 'London nonsense' if you tried to explain it to them. The nation indeed generally looks to the discussions in Parliament to enlighten it as to the effect of the Bills. But in this case neither party, as a party, could speak out. Many, perhaps most of the intelligent Conservatives, were fearful of the consequences of the proposal; but as it was made by the heads of their own party, they did not like to oppose it, and the discipline of party carried them with it.

There was a very small group of Tories, however, who were prepared to follow the same course of action as Cranborne. They included General Peel, 'whose eye', according to Disraeli, 'lit up with insanity' when the phrase 'household suffrage' was mentioned, and Carnavon, one of the rising hopes of the party. Among backbenchers, men like Sir William Heathcote, the senior member for Oxford University, persisted throughout the debates in arguing that the Reform Bill would destroy the influence of rank, property, and education by increasing the force of numbers. But men like Heathcote and Cranborne were intellectuals of the right, never unduly worried by tactical considerations within the House of Commons or by pressure from their constituents outside. Disraeli had already had to tell Heathcote in 1861 to think more of tactics and less of principles. 'After all, politics is like war – roughish work,' Disraeli had written then; 'we should not be over sensitive.' If the advice was not repeated in 1867, it was because Disraeli knew it would have no effect.

There was a third group of Conservative members of Parliament, distinct from both the country members and the intellectuals – the Conservative members for urban constituencies. It is clear that these men played a not inconsiderable part in the story of the passing of the second Reform Bill. The most important of them was Samuel Robert Graves, the member for Liverpool. Graves, who was a wealthy merchant and shipowner and had been mayor of Liverpool in 1860, saw Disraeli immediately after the government had decided to include a reference to reform in the Queen's speech and expressed delight at the proposals – 'an immense relief to him: only one opinion out of doors: settlement of the question'. Graves was called upon to second the reply to the address in the House of Commons. Throughout 1867 he led a group of Conservative members who were anxious for large-scale redistribution rather than a lowering of the franchise as the basis of comprehensive reform; and it was because of his pressure that Disraeli finally expressed his willingness to grant a third member to Liverpool, Manchester, Birmingham, and Leeds.

Another urban Conservative from the same area was also influential. Laird, the shipbuilder, who sat for Birkenhead, was in close touch with middle-class Conservative interests in Lancashire. So indeed was Derby himself. It has been said that Derby's local leadership during the cotton famine 'had not a little to do with turning Lancashire from one of the most Radical into one of the most Tory districts in England'. After the bill was passed, he welcomed the mass demonstrations in favour of the bill in the cotton areas. Towns like Blackburn and Salford were strong centres of urban conservatism. The pressure of constituency affected the character of the representatives selected. Conservatives were bound to become more 'democratic' when they sat for large towns.

It is difficult to estimate the strength of the urban Conservative group or the extent to which industrial activity influenced the attitudes of Conservative members. Fourteen Conservatives had interests in shipping, three in engineering, seven in metals, and one in building and contracting. Some of these members sat for small boroughs rather than for large cities, and the Graves group was supported throughout by men like Goldney, the member for Chippenham, and Jervis, the member for Harwich. Apparently, the inner core of the group consisted of about twenty-two men, but they were able to win over many county members as well. One hundred and fifty members of Parliament were present at a Conservative meeting held at the end of February, and the majority of them declared in favour of household suffrage with three years' residence and a personal payment of rates. The urban members succeeded in persuading the 'county caucus' present at this meeting that there was little point in preserving a constitution which maintained Whig supremacy in Parliament. As Malmesbury had pointed out as early as 1853, there were grounds for believing that if the five-pound householders were often Radical, the labourers were often Conservative; or, as Dudley Baxter, the electoral statistician, had told Disraeli, 'beer-barrel influence' would be most pronounced if the widest of all plans were adopted.

It was this decision of this meeting which had persuaded Disraeli that 'the bold line is the safer one, and, moreover, that it will be successful'. Throughout the whole reform struggle Disraeli, who had spoken disparagingly only a year earlier of 'the rule of mobs in great towns, and the sway of turbulent multitudes', leaned more and more heavily on the urban Conservative members. The results of the alliance with urban conservatism were not apparent until the end of the 1874 election, although at the general election of 1868, which the Liberals won, nineteen out of the thirty-two Lancashire seats returned Conservatives. In 1874 striking Conservative gains were recorded in great manufacturing towns, such as Manchester, Leeds, Bradford, Oldham, Newcastle-upon-Tyne, Nottingham, Stoke-on-Trent, Wakefield, Wigan, Warrington, Staleybridge, and Northampton, as well as in the large populous London districts such as Chelsea, Greenwich, Marylebone, Southwark, and, most important of all, the vast constituency of Tower Hamlets. The 1874 election showed that it was the

Whigs and not the Tories whose power had been challenged by the extension of the franchise and the redistribution of seats. Pure Whiggery had always survived with difficulty in a smoky atmosphere; now its continued existence came to be almost impossible. The great Whig Clarendon might write slightingly in 1868 that 'a demoralized nation admires the audacity, the tricks, and the success of the Jew'; but, by 1874, new Radicals, like Chamberlain, were as anti-Whig as they were anti-Tory. Probably Derby, who himself knew the vigour and vitality of the Lancashire workingmen's Conservative associations, and followed up the Reform Bill with 'Tory democratic' speeches at Manchester and Liverpool, was as far-sighted as Disraeli in foreseeing the long-term results of 1867.

6

Although the passing of the second Reform Bill was welcomed by most of the Conservatives, including some, like Lord Cairns, who had hitherto attacked all schemes of substantial reform, it was less happily received by influential Conservative sympathizers outside the immediate parliamentary circle. 'The gross hypocrisy', the aged Lord Shaftesbury called the bill. 'With the exception of a very few advanced Democrats, they all detest and fear the measure. But it is a sensual and self-seeking age, they hate trouble, they hate responsibility, they hate to look an evil in the face. "They crown their cups with roses, and their heads with folly and forgetfulness."' It was not the welfare of the realm or the security of national institutions which had prompted the measure but the seeking after place, the omnivorous desire for power and office. 'You practically banish all honourable men from the political arena,' added Cranborne; 'and you will find in the long run that the time will come when your statesmen will become nothing but political adventurers, and professions of opinion will be looked upon only as so many political manoeuvres for the purpose of obtaining office.' 'Derby has set himself to prove that dishonesty is the best policy,' wrote Lord Dalhousie. 'The Reform Bill may be a leap in the dark to him, it is none to me. Where we have lifted the sluices of democracy an inch, he and Dizzy have raised them a foot. My own private hope is that they will be the first to be washed away in the flood.' *Fraser's Magazine* described an incident at the Carlton Club. A message boy with a sense of humour stopped at the doors and asked, 'Is this the Reform Club?'

'No, you rascal,' was the reply, 'the Revolution Club.' Party discipline may compel votes, *Fraser's* concluded; 'it cannot compel conviction, hide regret, or cover shame.'

Writers like the prophet Carlyle and the poet Coventry Patmore were equally enraged. 'Traitorous politicians grasping at votes, even votes from the rabble', had tumbled the country over the precipice. Eighteen-sixty-seven was

> The year of the great crime,
> When the false English nobles, and their Jew,
> By God demented, slew
> The trust they stood twice pledged to keep from wrong.

Carlyle could see no hope for the future. 'Perhaps the sooner such a mass of hypocrisies, universal mismanagements, and brutal platitudes and infidelities ends, if not in some improvement then in death and *finis*, may it not be the better?'

Such profound gloom could not have been produced by an ordinary act of political legerdemain or the most clever political juggling. It emanated from a complete uncertainty about the future. Power was to be transferred 'tamely and miserably' – so it seemed to the critics – from the middle classes to the working classes, from the political *élite* to the masses of the large towns.

Some of the critics, like Shaftesbury, could claim that they knew the towns better than the makers of the act. They could see in them happy hunting grounds for the carpetbagging demagogues and shady corners for the corrupt wire-pullers. The masses themselves would become dangerous not because they were violent but because they were amenable to pressure – the pressure of socialists as well as of plutocrats. Shaftesbury's fears were shared by Lowe and by Bagehot. The extension of the franchise would open the gates to dangerous forces which had previously been kept under control. 'If the first work of the poor voters,' said Bagehot, 'is to try to create a poor man's paradise, as poor men are apt to fancy that paradise, and they are apt to think they can create it, the great political trial now beginning will simply fail. The wide gift of the elective franchise will be a great calamity to the whole nation, and to those who gain it as great a calamity as to any.'

'The leap in the dark,' Derby called the act. But was it not the first of a series of leaps in the dark which might go on for years to come? *Facilis descensus Averni.* 'The appetite for change can never be glutted,' said Cranborne; neither Disraeli not Bright could appease it.

When Mr Bright is preaching moderation and caution, Mr Beales [of the Reform League] will be just girding himself for the battle; and doubtless Mr Beales already numbers among his lieutenants politicians who look upon him as absurdly behind the age. The Girondist always has a Jacobin behind him ready to trip him up.

Behind such gloomy prophecies were the memories of twenty years of political controversy and the very real fears of the working classes. Was it not taking a big risk in 1867 to give the vote to large numbers of workingmen about whose real purposes the leaders of society knew very little? It did not need the icy eloquence of Lowe to emphasize the key importance of this question. As Homersham Cox, the moderate Whig reformer, put it:

The Earl of Derby 'hopes' that all will turn out well. Adventurous gamesters are always hoping for luck; that the right card will be dealt, the right number turn up on the dice, the right horse win. But hitherto it has not been considered good statesmanship to commit the destinies of our empire unreservedly to Fortune. We have been content to advance from precedent to precedent, to pass from the known to the unknown by slow and heedful steps. The policy of political 'leaps' remained to be invented by a government which called itself Conservative.

A period of measured discussion of politics and society had ended in a political gamble.

There were three possible grounds for optimism. The first

was general. Why fear the masses of the people? Working people were just as much entitled to the vote as of right as any other people. They *were* England. How, then, could they do anything against English interests? This democratic argument did not excite even philosophic Radicals like Mill or middle-class Radicals like Bright. Mill was increasingly afraid of the tyranny of majorities and of a 'governing majority of manual labourers' limiting competition in the labour market, taxing or restricting machinery, and protecting the home producer against foreign industry; while Bright feared the enfranchise-ment of a dependent class and was careful not to identify his arguments too closely with those of democracy. Disraeli, the author of the bill, was very careful to insist that democracy was a form of government with which his party had no sym-pathy.

The second ground was based on observation. The working classes were not dangerous or revolutionary; they fitted into the social system rather than aimed at its destruction. Their organizations, including the trade unions and the co-operative societies, were valuable voluntary bodies, subordinating indi-vidual selfishness to the good of the group. The state would gain from their active interest in politics. Far from the influence of liberal statesmen being diminished in the future, it would increase. Far from conservatism being blotted out, it would discover new support in the lower strata of the population. The deeper you penetrated the working classes, the more likely would you be able to find there a vein of gold and to encounter the presence of highly conservative feeling.

The third reason was closely associated with the second, though it depended on temperament rather than on calculation. If you were not melancholy but optimistic by nature, you might put your trust in the good sense of all groups in the community. Derby and Disraeli did this. Derby expressed 'the greatest con-fidence in the sound sense of my fellow-countrymen' and entertained 'a strong hope that the extended franchise which we are now conferring upon them will be the means of placing the institutions of this country on a firmer basis'. Disraeli talked also of strengthening the institutions of the country. To the members of a workingmen's club he wrote: 'None are so interested in maintaining the institutions of the country as the working classes. The rich and the powerful will not find much difficulty under any circumstances in maintaining their rights, but the privileges of the people can only be defended and secured by popular institutions.' This was not cant, though it may have been emotion calculated in tranquillity. Being good politicians, Derby and Disraeli knew that, once they had begun to tamper with the constitution, there was no natural barrier between them and the full concession of household suffrage. Disraeli knew, too, that his own ambitions for the future could be realized only if the country had a future also. He trusted the electorate. In the last resort it was Disraeli, the opportunist, who was the optimist, and Cranborne and Lowe, the men of principle, who were the cynics.

The passing of the Reform Bill in 1867 brought to a close a period of history. As soon as the act was passed, new political and social questions began to force themselves to the forefront. As Bagehot said:

A political country is like an American forest: you have only to cut down the old trees, and immediately new trees come up to replace them; the seeds were waiting in the ground, and they began to grow as soon as the withdrawal of the old ones brought in light and air.

Soon the landscape itself was to change. The intellectual and social climate of the 1870s was far more variable than that of the 1860s, and the new trees were no longer allowed to grow where the old ones had been withdrawn. An enlarged electorate was left to wrestle with the problems of a complicated world in which ideas and interests clashed and issues loomed larger than men.

CHAPTER ELEVEN

Epilogue

The last quarter of the nineteenth century witnessed a great transformation in the character of English politics and society. The Reform Bill of 1867 proved no more final than the Reform Bill of 1832, and in 1884 the vote had to be granted to the agricultural as well as to the urban labourer. With the emergence of a mass electorate, political ideas and organizations were bound to change, and the central issues of politics moved from the battle for the vote to the battle for what to do with it.

There was a change too in the economic atmosphere. From 1868 to 1872 the country passed through a roaring boom, what Disraeli described as 'a convulsion of prosperity', but in 1873 there was a dramatic financial crash, followed by a sustained fall in interest rates and commodity prices. The rate of increase of total industrial production fell also, although output per man continued to increase.

Against such a background, agriculture was the first industry to languish: prices dropped, rents fell, and many great country estates were in the doldrums. The mid-century power of land was partially broken; in the words of Lady Bracknell, in Oscar Wilde's *The Importance of Being Ernest* (1889): 'What between the duties expected of one during one's lifetime, and the duties exacted from one after one's death, land has ceased to be either a profit or a pleasure. It gives one position, and prevents one from keeping it up. That's all that can be said about land.' Farmers were swamped from the bad harvest of 1879 onward by a flood of cheap wheat from America. The acreage of home-grown wheat fell by a million between 1875 and 1884, and prices per quarter, which had soared to seventy-four shillings in 1855 during the Crimean War, dropped to as little as nineteen shillings in 1894. In such circumstances it is not surprising that there was a new demand for agricultural protection, even while John Bright was still alive. 'It is strange to hear after thirty years of silence,' wrote the *Echo* in 1878, 'issuing as it were from the tomb the assertions and fallacies which most people thought were buried beyond the hope of resurrection.'

Businessmen, too, were confronted with serious problems in the 1870s and 1880s – problems springing from increased foreign competition and falling profit margins. 'Chimneys still smoke and engines clank,' wrote J. A. Froude in 1890, 'and the volume of our foreign trade does not diminish, but if the volume is maintained the profits fall, and our articles must be produced cheaper and even cheaper if we are to hold our ground.' Some of the hardest-hit businessmen dropped all talk of free trade and talked of 'fair trade' instead; others abandoned their reliance on themselves and turned increasingly either to industrial combination or to the state. Against such a background, the appeal of Samuel Smiles was bound to diminish among employers as well as workmen.

As far as the workmen were concerned, although the employed continued to enjoy rising real wages and there was no general contraction of output, there were dangerous concentrations of unemployment in some areas and hard fights in some industries to maintain money wages. Sectional struggles within the labour movement were accompanied by increased antagonism in the relations of labour and capital. Large claims were made in the political as well as the economic field, as Bagehot had feared in 1867, and as Lowe had prophesied. 'We [labour],' wrote the editor of *Reynold's Newspaper* in 1882, 'have about as much real power as the child enjoys who tries to get hold of the stars. Nurse gives it a bit of coloured glass and the little silly goes comforted to sleep.'

It is no longer fashionable or in conformity with technical economic vocabulary to describe trends in the last quarter of the nineteenth century, even in farming, as a great depression, but there is something depressing about this course of events. The balance of the middle century was upset as the clamour of sectional interest groups began to prove stronger than the voice of the nation. When the new gospel of empire produced a noisy rallying-point in the last decade of the century, it was the turn of the intellectual to be disillusioned. Already he had begun to react strongly against mid-Victorian conceptions of authority in the moral as well as in the political sphere; now he often became disillusioned with the results. '*Fin de siècle*,' murmured Sir Henry in Wilde's *Picture of Dorian Gray*. '*Fin du globe*,' answered his hostess. 'I wish it was *fin du globe*,' said Dorian with a sigh; 'life is such a great disappointment.'

The conditions and moods of the last generations of Victorian England were more complicated than these bold generalizations suggest, but the contrast between the conflicts of the late nineteenth century and the balance of the middle century is real enough. The mid-Victorian balance had rested on a tacit acceptance of the fact that there were certain areas of life which should not be explored too fully. It was known that there was a 'vast deal of life that skulks or struggles ... (which) burrows in holes and corners where few know of its existence or care to follow it'. The social unconscious was only laid bare, however, when the stability of mid-Victorian society was shattered and the fragmentation of social studies permitted a more expert diagnosis of the social system. Likewise a late-Victorian revolt against authority preceded the discovery of the individual unconscious in the twilight years of the century.

Yet the historian must not use too strong colours if he wishes to be faithful to the continuities hidden behind the story. There was a real relationship between the mid-century period and that which followed it. Just as the world described in this book grew out of the troubled world of the 1840s – the context of the first initiating experiences in society and politics for Disraeli, Bright, Hughes, and Smiles – so, many of the new features of England after 1873 were prepared by hidden social erosion in the 1850s and 1860s.

The makers of the late-Victorian revolt had their origins in mid-Victorian society. What happened inside families then influenced what happened in many areas of public life later. If the 1870s were a divide, the year 1859 also may be seen as a turning-point. 'It would be difficult to name any one year in the whole history of mankind,' wrote the rebel Havelock Ellis, 'in which the human spirit was more profoundly stirred to more manifold original achievements' than the year 1859. The *Origin of Species* and the *Rubáiyát of Omar Khayyám* appeared in the bookshops in this year at the same time as *Self-Help*. So did Mill's essay *On Liberty*, which not only looked back to Benthamite individualism in the early century but forward also to that burst of late nineteenth century individuality which unsettled all existing intellectual systems and challenged all existing moral codes.

But Havelock Ellis saw a different 1859 from that seen by the characters described in this book; it was the *annus mirabilis* only of the young men and the future. For an older generation

> This double decade of the world's short span
> Is richer than two centuries of old.

It is difficult to believe that any of the Victorian people described in these pages could have traced their steps differently across the mid-century years. They walked with assured and measured tread – although they were not always certain of the road they were taking – towards different destinations. It was only after 1867, when the young men were talking of a new age of emancipation, that a few of the old were sure that they were journeying into the darkness.

BIBLIOGRAPHICAL NOTE

This bibliographical note is highly selective; it is designed primarily for the assistance of the reader who wishes further to pursue the subjects of the separate chapters. Several of the books have appeared since *Victorian People* was written.

1. INTRODUCTION

For a general narrative history of the period three volumes are of great value: Spencer Walpole, *History of England, 1815–1875* (6 vols., rev. ed.; London, 1890); Herbert Paul, *A History of Modern England* (5 vols.; London, 1904); and W. N. Molesworth, *The History of England, 1830–1874* (3 vols.; London, 1875). See also my general study *The Age of Improvement* (London, 1959).

Among books which signpost the changes in historical interpretation are Lytton Strachey, *Eminent Victorians* (London, 1918); G. M. Young (ed.), *Early Victorian England* (2 vols.; London, 1934); W. W. Rostow, *British Economy of the Nineteenth Century* (Oxford, 1948); Basil Willey, *Nineteenth Century Studies* (London, 1949) and *More Nineteenth Century Studies* (1956); *Ideas and Beliefs of the Victorians* (London, 1949), a useful symposium of radio talks; W. E. Houghton, *The Victorian Frame of Mind* (London, 1957); and G. Kitson Clark, *The Making of Victorian England* (London, 1962).

Élie Halévy's masterly *Histoire du peuple anglais* (6 vols.; Paris, 1912–47) has been translated into English. Although it does not cover the years described in this book, it is of fundamental importance in understanding the background of the period.

A recent well-documented survey is W. L. Burn, *The Age of Equipoise* (London, 1964).

2. THE CRYSTAL PALACE AND THE MEN OF 1851

Martin Tupper, from whom the introductory quotation is taken, was a poet-philosopher whose *Proverbial Philosophy* (London, 1850) was a best-seller of the day. A recent book about him is by Derek Hudson, *Martin Tupper; His Rise and Fall* (London, 1949).

Many books on the Exhibition of 1851 were published for its centenary celebrations, but a study of its *Official Catalogue* (London, 1851) is still the best source. *The Commemorative Album* (London, 1950) is extremely useful. See also Christopher Hobhouse, *1851 and the Crystal Palace* (London, 1937). In a 1950 edition, illustrated by Osbert Lancaster, Mr Lancaster contributes an interesting Preface on the changing attitude towards the Victorians. C. R. Fay's *Palace of Industry, 1851* (Cambridge, 1951) is an interesting scrapbook, and Yvonne Ffrench's *The Great Exhibition* (London, 1951) is a good popular study. Nikolaus Pevsner's *High Victorian Design* (London, 1951) is by far the best book on the 'taste' of the period.

There are few good studies of religion and politics in 1851. *The Letters of Queen Victoria: A Selection*, edited by A. C. Benson and Lord Esher (London, 1908), Volume II, gives perhaps the best overall picture. An interesting and well-documented article by G. H. Le May, 'The Ministerial Crisis of 1851', *History Today*, Volume I (June 1951), deals with the central political manoeuvres of the early part of the year; there is no full study of the dismissal of Palmerston. Edwin Hodder's *The Life and Work of the Seventh Earl Shaftesbury* (3 vols.; London, 1887) is useful for social as well as religious questions. See also, for different sections of the community, K. Inglis, *Churches and the Working Classes in Victorian England* (London, 1963) and F. M. L. Thompson, *English Landed Society in the Nineteenth Century* (London, 1963).

Sir Llewellyn Woodward has written a stimulating essay on '1851 and the Visibility of Progress', in *Ideas and Beliefs of the Victorians* (London, 1950).

3. JOHN ARTHUR ROEBUCK AND THE CRIMEAN WAR

P. E. Leader's *Life of J. A. Roebuck* (London, 1897) remains the only full study. For Roebuck's Radical background, including relations with Urquhart and Layard, see Simon Maccoby, *English Radicalism, 1857–1886* (London, 1938).

Some other personalities discussed in this chapter are described in Sir Edward Cook, *Delane of The Times* (New York, 1916). Cook has also written about Florence Nightingale, as has Mrs Cecil Woodham-Smith in *Florence Nightingale* (London, 1950). See also her account of the Crimean War, *The Reason Why* (London, 1953).

The classic book on the Crimean War is by A. W. Kinglake, *The Invasion of the Crimea* (9 vols.; 6th ed.; Edinburgh, 1887), but it is interesting to compare it with the volume by W. H. Russell, the war correspondent, *The Great War with Russia* (London, 1895).

The distant origins of Russophobia are discussed by J. H. Gleason, *The Genesis of Russophobia in Great Britain* (Cambridge, Mass., 1950), while the immediate background of public opinion and the war is sketched in Kingsley Martin, *The Triumph of Lord Palmerston* (rev. ed.; London, 1963). G. B. Henderson has produced an excellent series of essays on *Crimean War Diplomacy* (Manchester, 1947), and there is a lively essay by A. J. P. Taylor in *Rumours of War* (London, 1952). See also his *The Struggle for Mastery in Europe* (Oxford, 1954).

4. TROLLOPE, BAGEHOT, AND THE ENGLISH CONSTITUTION

Bagehot's *English Constitution* was first published in 1867; a second edition, with an important additional chapter, was published in 1872. His complete works have been edited by his sister-in-law, Mrs Russell Barrington, in ten volumes (London, 1915) The best recent study is N. St John-Stevas, *Walter Bagehot* (London, 1959), which includes a selection from his political writings.

By contrast Trollope has had many commentators; one of the ablest is Michael Sadleir, *Trollope: A Commentary* (rev. ed.; New York, 1947). It provides a full bibliography of his novels and a scholarly analysis of them. Trollope's own *An Autobiography* (London, 1883) is still an indispensable source.

For the political background of the period see Norman Gash, *Politics in the Age of Peel* (London, 1953); H. J. Hanham, *Elections and Party Management*, (London, 1959); and C. O'Leary, *The Elimination of Corrupt Practices in British Elections* (London, 1962). A fascinating nineteenth-century study is by Sir John Walsh, *The Practical Results of the Reform Bill of 1832* (London, 1860).

There is no full account of civil service reform, although one side of the picture is presented fully in an article by Edward Hughes, 'Civil Service Reform, 1853-1855', *History*, Volume XXVII (June 1942).

For the general background of English political thought see Crane Brinton, *English Political Thought in the Nineteenth Century* (Cambridge, Mass., 1950).

5. Samuel Smiles and the Gospel of Work

The most important source for the study of Smiles, who has received little attention from twentieth-century historians, is his *Autobiography* (London, 1905), edited by Thomas Mackay. For a picture of the radical milieu of his early youth see my article 'Ebenezer Elliott, the Corn-Law Rhymer', *Cambridge Journal*, Volume III (August 1950) and the collection of essays *Chartist Studies* (London, 1959), especially the chapter by John Harrison on Leeds. See also my introduction to the Centenary Edition of *Self-Help* (London, 1958) and for a gossipy story A. Smiles, *Samuel Smiles and his Surroundings* (London, 1956).

Success literature is more common in the middle of the nineteenth century than has usually been recognized. Three interesting English examples are *Success in Life; A Book for Young Men* (London, 1852), mentioned on page 127; *Men Who Have Risen; A Book for Boys* (London, n.d.); and *Fortunes Made in Business* (London, 1887). On the comparative American material see Richard Wohl, 'The Rags to Riches Story: An Episode of Secular Idealism', in *Class, Status and Power*, ed. Reinhard Bendix and S. M. Lipset (Glencoe, Ill., 1953). A valuable study providing general orientation is R. D. Altick, *The English Common Reader* (Chicago, 1957). See also P. Appleman, W. A. Madden, and M. Wolff, *Entering 1859, A Year of Crisis* (London, 1959).

6. Thomas Hughes and the Public Schools

A valuable detailed study of English public schools in relation to the main currents of national thought and life is the two-volume work of E. C. Mack, *Public Schools and British Opinion* (London, 1930 and 1941).

For a more popular picture of the history and buildings of each of the main public schools see F. A. M. Webster, *Our Great Public Schools; Their Traditions, Customs and Games* (London, 1937). It is from this book that the proud declaration, quoted on page 148 is taken.

By far the best work on Thomas Arnold is still A. P. Stanley's *The Life and Correspondence of Thomas Arnold* (2 vols., 12th ed.; London, 1881). When he wrote it, Dean Stanley was Regius Professor of Modern History in the University of Oxford. He and some of Arnold's other pupils are discussed at length in Frances J. Woodward, *The Doctor's Disciples* (Oxford, 1954). A popular modern picture of Arnold himself is painted by Norman Wymer in *Dr Arnold of Rugby* (London, 1953). D. Newsome, *Godliness and Good Learning* (London, 1961) gives excellent case histories.

On Thomas Hughes see the excellent recent study by E. C. Mack and W. H. G. Armytage, *Thomas Hughes* (London, 1952), which firmly sets Hughes in the middle of Victorian society. *Tom Brown's School Days* (1858) is obtainable in many different editions.

7. ROBERT APPLEGARTH AND THE TRADE UNIONS

The best general account of English trade unionism is that by Sidney and Beatrice Webb, *The History of Trade Unionism* (London, 1920 ed.) but there is much new material and many new ideas in the first part of H. A. Clegg, A. Fox, and A. F. Thompson, *A History of British Trade Unions since 1889* (Oxford, 1964). G. D. H. Cole has written an interesting essay called 'Some Notes on British Trade Unionism in the Third Quarter of the Nineteenth Century', *International Review of Social History* (Amsterdam), Volume II (1937).

On the engineers see J. B. Jeffreys, *The Story of the Engineers* (London, 1945); on the builders, carpenters, and joiners, see Raymond Postgate, *The Builders' History* (London, 1923).

None of the twentieth-century writers catches the full flavour of the Report of the *Royal Commission on the Organization and Rules of Trade Unions and other Associations* (1867-9), or the earlier *Report on Trade Societies* (1860) of the influential Social Science Association. Interesting mid-nineteenth-century surveys are T. J. Dunning, *Trade Unions and Strikes* (1860); J. M. Ludlow and Lloyd Jones, *The Progress of the Working Classes, 1832-1867* (London, 1867), and the Comte de Paris, *The Trade Unions of England* (London, 1869). This latter book had the distinction of being translated by the economist, Nassau Senior, and of being edited by Thomas Hughes. See also for the attitudes of a journeyman engineer who was quoted by Matthew Arnold as one of the finest examples of the working class, Thomas Wright, *Our New Masters* (1873).

There is only one life of Applegarth, that by R. Humphrey (London, 1913). For the attitude of English trade unionists to the American Civil War, see R. Harrison, 'British Labour and the Confederacy' in the *International Journal of Social History* (1957), and, for Sheffield, S. Pollard, *A History of Labour in Sheffield* (Liverpool, 1959). There are important essays by S. Coltham, R. Harrison, and H. Collins in the book edited by John Saville and myself, *Essays in Labour History* (London, 1960).

8. JOHN BRIGHT AND THE CREED OF REFORM

The best introduction to the politics of the period and a good link with the material in the previous chapter is F. E. Gillespie, *Labor and Politics in England* (Durham, N.C., 1927).

For John Bright himself see G. M. Trevelyan, *John Bright* (London, 1913), and a more recent and very useful book by J. Travis Mills, *John Bright and the Quakers* (2 vols.; London, 1935). G. B. Smith's *The Life and Speeches of John Bright* (2 vols.; London, 1881) is a basic book to study, as is John Morley's *Life of Cobden* (2 vols.; London, 1881). Much useful additional material is contained in *The Diaries of John Bright*, with a Foreword by Philip Bright (London, 1930).

It is interesting to compare Bright's creed of reform with the main current of reform ideas in the middle of the century. See a stimulating article by F. H. Herrick, 'The Second Reform Movement in England', *Journal of the History of Ideas*, Volume IX (April 1948). For the key years after 1859 see W. E. Williams, *The Rise of Gladstone to the Leadership of the Liberal Party, 1859–1868* (Cambridge, 1934), and, more recently, Sir Philip Magnus's superb biography, *Gladstone* (London, 1954).

Bright's attitude towards the United States is analysed sympathetically by J. G. Randall in an essay, 'Lincoln and John Bright', reprinted in *Lincoln, the Liberal Statesman* (New York, 1947).

9. ROBERT LOWE AND THE FEAR OF DEMOCRACY

There is no satisfactory biography of Robert Lowe. A. P. Martin's *Life and Letters of the Rt Hon. Robert Lowe, Viscount Sherbrooke* (2 vols.; London, 1893) deserves all the rebukes Lytton Strachey bestowed on heavy 'official lives'. It is one-sided and ponderous, but it does include Lowe's own typewritten memoir, produced in 1876,

A good account of his Australian experiences is given by J. F. Hogan in *Robert Lowe* (London, 1893,) while Viscount Bryce wrote stimulating essays about both him and Disraeli in *Studies in Contemporary Biography* (New York, 1903).

Lowe's political ideas are set out cogently and at times brilliantly in his *Speeches and Letters on Reform* (London, 1867); those of critics are similarly propounded in *Essays on Reform* (London, 1866). For his ideas on administration, foreign policy, and economic questions there are some interesting unpublished letters to and from Lord Granville and some useful comments on his views and personality in the *Political Correspondence of Mr Gladstone and Lord Granville, 1868–1876* (2 vols.; London, 1952).

For the background of the educational changes of the last century see G. A. N. Lowndes, *The Silent Social Revolution* (London, 1937).

10. BENJAMIN DISRAELI AND THE LEAP IN THE DARK

The monumental standard *Life of Benjamin Disraeli*, by W. F. Monypenny and George Earle Buckle (2 vols.; London, 1929), is the sourcebook for all Disraeli studies. It does not completely overshadow or supplement earlier books, however, of which the best written is by J. A. Froude, *The Earl of Beaconsfield* (London, 1890). Lewis Apjohn's *The Earl of Beaconsfield* (London, 1884) is also useful. The last days of the Earl are discussed in *Memorials of Beaconsfield* (London, 1881).

There is a dearth of good accounts of nineteenth-century conservatism or of the development of the Conservative party. The necessary material for such a survey is discussed in H. J. Hanham's *Elections and Party Management* (London, 1959) and scattered about in innumerable biographies, of which the most useful is Lady Gwendolen Cecil's *Life of Robert, Marquis of Salisbury*, Vol. I: *1830–1868* (London, 1921). There is no good biography of Lord Derby; the brief and ill-documented *Life* by George Saintsbury (London, 1892) is most inadequate.

On Lancashire, which is a key area in this story, see R. A. Arnold, *The History of the Cotton Famine* (London, 1865).

Index

314

Index